JESSE LIBERTY'S
from scratch
PROGRAMMING SERIES

Java Server Pages

from scratch

Maneesh Sahu

201 West 103rd Street,
Indianapolis, Indiana 46290

Java Server Pages from scratch

Copyright © 2001 by Que

International Standard Book Number: 0-7897-2459-6

Library of Congress Catalog Card Number: 00-107934

Printed in the United States of America

First Printing: October 2000

02 01 00   4 3 2

Trademarks

Warning and Disclaimer

Associate Publisher
Tracy Dunkelberger

Acquisitions Editor
Loretta Yates

Development Editor
Hugh Vandivier

Managing Editor
Tom Hayes

Project Editor
Leah Kirkpatrick

Copy Editor
Margaret Berson

Indexer
Kelly Castell

Proofreader
Harvey Stanbrough

Technical Editor
Lance Lavandowska

Team Coordinator
Cindy Teeters

Media Developer
Aaron Price

Interior Designer
Sandra Schroeder

Cover Designer
Maureen McCarty

Production
Stacey DeRome
Mark Walchle

Contents at a Glance

Contents

About the Author

Maneesh Sahu is a distributed-object consultant with IBM. He travels the globe helping customers develop and deploy enterprise applications. Prior to this he worked on the AlphaBeans team at IBM where he created XMLViewer and XML Beans that are available today on alphaWorks. He co-authored *Enterprise JavaBeans Development Using VisualAge for Java* and *Deploying Enterprise JavaBeans on IBM Servers*, both IBM Redbooks. He has also contributed several articles on XML and Servlets to *Webtechniques* and webreview.com.

Dedication

In memory of Dad, who first introduced me to computers.

Acknowledgments

It was in early February 2000, while I sat at my desk musing over 4 across of my daily crossword in Bangalore that I received a new mail notification. The mail was from the acquisition editor at Macmillan asking me whether I was interested in authoring this book. I jumped at the offer because not only did it give me an opportunity to explore the new features of Java Server Pages 1.1, it also gave me a chance to document information, largely in my head, for future reference.

Several moons and many sleepless nights later, I finally finished this book. It was written across two continents, four time zones, and six cities. This arduous task couldn't be accomplished without the help of my family and friends.

Thanks to Mom; my brother, Ashish; Urmila; and Roshan for their support.

Thanks to Deepa Jivan for her unbounded love and care.

Thanks to my friends in Austin—Koshy, Manjo, Bothra, and Band—for making me tea at times to keep me awake!

Thanks to David Gaertner for helping me obtain from IBM the necessary software for the book.

Thanks to the editorial team at Macmillan for their useful reviews and suggestions.

Special thanks to Kingshuk Bandopadhyay, who loaned me his computer when mine broke.

Graphics were developed with help from Lotus Freelance Graphics.

Thanks, Lord, for getting me here.

Tell Us What You Think!

As the reader of this book, *you* are our most important critic and commentator. We value your opinion and want to know what we're doing right, what we could do better, what areas you'd like to see us publish in, and any other words of wisdom you're willing to pass our way.

As an associate publisher for Que, I welcome your comments. You can fax, email, or write me directly to let me know what you did or didn't like about this book—as well as what we can do to make our books stronger.

Please note that I cannot help you with technical problems related to the topic of this book, and that due to the high volume of mail I receive, I might not be able to reply to every message.

When you write, please be sure to include this book's title and author as well as your name and phone or fax number. I will carefully review your comments and share them with the author and editors who worked on the book.

Fax: 317-581-4666

Email: quetechnical@macmillanusa.com

Mail: Associate Pulbisher
        Que
        201 West 103rd Street
        Indianapolis, IN 46290 USA

Introduction

The Web has changed the way we live and operate. Even the non-computer users have been affected by the Internet Revolution. It's hard to miss those dot com ads shown on the television and splashed on billboards all over the city and countryside. Chances are that you are interested in jumping on the Web bandwagon and are looking for the right technology to implement your Web application. Java Server Pages, or JSPs, could well be the right technology to use.

Learning a new technology is not an easy task. At first you will spend time searching for good resources on the topic and then grope with the syntax and techniques associated with it. In my case I had to go through the Java Server Pages specifications and the server technical manual before I became productive with developing an application. I hope to expedite your learning experience by sharing mine.

In this book, we will explore the JSP 1.1 specification by developing an application covering the different facets of JSPs—JSP elements, JavaBeans, custom tag libraries, JavaMail, Servlets, Enterprise JavaBeans, and JDBC. You will also learn some powerful techniques for Web-based application development so you can easily incorporate them in any other application.

Life, the World Wide Web and Everything After

There are about 170 million people connected to the Internet. They are accessing it from their office workstations or servers connected to Local Area Networks or from their home PCs and laptops via phone and cable modems. Now there are even wireless, handheld devices so people on the move can access the Internet without any strings attached.

Figure I.1 shows the Web of interconnected Internet devices. The world was not always like this. Centuries ago the only means of communication was by sending messages using homing pigeons or in bottles thrown into the sea. It was in the mid-nineteenth century that the first transatlantic cable was laid to connect the U.S. with Europe. Almost a century later, the U.S. Department of Defense conceived the ARPAnet: a communication network for computers structured to provide reliability in the event of failure among nodes in the network. The hub-based design ensured that defense information could be rerouted to reach its destination in the event of loss of a node during a potential war.

Figure I.1

Internet enabled devices

ARPAnet eventually developed into the Internet, a global network that was initially used mostly by scientists and universities for sharing information. By the 1970s, text-based services such as remote login, email, and file transfer were available on the Internet.

 Remote login, or *Telnet*, is a protocol allowing users to log on or work remotely on another machine on the network.

In 1980, Timothy Berners-Lee, a consultant at CERN (*Centre European pour la Recherche Nucleaire*—French for the European Laboratory for Particle Physics) got frustrated with the fact that his information, which was scattered across different machines, was hard to retrieve simultaneously. He then envisaged a system called "Enquire" to quickly summon information by means of some "random associations between arbitrary pieces of information." In 1989, he wrote a paper proposing that CERN create a hypertext-based system for information management.

It was this system that became the World Wide Web. The first *Hypertext Markup Language*, or *HTML*, was published in August of 1991, but most users were able to experience it only by using text-based browsers, such as Lynx, that allowed basic text-based formatting such as bold and italics and allowed users to "jump" between links. In 1993, a software program out of the National Center for Supercomputing Applications, or NCSA, at the University of Illinois-Urbana/Champaign added something to the mix. Mosaic did everything that Lynx did. It ran on Windows and the Macintosh as well as UNIX, and it had one very important improvement: It displayed images. Suddenly there was a creative element to this new World Wide Web.

In the mid-1990s a new meta-language, *XML*, short for the *eXtensible Markup Language*, arrived on the Web landscape. It allowed the creation of a new set of documents that could be marked-up and structured syntactically. This allowed documents to provide descriptive information instead of the formative data. It opened doors for new sets of Web applications such as document and Electronic Data Interchange (EDI).

Electronic Data Interchange has benefited with the use of XML. Using XML you can represent your information in custom tags stored according to a predefined structure. For example, if you wanted to pass information, such as user information, using HTML you could only use tables. Using XML you can specify a structure as shown in Table I.1.

Table I.1   Comparison of HTML and XML Techniques in Passing User Information

HTML	*XML*
`<table>`	`<person>`
`<tr><td>First Name:`	`<firstname>Joanna</firstname>`
`</td><td>Joanna</td></tr>`	`<lastname>Jivan</lastname>`
`<tr><td>Last Name:`	`</person>`
`</td><td>Jivan</td></tr>`	
`</table>`	

You can develop a program using one of the standard parsing techniques that can easily understand the structure and extract the information.

In 1997 Nokia, Ericsson, and Motorola along with Phone.com (formerly Unwired Planet) formed the Wireless Access Protocol (WAP) forum for defining a set of protocols for developing applications over wireless communication networks. This enabled the proliferation of the Internet to wireless devices, such as handheld devices, cellular phones, and PDAs. The growth of the cellular industry has been *nonpareil*, with the numbers of such devices connected to the Internet expected to overtake those of personal computers in the coming years.

The number of other devices connected to the Net is on the rise. There is one refrigerator company that's developing a Net-enabled refrigerator that would place orders with a grocery store, settle bills for expenses incurred on the new orders, as well as warn users about approaching expiry dates on food products stored in the fridge!

The Growth of Java

On May 23, 1995, Sun launched Java, a new distributed, portable, robust, object-oriented programming language. The initial focus of Java was on client-side programs, called *Applets* that could be embedded within HTML pages and viewed on a browser. The language's appeal grew when IBM, HP, and other operating system vendors ported the Java Virtual Machine to their platforms, thus including mainframes, AS/400, AIX, HP-UX, and others within the platforms supported by the cross-platform language.

 Applets are Java programs compiled into bytecodes and interpreted on a Java Virtual Machine, or JVM, in a browser. They can be downloaded from a browser along with the HTML pages they are embedded in.

how tōō pr̄o nouns' it	Applets: *APP-lets*

The real potential of Java was realized when specifications were drafted for its use on the server side in mid-1996. These specifications included database access from Java programs (JDBC), a distributed application development using the Remote Method Invocations, or RMI. The "Write Once Run Anywhere" feature of Java caught the fancy of IT managers and developers. The very idea of a robust application that could be developed on one platform and deployed on another without the need for any porting became a big hit with the industry. The amount of effort saved in the portability of server-side applications could be translated into many man-years.

Performance enhancements also grew along with the language. Java applications are basically compiled into a platform-neutral format called *bytecodes*. These bytecodes are then interpreted within a Java Virtual Machine (JVM) when run. Interpreted code is a bit slower than natively compiled code due to the extra interpretation stage. New advancements in compiler technology, such as optimizations in compiled code, faster virtual machines, Just-in-time or *JIT* compilers, have resulted in performance comparable to programs written in C++.

JIT features of the JVM boost the execution speed of Java applets and applications by instantly converting Java bytecode to native code on-the-fly unlike the normal compilers and run time that interpret the bytecodes at all time. JIT is now an integral part of most virtual machines and almost all vendors support it.

While this book was being written, Sun released the next version of its JDK, version 1.3, featuring the HotSpot technology. The HotSpot performance engine performs on-the-fly adaptive optimizations to accelerate code. It identifies critical sections of the code, known as *hotspots*, and devotes its time aiming to optimize these sections during the compilation process.

how tōo prō nouns' it	JIT: *jit* (rhymes with the verb '*hit*')

Dynamic Content and Java Server-Side Technologies

When the World Wide Web burst on to the already-established Internet scene in the early 1990s, it was a static medium. A Web page was nothing but a file of text, albeit text specially marked up with HTML tags. It couldn't change or adapt to user input or conditions.

HTML is a way of formatting documents by marking it up with tags. For instance, a simple page of information might look like Listing I.1:

Listing I.1   A Simple HTML Page

```
<HTML>
<HEAD>
    <TITLE>My Home Page</TITLE>
</HEAD>
<BODY>
    <H1>Welcome!</H1>
    Welcome to my little <B>nook</B> across the Intergalactic Information
 Superhighway. Glad you could stop by. Check out my
 <A HREF="/misc/links.html">links</A> for
a really cool surfing experience.
</BODY>
</HTML>
```

A browser takes this text and formats it and displays it according to the markup tags as shown in Figure I.2.

The static pages were great for information sharing but there was no way that one could submit data or search for specific information.

Figure I.2

Page rendered in Microsoft Internet Explorer

The Hypertext Transfer Protocol was then enhanced to its current version (HTTP 1.1) to support this dynamic model of the Internet. It enabled users to submit data to the Web server as requests and the Web servers to respond to the request in turn. The *Common Gateway Interface*, or *CGI*, emerged to enable applications to process the requests and produce responses. It enabled the Web server to delegate requests to an application and obtain responses as output from it.

CGI gave developers the flexibility to develop those applications using their choice of programming languages such as C, C++, or scripts such as Bourne shell or Perl.

The CGI model, however, has its deficiencies. The Web server has to run a new instance of the application in order to delegate a new request. The creation of a new process is quite an expensive operation that requires loading the application into the memory, passing the parameters, running the instance in memory, and shutting down the process. If a thousand requests arrive at the same time, a thousand new processes need to be started, run, and subsequently shut down. It would surely cripple the system as the number of requests increased substantially.

Several proprietary solutions from different vendors, such as Microsoft's ISAPI and Netscape's NSAPI, were produced to remedy the situation. These applications were executed under the same process as that of the Web server and therefore saved the overhead of starting a new process. The problem was that a truant application handling the requests could bring down the entire Web server along with it.

Java's Servlet Mechanism finally provided the complete solution to the problem. *Servlets* are loaded into memory only once during initialization and a new thread is created to serve a new request. They're lightweight because they share the same address space as the process that created it. The application doesn't bring down the Web server too, as it operates independently of it.

In operating systems (OS) parlance, a *thread* is a lightweight process created within a process. In a multiprocessing OS, slots of CPU time need to be assigned to every process loaded into memory so that each process can be executed simultaneously, or at least made to seem so to the user. The switch from one process to another when the CPU is assigned to another process requires that the heap space, stacks, and registers for the old process be unloaded and the ones for the new process be loaded. Because threads share the same address space as the process, the switch is easier.

Servlets, like their CGI counterparts, produce dynamic content within the program. Thus, even trivial cosmetic changes to the HTML output require a change to the program, followed by its recompilation and reloading. The task of generating the HTML output also lies with the programmer.

Sun subsequently released the Java Server Pages (JSP) specifications to address that issue. JSPs are precompiled servlet codes that look like HTML pages. JSP allows you to generate dynamic content by embedding tags and Java code within HTML pages. This way a Web page designer could create the static part of the page, and all you need to do is intersperse JSP tags and code that represents the dynamic content within it. JSPs are compiled into Java Servlets by a container and executed within a servlet runtime. Changes made to the JSP are detected by a difference in the time stamps of the file and the associated servlet. If a change occurs, the JSP is recompiled and reloaded by the container into the runtime.

I have personally been involved in different Web-based applications and used myriad technologies to implement them. About half a decade back, when the Net was still in nascence, we decided to implement our dynamic Web applications using C programs. The program had to deal with low-level bytes to extract and decode information and use standard input/output to generate Web pages. We ended up spending more time implementing the CGI protocol than on the business task at hand. Proprietary C libraries emerged to handle this task, and more discoveries ensued to learn about their quirky functionality and integration with our programs. The lengthy compile, link, transfer, and execute cycle associated with C programs also made the job of creating our perfect Web application a tedious task.

I then got to use UNIX *shell scripts* for developing another simple Web application. Shell scripts are batch programs containing a sequence of commands. Web applications were easier to create and modify as changes made to the scripts were readily available without the need for any compilation and linking. The limited programming capabilities offered by these shells and the lack of database integration within the shell scripts became a major handicap in building enterprise applications.

Perl arrived on the scene. It provided scripts with rich string manipulation capabilities, a cross-platform appeal, and additional database modules to overcome the shortcomings of their shell script counterparts. The fact that Perl used the CGI model was its major disadvantage.

 Perl stands for *Practical Extraction and Reporting Language*. It was developed by Larry Wall primarily to provide expert string-handling manipulation capabilities, such as regular expression or pattern matching that is quite unmatched.

I also found an exciting tool, Lotus Domino, that I could use to rapidly develop Web-based forms and database views. I could visually create forms, views, provide full text search facilities, and set user permissions and security roles without having to write a piece of code. Standard tasks were easy to implement, but customizing the output implied delving into proprietary scripting.

With Java Servlets and JSPs I found an excellent object-oriented solution and a clear-cut application development model that I could easily apply to all my programs. I am sure you will find the advantages of them through the course of this book as well.

What You're Going To Do

In this book you are going to build a Web site for a fictitious Auction house called "Auction Station." This site doesn't attempt to rival the more complex sites, such as eBay and Yahoo! Auctions that are already devoted to the task.

The task of building the auction site might appear complex but you can break it into smaller, more manageable modules by applying the divide and conquer strategy. One such way of breaking it into manageable and cooperating modules is shown in Figure I.3.

Figure I.3

Modules in the Auction Station application

- **User Registration module**—This module handles new user registration and user authentication.

- **Auction module**—It allows registered users to bid, sell, and browse items on the site. The application is also responsible for closing the bids.

- **Calendar of Events module**—This allows users to add to and view events on a calendar using a Web-based interface.

- **Messaging and Mail module**—This is used by the different modules to send email.

- **Personalization module**—This customizes content for registered users.

- **Content module**—This provides static content such as news and information that can add value to the site.

In implementing these modules, you'll learn the following topics necessary for developing any Web application:

- **HTML**—This is the minimum requirement for building any Web-based application, and this book will provide you with examples of some tags and structures that you will typically use. This book, however, doesn't serve as a reference guide for HTML and JavaScript.

- **Using JSP elements**—You will learn how to use elements like directives, include tags, forward tags, declarations, scriptlets, and implicit objects.

- **Using JavaBeans**—Occasionally, you will need to develop and use JavaBeans, which are portable Java components, when you come across situations when you can't use the implicit objects. You will create and use beans for handling requests and for sending email.

- **Using tag libraries**—You will learn about this exciting, new feature of JSP 1.1 that allows you to create portable and easy to use custom tags within your JSPs.

- **Database access**—JSPs and Java make it easy for you to bring your database to the Web. I will cover some very basic *Structured Query Language*, or *SQL*, and database access techniques provided by Java and JSPs.

- **Personalization**—You will learn how to personalize Web content using cookies.

- **Wireless Markup Language (WML)**—For delivering content to the wireless world you will need to know about WML and WAP. This book will cover them but not to the extent of serving as a reference.

What You Aren't Going To Do

To keep focus on Java Server Pages and to prevent the book from resembling the unabridged Webster's dictionary, this book will not delve into the following topics:

- OOAD
- CORBA
- Database and Web-server Administration

System Requirements

For developing the Web application, you can use any platform that has a Java Development Kit version 1.1.7 and higher. As of today that includes Windows 95/98/NT, Linux, the different flavors of UNIX, AS/400, Mainframes, and more. The application created in this book has, however, been built, tested, and run on a Windows NT machine alone, so some additional steps and changes might be required to run it on another platform.

The hardware requirements of the JDK govern those for the application. The software requirements are shown in the following sections.

Authoring Pages

As with HTML, all you need to write Java Server Pages is a text editor, such as Notepad or vi. If you have an HTML editing tool, such as Netscape Composer or Websphere Studio, you can rapidly develop HTML and JSP pages. This book assumes that you will be using only a simple text editor.

Developing JavaBeans and Classes for Database Access

To develop the JavaBeans and classes you can write the code using a simple a text editor, and compile and run it using Java Development Kit (JDK) version 1.1.7 and higher. You can also use a development tool, such as VisualAge for Java, to ease a lot of your development and debugging efforts. The examples in this book will, however, assume that you only have a plain-text editor and the JDK.

Serving Pages

After you write a Java Server Page, it needs to be served or executed by a Web server. You require a JSP container and a servlet runtime to execute those pages. The fact that you are using Java technology implies that you have a host of operating systems to choose from for running your Web application.

Next Steps

In Chapter 1, we get ready for Web application development. We need to plan for our application and design it. We look at some popular tools that can aid in application development and also develop an HTML-based start page for our application.

Chapter 1

Planning and Designing a Web Application

This chapter introduces you to the requirements for planning for your application, identifying the roles of the players on your development team, and equipping yourself with some power tools you can use. It also introduces you to the basics of creating simple Web pages.

Why Plan?

I am sure that you are itching to get some code written for your Web application. If you have gone through a Web project lifecycle before, you might want to skip to Chapter 2, "Developing a Monthly Calendar Using Java Server Pages," and get started with developing Web applications using Java Server Pages (JSPs). You might be under pressure from the higher-ups in your organization to get that application rolling, or from venture capitalists whose funding is drying up for your dot-com idea.

In a typical project, schedules are usually tight, resources are limited, and you want to show some outputs that can make it to your weekly status report. However, it would be a big mistake to start typing out the code right away without designing your application. For small Web applications, you can get away without doing any design or planning, but as you change and enhance your application, your code can get patchy and unwieldy—and surely prone to errors.

Web application development can be compared to the task of building a house. You can build a small birdhouse by nailing a few wooden boards together in a few minutes. (It's another matter whether your canaries want to move in to such a hastily built accommodation.) For building a house, however, you need to have a plan, design the house, create a blueprint, and then proceed with the actual construction in accordance with your plan. You will also require the help of a team in case you want that building constructed in your lifetime.

The Application Development Lifecycle

A typical object-oriented application development lifecycle consists of four parts, as shown in Figure 1.1.

Figure 1.1

The application development lifecycle

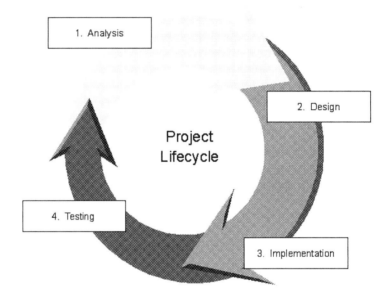

1. **Analysis**—Define the scope and understand the business at hand.
2. **Design**—Plan for the project and define the features.
3. **Implementation**—Build the product according to the requirements.
4. **Testing**—Test whether the application meets the requirements and matches the expectations.

In application development, the first step is to work against a problem statement. A problem statement can be a one-liner, for example, "To develop an auction site", provided by the top-level management, or a well-written abstract that you developed yourself. To find out exactly what the author of the problem statement had in mind, you need to gather the requirements. You can do that by asking "what" and "who" questions: "What kind of an auction do you want?" and "Who will be able to use the application?" and go more into detail, for example, "How does a user close an auction?" You might also consult a business domain expert to obtain some of the answers.

After you have finished gathering the requirements, you create use-case models to represent the interactions of the users of the system with the system to be developed. Use-case models contain different users, also known as *actors*, within the system. In the case of an auction application, there are five discernible actors:

- A casual user or guest who browses through the site and the auction items
- A registered user who places items for auction
- A registered user who bids on different items
- An administrator who manages the auction site
- An automated agent responsible for closing the bids

You also define the actions performed by an actor for each use case. For example, for placing an item for auction, a user first logs on to the system. After a successful logon, the user then navigates to the specific part of the site and lists the item by providing the requisite details for the product.

After you have described the use cases, you break down the details of the cases into sequence diagrams specifying interactions between objects (actors) in the system. The actors become objects, and the interactions become methods on the targeted objects. These interactions then result in class diagrams.

In the implementation phase of the Web application, the actor's interactions are translated into forms accepting different values at the client end, and applications processing the request on the Web-server end to update a database and to respond adequately to the requests.

Finally, in the testing phase, the implementations are checked to see whether they match the requirements and expectations. The feedback from this phase in the form of defects or updates is sent for incorporation in a new cycle of analysis, design, implementation, and testing. The refinement process can continue for several cycles until either Quality Assurance (QA) is satisfied or the project funding runs out.

The folks at Rational Corporation refer to a lifecycle as inception, elaboration, construction, and transition containing different iterations of analysis, design, development, and test workflow. The lifecycle also features many intermediate iterations and releases of the application.

Define Roles and Responsibilities

Web application development traverses a wide range of skills: programming, creativity, tenacity (read testing capacity and ruthlessness), managerial, and (last but not least) Web-based skills. You may be able to execute your application singly for a smaller project, but as the complexity and requirements of the application increase, you will need to work with a team that has varied expertise to complete the application in the desired timeframe.

A Web development project can be partitioned into several phases, as you saw earlier. Roles can be clearly demarcated in these phases, and either you or any other member of the team can adopt a role or a set of roles based on your or their skills.

Architect

An *architect* analyzes the problem, gathers the requirements for the application, and designs a high-level solution. The architect examines the problem statement at hand, determines the "what" and "who" of the problem, and documents the results as the application architecture.

For example, the problem statement could read, "Develop an online Calendar of Events application." The architect examines the "what" and "who" of the statement: "What does the Calendar of Events application do?" and "Who are the people interacting with the application?" To do this, the architect gathers the requirements, sometimes along with a business analyst who has domain knowledge in the area where the problem lies. In Object-Oriented Analysis and Design (OOAD), this phase typically ends in the creation of a use-case model that defines use cases or sequences of interactions between the actors within the proposed system.

The high-level solution provided by the architect does not deal with the nitty-gritty of Web-based development, but outlines the real-world scenario. This analysis is essential in determining the entities in the application, the data flows, and the interactions between the entities. The analyst provides consultation and reviews the work of the developers during the design phase of the project.

The analysis of the Calendar application may result in the identification of two entities: the user and the Calendar application. The attributes of each entity are also identified at this stage. For example, the user has a name, address, date of birth, and ID as well as a password for authorization. The user views the calendar entries for a given month, and authorized users can add, modify, and delete entries in the Calendar.

Data Modeler

A *data modeler* designs the databases and the tables in them. After the analyst has finished the analysis and determined the entities in the application, the data modeler uses the information to design the Entity Relationship (ER) model. In the development phase, the ER model is translated into databases and tables.

For example, from the entities identified by the architect, the data modeler eventually translates them into tables, such as the User table and the Calendar of Events table, with the attributes translated to columns in the table.

Server-Side Developer

A *server-side developer* creates the server-side business logic plus code for accessing data stores. This involves designing and implementing the use cases. This will involve accessing the database; invoking any create, retrieve, update, or delete operations on the database tables; and returning results that can be easily consumed as JavaBeans by the Web integrator.

For example, to implement the Add Entry to Calendar use case, the server-side developer designs and creates objects that first authenticate the user, using the name and password, and then insert a row in the Calendar of Events table representing the event to be added. Finally, the program returns the status of the operation as well as any error messages encountered during the operation.

Web Interface Designer

A *Web interface designer* produces the page interfaces, layouts, and art design. This comprises the artistic part of the Web application, involving aesthetics and creativity to reflect the type of application being developed and the corporate culture. This ultimately results in the development of templates into which content, both static and dynamic, can be inserted.

The Web designer designs "themes" represented by images, banners, navigation bars, fonts, colors, and interface layouts. Intuitiveness and consistency of the user interface are important aspects of Web interface design.

Web Integrator

A *Web integrator* embellishes Web pages developed by the Web designer with JSP tags, as well as with the JavaBeans developed by the server-side developer, to develop the client side of the Web application. The Web integrator describes the data flows using HTML forms, adding JSP tags to the Web pages for passing and retrieving information to and from the objects created by the server-side developer.

Project Manager

A *project manager* keeps the act together and ensures that the project is executed without a hitch. One important phase occurs during the analysis, when the project manager does a risk analysis along with the architect to find out what parts of the project are feasible with the constraints of time and resources. The rest of the job description includes chalking out proper and realistic schedules, managing resources, ensuring that deadlines are met, and also handling nontechnical issues, like doling out hefty paychecks to ensure that employee satisfaction is high!

Tester

A *tester* checks whether the application matches the expectations it was built for. The tester performs a black box verification of functionality provided by the server-side developer, Web integrator, and Web interface designer.

The tester designs and creates test cases for the interfaces designed by the developers. For the server-side developer, the test process involves passing different types of parameters, including incorrect and incomplete inputs to check whether the application breaks and to check whether the return values are coherent with the input parameters.

For the Web interface designer, the test process implies testing the application on different platforms, browsers, and screen resolutions. It also includes testing for usability, consistency, and conformance with user interface guidelines—and most importantly, broken links!

For the Web integrator, the test process implies passing values in the forms and URLs and checking for conformance. Incorrect values or incomplete fields in the form are also passed to check whether adequate error information is provided to help the user in finding the problem.

Figure 1.2 shows the utilization of the different team members in different phases of the project. Remember that one person may adopt more than one of the roles and the reverse, depending on the requirements of the project and the skill of the person(s).

Figure 1.2

Utilization of roles in the different phases

Role	Analysis Phase	Design Phase	Development Phase	Testing Phase
Architect	Gather Requirements, Analysis, Architecture	Design use cases, data flows	Consult and Review	Consult and Review
Data Modeler		Design Databases	Create Database and tables	
Server Side Developer		Design business logic and database access	Create EJBs, JavaBeans and Servlets	
Web Interface Designer		Design Site Layout, Page Layout and Art work	Create site, HTML pages and art work (images)	
Web Integrator		Design forms and scripts for handling data flows and dynamic content	Integrate work of server side developer and Web designer	
Project Manager	Risk Analysis, Manage	Manage	Manage	Manage
Tester			Create Test Cases	Test Server Side, Client side logic and site structure for problems

Identify Tools, Software, and Platforms

In developing a house, you require power tools like drills, necessary wares like wooden planks and bricks, and of course a plot of land to build the house on. In Web development, too, you require power tools, software, and a platform to develop and run the application. In this section we will look at these elements necessary for Web application development and deployment.

Tools

During the different phases of the project, you might want to use power tools to increase productivity. Different tools can help in any of the following areas:

- Reducing the complexity of the task; for example, a tool can ease development by visually presenting activities for manipulation.

- Automating repetitive or cumbersome activities, like testing for broken links—which beats manually testing for 404s!

 404 is the HTTP error code indicating that a Web resource could not be found using the specified URL. Now humorists also use the term to describe people who are lost to the present!

- Documenting artifacts such as use cases, object models, and data models as well as Web pages.

Analysis and Design Tools

Object-Oriented Analysis and Design (OOAD) tools such as Rational Rose for Java/C++ and TogetherSoft's Together/J can be used for creating and documenting use cases, class diagrams, and object interactions.

Data modeling tools such as Computer Associates' ERwin and Emberacadero's DBArtisan can be used for designing database schemas or Entity Relationship models.

Text Editors

Because HTML documents and Java source files are text-based, you can create and edit them using any standard text editor.

Text editors are usually shipped along with the operating system, so you may not need to purchase or download the software. Some of the editors include the following:

- Edit and Notepad on Microsoft Windows95/98/NT/2000
- vi and emacs on Unix/Linux
- Helios' TextPad
- Visual SlickEdit

You can use these tools to create and edit HTML files, as shown in Figure 1.3, and also to edit source code.

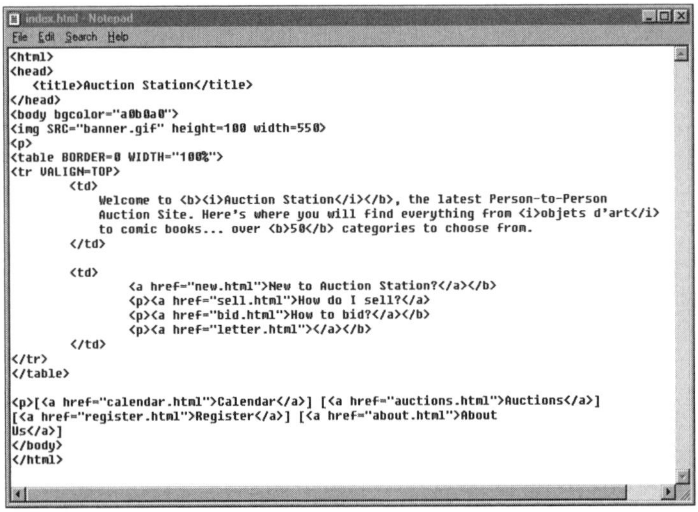

Figure 1.3

Using Microsoft Notepad for editing a Web page

```
index.html - Notepad
File  Edit  Search  Help
<html>
<head>
    <title>Auction Station</title>
</head>
<body bgcolor="a0b0a0">
<img SRC="banner.gif" height=100 width=550>
<p>
<table BORDER=0 WIDTH="100%">
<tr VALIGN=TOP>
        <td>
            Welcome to <b><i>Auction Station</i></b>, the latest Person-to-Person
            Auction Site. Here's where you will find everything from <i>objets d'art</i>
            to comic books... over <b>50</b> categories to choose from.
        </td>

        <td>
            <a href="new.html">New to Auction Station?</a></b>
            <p><a href="sell.html">How do I sell?</a>
            <p><a href="bid.html">How to bid?</a></b>
            <p><a href="letter.html"></a></b>
        </td>
    </td>
</tr>
</table>

<p>[<a href="calendar.html">Calendar</a>] [<a href="auctions.html">Auctions</a>]
[<a href="register.html">Register</a>] [<a href="about.html">About
Us</a>]
</body>
</html>
```

Page-Editing Tools

Professional Web page designers use WYSIWYG tools for editing Web documents. These tools enable even HTML-challenged users to create Web pages. The visual feedback and rapid page development that these tools provide have enamored even the hard-core HTML *cognoscenti*.

WYSIWYG stands for What You See Is What You Get, a document- or image-editing mechanism where you get visual feedback as you make changes to the document or image.

**how tōo
prō nouns′ it** | WYSIWYG: whi-zee-wig

Figure 1.4 shows how a Web page can be visually edited using a page editor. The following are some popular page-editing tools:

- Adobe PageMill
- Allaire HomeSite
- Lotus WordPro
- Microsoft FrontPage Express
- Netscape Composer
- Sausage Software's HotDog
- SoftQuad HotMetal Pro

Figure 1.4

Using Netscape Composer for visually editing a Web page

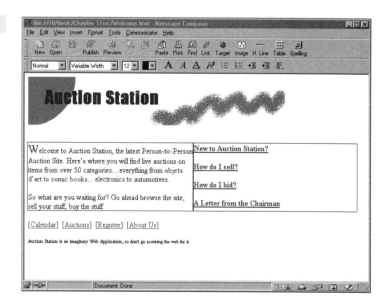

The Web interface designer and Web integrator can use these tools to create and edit HTML pages.

Site-Editing Tools

You can use site-editing tools for creating, editing and managing Web sites. They allow you to structure a Web site and provide a site-wide look for it as well. For example, NetObjects Fusion allows you to define the site structure as a hierarchy of pages as shown in Figure 1.5.

Figure 1.5

NetObjects Fusion's site outline view

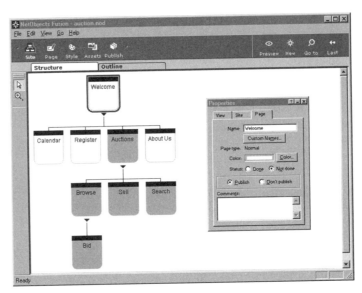

Some of the great features of these tools include the following:

- Pluggable themes for changing the entire site's look by switching site styles
- Automatic hyperlinking between pages as defined by the site structure—beats hard-coding filenames in Web pages
- Automatic generation of banner images, navigation bars, and links

Figure 1.6 shows how the Welcome page is represented using a site-editing tool. Specifying a different *theme* can change the page's look. Site-editing tools have built-in page-editing features, so you need not invest in a page editor if you have a site editor. A Web interface designer can use this tool for structuring and creating the Web site.

A few of the site-editing tools in the market today include the following:

- Adobe GoLive
- Microsoft FrontPage
- Macromedia DreamWeaver
- NetObjects Fusion

Figure 1.6

Welcome page developed using the Flow theme of NetObjects Fusion

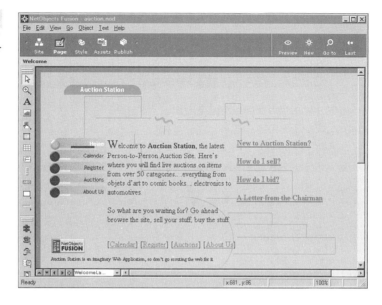

Scripting Tools

Scripting tools provide a visual mechanism for adding both client- and server-side scripts to the Web page. Client-side scripts can be written in JavaScript, an object-based language commonly used for validating forms and for providing dynamic behavior. Server-side scripts include the JSP tags that you will learn more about in this book. Figure 1.7 shows how you can use scripting tools to visually embed scripts, such as JSP tags, in this case in a Web page.

Figure 1.7

IBM's WebSphere Studio Page Designer in action

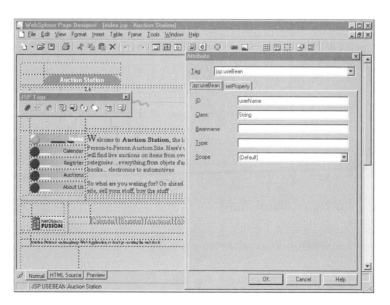

Some of the popular JSP script-editing tools in the market include the following:

- IBM's WebSphere Studio
- Macromedia Drumbeat 2000 JSP
- NetObjects ScriptBuilder (formerly Acadia Infuse)

Tools for Designing and Editing Images

Whoever said "A picture speaks a thousand words" must have had Web pages in mind. To enhance the look of your Web application and make it visually appealing, you will need to sprinkle images all over your site. You can create and edit these images with an image-editing tool. Several formats for storing these images exist on the Web today. CompuServe's GIF and Joint Photography Extension Group's JPEG are the most popular of those formats. The following are some image-editing tools that support them:

- Adobe Photoshop
- CorelDRAW
- JASC PaintShop Pro
- Macromedia FreeHand/Fireworks
- NetStudio 2000

 The JPEG (Joint Photography Extension Group) format is usually used for representing high-resolution photographic images because of the higher compression it provides. CompuServe's Graphics Interchange Format (GIF) is typically used for representing banner images, navigation bars, buttons, and other low-resolution images.

how too pro nouns' it	JPEG: jay-peg
	GIF: gif

For a Web application, you use an image editor to create banners, navigation buttons, backgrounds, logos, advertisements, and other works of art. Figure 1.8 shows how you can create an ad banner by putting together stylized text, figures, and colors in NetStudio 2000.

Version Control Tools

If you work in a team, you may operate on common documents and source files during application development. It is highly recommended to use a version control tool to provide some control in this team environment. This tool allows only a single user to operate on an "owned" document or source code at a particular time and subsequently check the source back into the repository to make available the latest release.

Figure 1.8

Creating an ad banner using NetStudio 2000

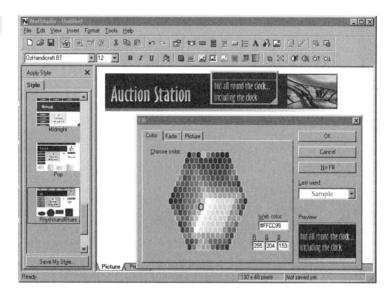

This tool also allows you to track changes and manage the files in the project through the intermediate iterations as well as the increments.

Some of the popular version-control tools in the market include the following:

- IBM VisualAge Team Connection
- Microsoft Visual SourceSafe
- CVS
- Rational ClearCase

Almost all the members of the Web application development team can use this type of tool to manage their text-based Web assets.

Java Integrated Development Environment

Sun's Java Development Kit (JDK) provides you with a compiler, debugger, and Java archive utility (JAR), as well as a runtime environment. You might consider using an Integrated Development Environment (IDE) for extra features: code editing, building project files, visual debugging, code inspection, integration with version-control tools, creating and unit testing JavaBeans, Applets, Servlets, Enterprise JavaBeans, and lots more. With all the many features incorporated into these tools, it's no wonder that this is called an *Integrated* Development Environment, a one-stop tool to help you develop and test your entire application—it does everything but make your coffee!

**how too
prō nouns′ it** | JDK, IDE: as you spell them

These are some of the popular IDEs that exist in the market:

- IBM VisualAge for Java
- Inprise JBuilder
- Symantec Visual Café
- Oracle JDeveloper

Server-side developers can use the IDE to create and unit-test JavaBeans, database access Java classes, Servlets, and Enterprise JavaBeans. Testers can also use this tool for creating test cases.

 Black box testing is a testing technique attempting to break the application by subjecting it to different test cases. The difference between black box testing and unit testing is that the tester is not aware of the boundary conditions of the code implemented by the user, and checks it using a combination of different parameters and checks for durability.

Figure 1.9 shows how you can debug Java code and inspect the values of variables at runtime using IBM's VisualAge for Java.

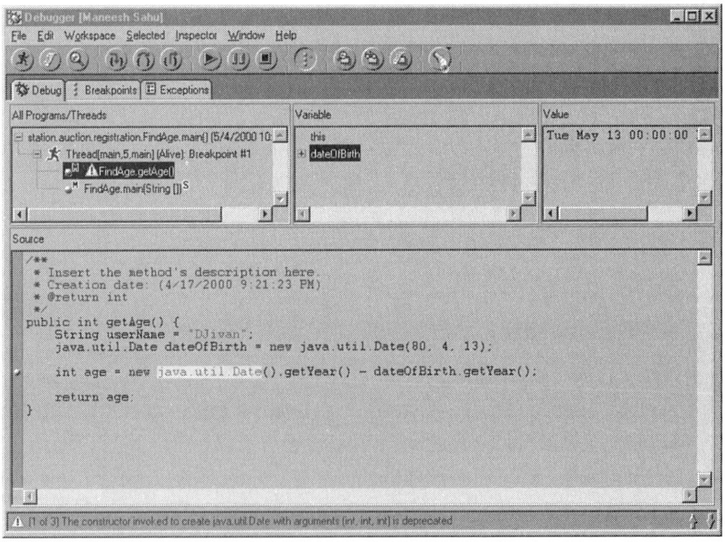

Figure 1.9

Debugging code and inspecting variables in IBM's VisualAge for Java

Browsers

Finally, you will need browsers to view and test the Web pages you develop. During unit testing, the Web interface designer and the Web integrator will need to check whether the pages are being rendered as they are supposed to. A tester will double-check the results using different browsers.

The following are some of the popular Web browsers:

- Microsoft Internet Explorer
- Lynx
- Netscape Navigator/Communicator
- Opera

Software

After you have completed your development, you will need to test and run your program. For running a Web application, you will need the following software:

- An HTTP server
- Browsers
- A database
- An application server

 The process of migration from a development and test environment to a working or production one is known as *deployment*.

HTTP Servers

The basic requirement of any Web Application is an HTTP server. The HTTP server acts as a request-response server. By using a Uniform Resource Locator (URL), clients request a file (HTML page, image, or any other file type) that resides on local or remote machines. The URL usually maps to a file on the file system or a dynamically generated page. The HTTP server responds to these requests by sending back the required data.

Figure 1.10 shows how a Web page addressed by a particular URL is sent to the browser.

A Web URL consists of two parts:

- A hostname or IP address
- A file location or the name of the program/script generating the dynamic code appended with the request parameters

Figure 1.10

How a page at
`http://www.auction.`
`station.net/index.`
`html is served`

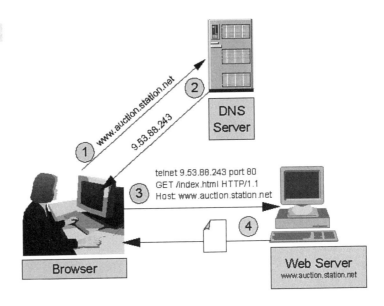

These are some of the popular Web servers:

- Apache
- IBM HTTP Server
- Lotus Domino 4.6 or R5
- Microsoft Internet Information Server (IIS)
- Netscape Enterprise Server

Databases

If you are building an industrial-strength Web application, it's very likely that you
will need a relational database. Databases allow you to store incredibly large amounts
of data, terabytes in some cases, while providing extremely fast retrieval rates. A
database allows you to focus on developing the business portions while taking care of
the data management aspects: storing, indexing, searching, retrieving, and updating
data on the file system.

Another feature of a database is the transactional integrity that it provides. A *transaction* is a set of create, retrieve, update, or delete operations performed on one or
more data sources meant to operate as though they were a single autonomic operation. For example, a money transfer transaction of a bank can be thought of as a single operation performing a debit in one bank account and a credit in another. If at
any time during the transaction, any of the operations—such as the debit or credit—
failed, the database would bring it back to a consistent state by rolling back both

operations. Only on the success of both operations would the transaction be committed into the database and made visible to the other users. This way, the transaction doesn't debit money in one account and miss crediting the other.

The world's database market is divided into some of these major players:

- Oracle
- IBM's DB2
- Informix
- Microsoft SQL Server
- Sybase

Application Servers

In the distributed world, one host typically requests information from another. This model is commonly referred to as the *client-server* or *two-tier architecture*. The data requested by the client may also reside on a data store, such as a database. This scenario is called *three-tier architecture*, and is used extensively in Web-based applications. The client is a machine with an HTML browser requesting data from a data store. The application server accepts requests via the HTTP server, understands them, and fetches the data from the data store. Application servers allow you to use your code for interpreting and responding to the requests.

Some Web-based application servers that allow you to use your Java code are the following:

- BEA WebLogic Server
- IBM WebSphere Application Server
- iPlanet Application Server
- Secant
- Powertier

Platforms

In addition to the tools and software that you decide to use, you will also need to decide which platforms you intend to use them on. The world of platforms is quite diverse, with operating systems ranging from DOS to high-end Unix boxes and mainframes, each having its distinctive edge over the other.

Each platform has carved a niche for itself in the market. The Apple Macintosh is widely regarded as the ultimate desktop publishing platform. Windows NT has a wide range of tool support and is a good choice as a development platform for creating applications. The various flavors of Unix (AIX, Solaris, HP-UX, Digital, and IRIX) are unmatched for their number-crunching operations, statistical operations, and image and multimedia processing. They also scale well to support a large number of users, and hence are an excellent choice as a Web server as well as an application server. Linux, touted as the biggest threat to Windows in the workstation arena, provides an inexpensive alternative for hosting Web applications. Mainframes are platforms that support a large number of concurrent users and transactions, appropriate for running database and transaction processing monitors.

Software companies such as IBM have also painstakingly ported their tools and software across the different platforms, so you have a choice of platforms on which to develop and deploy your applications. With the coming of Java, you can make applications written in Java instantly available to different platforms without the need for any ports. This is especially true for server-side applications, such as Web application servers, that provide the runtime for Servlets and Java Server Pages. As the demands increase, inferred by the number of hits, you will need to upgrade your memory and CPU. When the system cannot scale to meet the demands, you might want to deploy the same application on a higher-end machine, such as a Unix server. With Java technology, this switch to a totally different platform is a cinch.

Define Guidelines

After you have decided on your tools, software, and platforms, and before you are ready to begin work on the project, it's best to define and conform to guidelines in various areas of Web application development.

Site Structure Guidelines

On a Web server, static HTML pages are served off the file system. A directory on the file system is configured as the root Web directory in the Web server. All files that need to be available on the Web must be stored in the directory structure within the root. A Unified Resource Location (URL) of a file is mapped to its location relative to the root directory.

As with organizing your folders, you should also organize your site into logical sections. Allow for easy accessibility or navigability from one section to another by the use of navigation links.

 There are two types of URLs: absolute and relative. An absolute URL has the format *protocol://hostname/locator information*—for example, `http://www.auction.station.net/auctions/bid.html` and `new://news.software.ibm.com/vajava.ide`. A relative URL describes the location of the file relative to the current URL—for example, `../registration/newuser.html` or `closebid.html`. There are also root-relative URLs that describe the location of the file relative to the root, for example `/registration.html`.

Page Design Guidelines

While you are developing your Web application, you must keep in mind the potential clients that can view them. For example, your Web page could be viewed by different browsers as well as on different platforms.

You must also understand that a lot of incompatibilities exist between the different browsers. The market share of each browser is also too substantial to be ignored. Hence you should design your HTML interface so that the browsers can render them uniformly.

How do you design the HTML interfaces uniformly? Well, the World Wide Web Consortium, W3C for short, has created standards for structuring HTML documents. Each browser is also expected to comply with these standards and render them accordingly. When you create your documents, adhere to these standards (HTML 3.0 or 4.0) and avoid using browser-specific tags.

You could also have different hosts that run different operating systems viewing your application. You should therefore avoid any platform-specific components embedded in your pages, ActiveX components for instance.

The next task is determining the screen resolution for which you design your Web interfaces. Screen resolutions range from 470×300 pixels up to and beyond 1280×1024 pixels. If the resolution you design is too high, a user having a lower-resolution monitor will have to scroll the page to view the entire document. While creating images, you may decide to design against a targeted 800×600-pixel or 1024×768-pixel resolution; a majority of the internet browsers have these resolutions for their monitors.

An important guideline while designing Web pages is to maintain a simple and consistent design. You should provide for easy readability by displaying text with a large enough font, left-justifying the text, and avoiding all-uppercase text as much as possible. Avoid distracting the user by using blinking characters, non-contrasting colors (light-colored text on a white background), and overwhelming the user with a lot of visual elements. You should also spare the users from having to download a lot of large images. You can find a more comprehensive set of guidelines in any book on human-computer interaction (HCI). You can find more information on the subject in IBM's "Ease of Use Web Design Guidelines" located at `http://www.ibm.com/hci`.

You can also add client-side scripts to your page to provide some additional functionality, performing some event based on an action, such as showing a dialog or pressing a button. There are many client-side scripts; notable among them are those written in JavaScript, an object-based scripting language. Some browsers may not have the capability to run those scripts or may have the feature disabled. You must therefore keep the target audience in mind before adding client-side scripts. Within an organization, you can expect some consistency in the browsers; hence, intranet applications can be well-endowed with scripts. You may, however, want to minimize such scripts in Internet applications for the sake of providing universal access.

Coding Guidelines

As a part of the JSP development, you will also need to write some Java programs. To allow maintainability of the code, I recommend adhering to some coding guidelines. Some standard guidelines include indenting code within control blocks, and naming variables, constants, methods, and class names so that you can easily recognize them.

You can follow Javasoft's coding standards (`http://java.sun.com/docs/codeconv/html/CodeConventionsTOC.doc.html`) if you need to look at some industry-defined standards.

Develop a Web Interface

HTML, or Hypertext Markup Language, is a way to format a page by enclosing text with formatting information that a browser can understand and render. There is a great deal of literature already devoted to this topic, and this book will not attempt to provide a complete reference. It will, however, give you enough to get you on terra firma. If you are a Web interface designer or Web integrator, you should get your gear ready!

Getting Ready

The first things you need to have before you start churning out those Web pages are the mandatory computer and a text editor. You could also use any of the page-editing or site-editing tools that were described in the Tools section, but there's no better way of getting your hands dirty with HTML than working with the bare-bones text editor. What you need to keep in mind while working with a text editor is that you won't be saving your documents with the extension .txt on your file system but instead with an .html extension to identify it as an HTML page. You might have noticed some Web pages on the Web with the extension .htm; this is due to the three-letter restriction imposed by earlier file systems.

Home Is Where Web Scripting Begins

Let's begin with your first Web page if you haven't already created one. This page will also act as your home page. Type the lines of text shown in Listing 1.1 in your editor and save the file as `index.html`.

Listing 1.1   Source of the Home Page

```
Welcome to Auction Station, the latest Person-to-Person Auction site.
Here's where you will find live auctions on items from over 50
categories...everything from objets d'art to comic books...
electronics to automobiles.
```

Save the file, fire up your browser, and open the file you just created, `index.html`, in it. Figure 1.11 shows how the page is rendered in Netscape.

Figure 1.11

The bare-bones home page rendered in Netscape Navigator

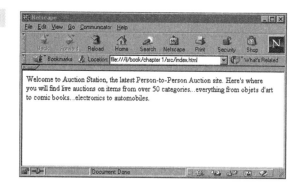

HTML Tags

Now you must be wondering what's so "hypertext" and "marked up" about the Web page you created. I just wanted to show you how trivial creating Web pages can be! Let's make some text bold, like the site name, "Auction Station," and some text italicized, like "objets d'art," because it is a common practice to italicize non-English words. You can provide this formatting information in the file you created by enclosing the targeted text within HTML tags. These tags have the following structure, containing an opening tag and a closing tag:

`<tag-name>``text to be formatted `**`</tag-name>`**

There are also some tags that only specify a page layout instruction and do not affect enclosed text, such as the horizontal rule (`<hr>`) and line break (`<br>`). These tags do not require closing tags and can represented as:

`<tag-name>`

or

`<tag-name/>`

or even

`<tag-name></tag-name>`

Table 1.1 provides a list of commonly used tag names that can be used in the body of an HTML page.

Table 1.1 Some Commonly Used HTML Tags

Tag Name	Description
<b>, <emph>	Makes the enclosed text bold
<i>	Italicizes the enclosed text
<h1>, <h2>, <h3>, <h4>, <h5>, <h6>	Makes the enclosed text a header

You could even nest tags to obtain a combination of effects. For example, to make text both bold and italicized, you nest the text within a bold tag and the bold tag within the italic tag, as long as you don't overlap them.

Listing 1.2 shows the correct way to nest your tags.

Listing 1.2 The Proper Way to Nest Tags

```
<b><i> text to be bold and italic </i></b>
<i><b> text to be bold and italic </b></i>
```

It would be incorrect, however, to overlap the tags as in Listing 1.3. The output of such overlapped tags is uncertain and is dependent upon the browser's ability to interpret this information.

Listing 1.3 Incorrect Nesting of Tags

```
<b><i> text to be bold and italic </b></i>
<i><b> text to be bold and italic </i></b>
```

After you apply your formatting information to the document, you will end up with the page's source as shown in Listing 1.4.

Listing 1.4 Source of the Marked-Up Home Page

```
Welcome to <b><i>Auction Station</i></b>, the latest Person-to-Person
Auction site.
Here's where you will find live auctions on items from over
<b>50 categories</b>everything from <i>objets d'art</i> to comic books...
electronics to automobiles.
```

To view the changes that you made to your file, click the Reload or Refresh button, and you should see your browser display the latest contents, as in Figure 1.12.

What you have actually created so far in this chapter is just the body of an HTML document. The specifications provided by W3C (World Wide Web Consortium) dictate that an HTML document have the structure shown in Listing 1.5.

Figure 1.12

The marked-up page rendered in Netscape Navigator

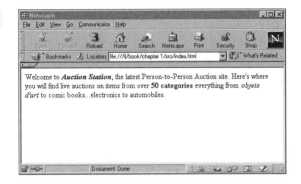

Listing 1.5   An HTML Document Skeleton

```html
<html>
<head>
<title></title>
</head>
<body>
</body>
</html>
```

As shown in Listing 1.5, an HTML document should start with an outer level `<html>` tag followed by a `<head>` and a `<body>` tag. The text of the page that you created earlier should be placed between the `<body>` and `</body>` tags of the HTML.

Your browser can display documents that did not conform to the specifications because the browsers are built to be highly tolerant. Thus, you could use uppercase for the tags or forget to end tags, and the browser will still attempt to display the remainder of the document after performing some error recoveries. You must also not assume that all browsers will be able to suppress such errors. Machines that have lesser memory, for example, hand-held computers, do not include error-recovery modules in their Web browsers. There are plenty of HTML conformance checkers in the market (also called HTML syntax checkers), and ideally you should run your pages through one to find any errors before putting them on the Web.

Images

Now you want to spruce up your home page. Adding images would be a good way to do that. You can start out by creating a banner image. You can use image-editing tools to create these images. You can also use site-editing tools to automatically generate banner images for a specified theme.

For your home page, you can include a banner image at the top of the page. You do this by adding an `<img>` tag and specify the image location as its `<src>` attribute.

```html
<img src="banner.gif" alt="Auction Station">
```

Figure 1.13 shows how the Web page will look with the embedded image.

Figure 1.13

Including an image in the home page

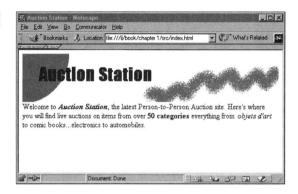

You can also specify the location using an absolute URL, such as the following:

```
<img src="http://www.auctionstation.com/images/banner.gif"
alt="Auction Station">
```

Note   It is a good practice to specify the alternate text, `alt`, property for an image. The alternate text specifies text that can substitute images. This way, even browsers that are not capable of rendering images, such as text browsers, can provide the information provided in `<img>` to the user.

You can add an image to an HTML page by including an `<img>` tag within the body. You could also set it as the background for a table or the entire page: `<body background="image.gif">`. When you do this, the image is tiled to cover the display area.

Links

You can add links to a document so that another file can be reached from it by adding hyperlinks within it. You can specify the URL you are linking to by specifying its URL within the anchor tag

```
<a href="../home.html">Home</a>
```

or to a file specified by an absolute URL:

```
<a href="www.auctionstation.com/home.html>
```

In the home page, you can add navigation links at the bottom of the page to reach parts of your site, as shown in Listing 1.6. The resulting appearance is shown in Figure 1.14.

Listing 1.6   Adding Navigation Links to the Page

```html
<html>
<head><title>Auction Station</title></head>
<body>
<img src="banner.gif" alt="Auction Station"><br>
Welcome to <b><i>Auction Station</i></b>, the latest Person-to-Person
Auction site. Here's where you will find live auctions on items from over
<b>50 categories</b> everything from <i>objets d'art</i> to comic books...
electronics to automobiles.

<p>[<a href="calendar.html">Calendar</a>]
   [<a href="auctions.html">Auctions</a>]
   [<a href="register.html">Register</a>]
   [<a href="about.html">About Us</a>]
</body>
</html>
```

Figure 1.14

Home page containing navigation links

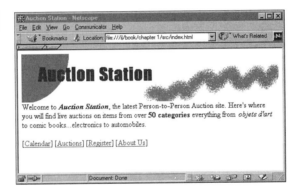

 Note   You can specify either relative or absolute URLs while creating hyperlinks. You should use relative URLs when the file is located on the same host. This way you can easily shift the site to another location without having to update the absolute or hard-coded URLs in your document.

If the file resides on another host, the link will need an absolute URL.

You can also set a link on an image by including it within the anchor start and end tags, as shown in Listing 1.7.

Listing 1.7   Hyperlinking a Document Using an Image

```html
<a href="../home.html">
      <img src="../home.gif" alt="Home">
</a>
```

Tables

You have seen how to format text using HTML tags. You can also format the document structure, using tables that allow you to lay content out in a tabular fashion. Tables allow you to arrange text and images, including other tables, within rows and columns.

To create a table, you need to add a `<table>` tag. You then need to nest as many table row, `<tr>`, tags within the `<table>` tag as the number of rows you need to create. You can then add either table data, `<td>`, or table heading, `<th>`, tags nested within the `<tr>` tag to specify columns within the individual rows. The text you want to display in a cell should be placed within the `<td>` or `<th>` tags.

Listing 1.8 contains the source for a table with three rows containing two columns. Figure 1.15 shows its rendering in a browser.

Listing 1.8   HTML Source for a Table Containing Three Rows and Two Columns

```
<table>
<tr>
        <th>caption 1</th>
        <th>caption 2</th>
</tr>
<tr>
        <td>data 1.1</td>
        <td>data 1.2</td>
</tr>
<tr>
        <td>data 1.1</td>
        <td>data 1.2</td>
</tr>
</table>
```

Figure 1.15

The table as rendered in Internet Explorer

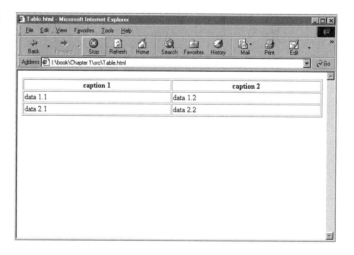

Putting It All Together

Listing 1.9 shows the complete source for the welcome page, and Figure 1.16 shows how it looks when viewed in a browser.

Listing 1.9 HTML Source for the Completed Home Page

```html
<html>
<head>
    <title>Auction Station</title>
</head>
<body bgcolor="a0b0a0">
<img SRC="banner.gif" height=100 width=550>
<p>
<table BORDER=0 WIDTH="100%">
<tr VALIGN=TOP>
      <td>
              Welcome to <b><i>Auction Station</i></b>, the latest
              Person-to-Person Auction Site. Here's where you will find
              everything from <i>objets d'art</i> to
              comic books... over <b>50</b> categories to choose from.
      </td>

      <td>
              <a href="new.html">New to Auction Station?</a></b>
              <p><a href="sell.html">How do I sell?</a>
              <p><a href="bid.html">How to bid?</a></b>
              <p><a href="letter.html"></a></b>
      </td>
</tr>
</table>

<p>[<a href="calendar.html">Calendar</a>] [<a href="auctions.html">Auctions</a>]
[<a href="register.html">Register</a>] [<a href="about.html">About
Us</a>]
</body>
</html>
```

Figure 1.16

The completed home page as viewed in Internet Explorer

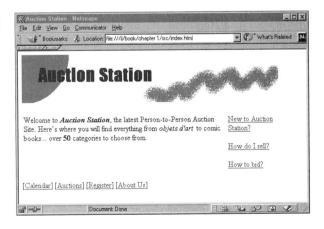

Summary

In this chapter you learned about planning for your application, identifying the different roles involved, and using some power tools for Web application development.

You also learned how to create a basic Web page using different HTML elements:

- Text
- Text formatting tags
- Images
- Hyperlinks
- Tables

Next Steps

The Web page you created is static, and its output will not change unless you alter its source. In the next chapter, you will learn how to develop dynamic content using JSPs by creating an online monthly calendar.

Chapter 2

Developing a Monthly Calendar Using Java Server Pages

In this chapter, you will dive right into the world of Web application development and create Auction Station's online monthly calendar.

What You Are Going To Do

You will start with displaying the current month's calendar. In the chapters to follow, you will add functionality to ultimately create an interactive calendar of events application.

This project will be done in a phased manner, with planned increments. Table 2.1 shows the development plan.

Table 2.1   The Calendar Application Increments

Version	Functionality
Version 1.0	Develop a monthly calendar for the current month
Increment 1 (Version 1.1)	Allows users to specify the month and year for the calendar
Increment 2 (Version 2.0)	Allows users to add events that will be displayed in the calendar

Don't be confused by the quirky naming pattern for the increments. It's not a typo for one! In a typical software lifecycle, products and applications go through various increments, starting out with the initial release or the 1.0 version. If a new release containing minor changes or bug fixes is then brought out, the version number is updated by .01, so it would be version 1.01. If additional functionality is introduced without re-engineering the original product, the version number is incremented by .1. That's how the first increment is numbered Version 1.1. You need to modify the initial application to display the calendar for a given month rather than for the current one. If the product is overhauled with some major changes, the version number is incremented by 1. In increment 2, you will be drastically changing the calendar application to support features such as adding, deleting, and modifying events in the calendar.

Using Apache Software Foundation's Tomcat Version 3.1

You need a JSP container and a Servlet runtime to run your Web application. Several commercial servers containing the JSP container and runtime exist. These products are commonly referred to as *application servers*.

For this book, we use an open-source implementation from the Apache Software Foundation (www.apache.org). The Apache Software Foundation recently released an open-source reference implementation of Sun's Servlet 2.2 and Java Server Pages 1.1 specifications, called Tomcat, that is a part of the Jakarta project. The Foundation is best known for producing the open-source Apache Web Server, which accounts for more than half of the Web servers today on the Net.

The Jakarta project attempts to create an ideal implementation from the JSP and Servlet specifications in the form of Tomcat. The advantage of using a reference implementation such as Tomcat is that it is being developed under the aegis of industry leaders from companies such as IBM and Sun as well as eminent personalities in the computing field.

The other advantage of using Tomcat is that you can develop and test your JSPs and Servlets using this cheap and effective server and can then deploy it seamlessly onto another server that is JSP 1.1–and Servlet 2.2–compliant.

You can learn more about the foundation and the Jakarta project by logging on to their Web site at http://jakarta.apache.org/ (shown in Figure 2.1).

Figure 2.1

Apache Software Foundation's Jakarta home page

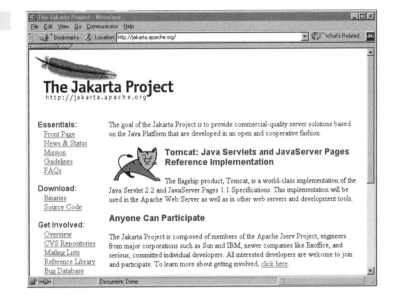

Installing Tomcat

At the time this book was being written, the Apache Software Foundation released Tomcat Reference Implementation version 3.1. More updates can be expected in the coming months, so you can always download the latest release directly from their Web site at `http://jakarta.apache.org/`.

The archive is available as a zip file for Windows 9x/NT/2000 and a zipped tar file for Unix and Linux. You can extract the archive using any of your standard unzipping tools. For Unix and Linux, you can use the tar utility that is provided with the operating system. If you don't have any unzipping tool, you can always use the JAR, (Java archive utility), provided with the JDK. You can extract the archive using JAR by typing the following command at the command prompt:

```
jar -xvf jakarta-tomcat.zip
```

This command extracts the contents of the archive within the current directory containing the archive. After the extraction completes successfully, you will have a directory structure created within the current folder as shown in Figure 2.2.

The `bin` directory contains batch files for Windows and shell scripts for Unix and Linux that you need to run in the command window in order to operate the JSP and Servlet runtime (as shown in Table 2.2).

Figure 2.2

Directory structure created upon extracting the Tomcat archive

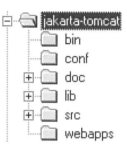

Table 2.2   The Tomcat Batch Files

Batch File/Shell Script	Description	Usage
Startup.bat/startup.sh	Starts the Tomcat server	Startup
Shutdown.bat/shutdown.sh	Shuts down the Tomcat server	Shutdown
Tomcat.bat/tomcat.sh	Can be used for starting up and shutting down the server as well as precompiling the JSPs in a batch mode	Tomcat start Tomcat stop Tomcat jspc

You can start the Tomcat server by running the startup batch file (shown in Figure 2.3). Tomcat has a built-in HTTP server, so you don't need to worry about downloading and installing one. Tomcat also allows you to configure the server with an existing HTTP server.

Figure 2.3

Starting the Tomcat server

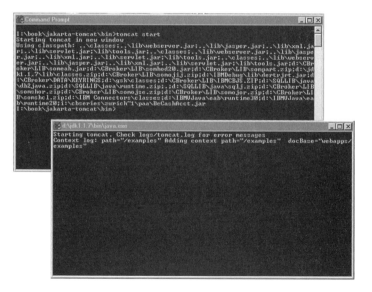

You can verify whether the server is operational by launching your browser and viewing the page referenced by the URL `http://localhost:8080/`. Make sure your browser's Internet settings recognize `localhost` as a valid local address. If your browser doesn't recognize it, you can switch to using a direct connection in your browser. If all went well, you will see the default Tomcat home page, as shown in Figure 2.4.

Figure 2.4

Tomcat's default Web page

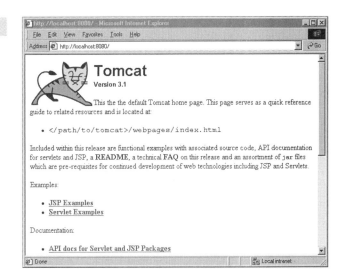

Preparing the Tomcat Server for Deploying Auction Station

You may want to deploy the HTML page that you created in the previous chapter in a Web server, like Tomcat, so that it is available via HTTP to other Web clients. Tomcat not only serves HTML documents but also acts as a container for Servlets and Java Server Pages for producing dynamic content.

You will need to create a subdirectory, AuctionStation, within the `<jakarta-tomcat>/` webapps folder. You can store your files (HTML files, images, JSPs, and other Web artifacts) with the AuctionStation directory as the root, organized according to your site structure guidelines. Your home page will then be identified by the following URL:

`http://localhost:8080/AuctionStation/index.html`

Sketching Out the Online Calendar Using HTML Elements

Let's develop the interface of the online calendar using some of the tags that you saw in Chapter 1. You need to create a table to format the days, containing eight rows for displaying the weeks in the month as well as the names of the days, and seven columns for the days in a week. Some parts of the table are static—for example, the names of the days in a week—and the others are *dynamic*; they need to be computed for display, such as the days in the month.

The Calendar Java Server Page (JSP) will generate the dynamic parts. A JSP is essentially an HTML page, with the extension .jsp, with some additional tags. Let's start with developing the static parts, as shown in Listing 2.1. Figure 2.5 shows the month.jsp displayed in a browser.

Listing 2.1   month.jsp: Skeleton of the JSP Containing the Static Portions

```
<html>
<head>
<title>Calendar</title>
</head>
<body>
        <table border="1">
        <tr>
                <td colspan="7"> 
                <!- HTML Comment: The Month's name goes in here  ->
                </td>
        </tr>
        <tr bgcolor="#BBBBBB">
                <td>Sunday</td>
                <td>Monday</td>
                <td>Tuesday</td>
                <td>Wednesday</td>
                <td>Thursday</td>
                <td>Friday</td>
                <td>Saturday</td>
        </tr>
        <%- Hidden Comment: The days go in here  -%>
        </table>
</body>
</html>
```

Adding Comments

In a team, the Web interface designer sketches out the JSP with the static parts. The designer intersperses comments within the JSP to provide information to the Web integrator indicating the desired placement of dynamic content, the days in the month for example. There are two types of comments:

- **HTML comments**—These comments are sent to the browser but are ignored while rendering the document. They have the following format:

  ```
  <!-- Text (Including dynamic text generated using expressions) -->
  ```

- **Hidden comments**—These comments are not sent to the browser. They have the following format:

  ```
  <%-- Text --%>
  ```

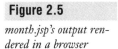

Figure 2.5

month.jsp's output rendered in a browser

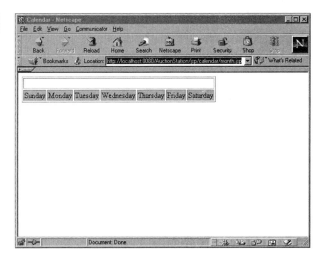

Including a Footer Containing Navigational Links

You may want to include a common footer in your site's pages. You can create a footer that includes links to special sections in the site as well as text specifying a caution. Because the output of the footer will be included in another page, you should not describe the complete HTML structure with the <html>, <head>, and <body> tags, but instead you should only specify data that—ideally—would be placed within the <body> tag.

Listing 2.2 displays the source for the footer containing navigational links and a disclaimer.

Listing 2.2   footer.jsp: Source of the Footer JSP

```
<br>
[<a href="month.jsp">Calendar</a>]
[<a href="auction.jsp">Auctions</a>]
[<a href="register.jsp">Register</a>]
[<a href="about.jsp">About Us</a>]
<br>
<font size="-4">
Auction Station is an imaginary site. Don't go scouting the Web for it</font>
```

To include the footer in the output, you need to modify month.jsp to include a *page include* directive. There are two ways you can do this:

- **Include directive**—The contents of the file specified in the directive are included directly in the JSP's source. The resulting file containing the JSP and the included file content is then parsed and translated to generate content. The following is the syntax of a page include directive:

  ```
  <%@ include file="relativeURLspec" %>
  ```

- **JSP page include tag**—The output of the page specified in the tag is included in the JSPs output at run-time. If the specified page was a JSP, it would first be parsed and translated and its output would be included in the embedding JSP's output. The following is the syntax of the simplest JSP include tag:

```
<jsp:include page="relativeURLspec"/>
```

To include the output of footer.jsp as the footer in month.jsp, you can use either of the include mechanisms just described. Each has its own pros and cons: the include directive results in a faster output because the contents of the file are statically included at translation time. The con is that changes are not reflected in the embedding page when the included file is modified. You can use the JSP include tag if you expect changes to be made often.

In this case, the footer is mostly static and you would not make changes to it very often. Therefore, it would be better to use an include directive. The directive includes the footer page's source in month.jsp and should be placed at the end of the `<body>` tag, where footers usually go, as shown in Listing 2.3.

Listing 2.3   index.jsp: Specifying the Include Directive in the JSP

```
<html>
<head>
<title>Calendar</title>
</head>

<body>
    <table border="1">
        <tr>
            <td colspan="7"> 
            <!-- HTML Comment #1: The Month's name goes in here -->
            </td>
        </tr>
        <tr bgcolor="#BBBBBB">
            <td>Sunday</td>
            <td>Monday</td>
            <td>Tuesday</td>
            <td>Wednesday</td>
            <td>Thursday</td>
            <td>Friday</td>
            <td>Saturday</td>
        </tr>

        <!-- HTML Comment #2: The days go in here -->
    </table>
<%@ include file="footer.jsp" %>
</body>
</html>
```

Figure 2.6 shows the output of index.jsp displayed in a browser.

Figure 2.6

Modified Calendar's output containing the footer links

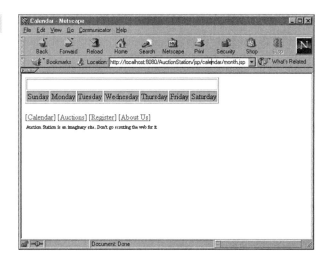

Generating Dynamic Content

You have seen a few of the JSP tags, such as comments and include directives. In this section, you will learn how to generate dynamic content, such as the days of the current month.

Handling Dates with Java Classes

Before you add the tags to the JSP, you might want to know about some Java classes used for handling dates. Table 2.3 shows some classes that you will require.

Table 2.3   Java Classes for Handling Dates

Java Class	Description
java.util.Date	Represents a specific instance in time, with millisecond precision. Creating a new date without any arguments creates an instance representing the current time and date.
java.util.Calendar	An abstract class that performs date arithmetic and can also be used for extracting information from the Date instance.
java.text.SimpleDateFormat	Used for formatting Date instances according to user-specified patterns.
java.text.DateFormatSymbols	Encapsulates locale-specific information, such as the month and day names.

When creating global Web applications, you must learn to incorporate two important concepts: *internationalization* and *localization*. Internationalization, or I18N for short, means that you are supporting multiple locales (languages and regions) and not hard-coding text such as month names for only a single locale, for example, U.S. English. Localization, L10N, implies that you are supporting a particular locale by providing specific values for that locale in the internationalized application.

The numbers in the shorthand notations, I18N and L10N, represent the number of characters between the start and end letters of the term.

Using Java Classes Within the JSP

To use the classes to handle dates within the JSP, you need to add extra JSP tags.

Adding Page Directives for Importing the Java Classes

At the top of the JSP, you need to add a page directive for importing the Java packages and classes. You can also use the page directive for specifying the content type and character sets:

```
<%@ page import="java.util.*,java.text.DateFormat,java.text.DateFormatSymbols"%>
```

The packages and classes that you need to import are specified in the import parameter, and you can use commas to separate the multiple entries. In the absence of the page directive, the JSP container imports the java.lang.* package classes.

The other values provided by default in the absence of this tag are shown in Table 2.4.

Table 2.4   Parameters in the Page Directive

Parameter	Description	Default Value
autoFlush	Specifies that the buffer be automatically flushed when it reaches its maximum size	true
buffer	Specifies the size of the buffer to be used while writing the content out	8kb
extends	The class the compiled JSP extends from	org.apache.jasper. runtime.HttpJspBase
contentType	The MIME type of the output generated by the JSP	text/html
charset	The character set to be used to encode the text	ISO-8859-1
errorPage	The page to be redirected to when an exception occurs	None
import	The packages and classes that need to be imported	java.lang.* package classes

Parameter	Description	Default Value
info	Textual information about the page	None
isErrorPage	Whether the page is designated as an error page	false
isThreadSafe	Whether multiple threads can access the page	true
language	The language used for scripting the dynamic parts	java
session	Indicates that the page takes part in an HTTP session	true

Declaring Variables for the Calendar

After you have specified the classes and packages to be imported, you need to declare the variables that you will use within the JSP. In this case, you will need an instance of the `Calendar` class for obtaining information about the current month. For determining the number of days in a month, you also need to specify an array of integers representing the number of days in a month and the array of month names.

Listing 2.4 shows the declarations of month.jsp for the `cal` and `monthNames` variables and the `DAYSINMONTH` constant.

Listing 2.4   month.jsp: Declaring Variables for Obtaining Information About a Month

```
<%! Calendar cal = Calendar.getInstance(); %>
<%! String[] monthNames = (new DateFormatSymbols()).getMonths(); %>
<%! public final static int[] DAYSINMONTH =
            { 31, 28, 31, 30, 31, 30, 31, 31, 30, 31, 30, 31 }; %>
```

 Note   You need not import the packages and classes if you fully qualify the classes for the variable you define in the JSP with their package names. Thus you can also declare the `cal` variable to be an instance of `java.util.Calendar` and use `java.text.DateFormatSymbols` for obtaining the month names.

JSP declarations can also be used to declare methods. You can declare a method that returns an array of `Strings` representing month names for a particular locale as shown in Listing 2.5.

Listing 2.5   month.jsp: Defining a Method That Returns the Month Names for a Specified Locale

```
<%! String[] getMonthNamesForLocale(String language, String country) {
        Locale aLocale = new Locale(language, country);
        DateFormatSymbols symbols = new DateFormatSymbols(aLocale);
        return symbols.getMonths();
} %>
```

If you need to perform a one-time initialization for a variable and you don't want to declare extra variables and also don't want to declare an extra method, you can perform the initialization within the predefined jspInit method as shown in Listing 2.6.

Listing 2.6   month.jsp: Initializing the Month Names with Ones Specified for the Japanese Locale

```
<%! public void jspInit() {
    Locale jpLocale = new Locale("JP", "JP");
    DateFormatSymbols jpDateSymbols = new DateFormatSymbols(jpLocale);
    monthNames = jpDateSymbols.getMonths();
} %>
```

Generating the Current Month's Name Using an Expression

After you have declared the calendar variables, you can generate the current month's name within the body of the JSP page using an expression. When you declared the Calendar instance using Calendar.getInstance(), you automatically set the current date and timestamp in the calendar. Thus you can obtain the current month's number (0 for January, 1 for February) by invoking the get(Calendar.MONTH) method on the Calendar instance. The output of the expression is placed along with the static content:

```
<%= monthNames[cal.get(Calendar.MONTH)]%>
```

Listing 2.7 shows the source of your JSP after you include the declaration and expressions.

Listing 2.7   month.jsp: Using an Expression to Generate the Current Month's Name

```
<%@ page import="java.util.*,java.text.DateFormat,java.text.DateFormatSymbols"%>
<%! Calendar cal = Calendar.getInstance(); %>
<%! String[] monthNames = (new DateFormatSymbols()).getMonths(); %>
<%! public final static int[] DAYSINMONTH =
        { 31, 28, 31, 30, 31, 30, 31, 31, 30, 31, 30, 31 }; %>
<%! String[] getMonthNamesForLocale(String language, String country) {
        Locale aLocale = new Locale(language, country);
        DateFormatSymbols symbols = new DateFormatSymbols(aLocale);
        return symbols.getMonths();
} %>
```

```html
<html>
<head>
<title>Calendar</title>
</head>

<body>
      <table border="1">
      <tr>
              <td colspan="7"> <font size="+2">
              <%= monthNames[cal.get(Calendar.MONTH)]%></font>
              </td>
      </tr>
      <tr bgcolor="#BBBBBB">
              <td>Sunday</td>
              <td>Monday</td>
              <td>Tuesday</td>
              <td>Wednesday</td>
              <td>Thursday</td>
              <td>Friday</td>
              <td>Saturday</td>
      </tr>
      <%-- Hidden Comment: The days go in here --%>
      </table>
<%@ include file="footer.jsp" %>
</body>
</html>
```

Figure 2.7

Calendar displaying the current month's name

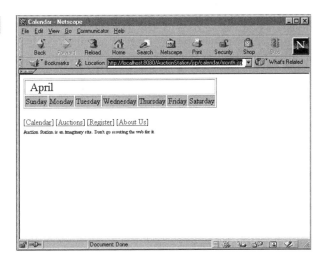

Using Scriptlets and Implicit Objects to Print the Month's Information

In the previous section, you generated dynamic content using expressions. An *expression* is the equivalent of invoking a method on an object, passing the necessary parameters, and placing the result in the output page. For a single method, expressions serve the purpose well, but for more complicated logic requiring more than a single object invocation, you will need to generate the content using scriptlets.

Scriptlets also allow you to embed Java code within the HTML source. Content can be outputted from the Java code by the use of the *implicit object*: out. Implicit objects are predefined variables provided by the JSP. The out implicit object is an instance of javax. servlet. jsp. JspWriter, and you can invoke the print and println methods on it to print content. It is made available by the JSP container for use within scriptlets for every JSP.

The format of a scriptlet follows:

```
<% //Your java code goes in here %>
```

We will extend the JSP created so far to print the following information:

- The current year
- The current month
- The current day
- The number of days in the current month

Information such as the year, month, and day of the specified date can be obtained from the java.util.Calendar instance that we declared earlier. The Calendar provides a get method that can provide a host of information, depending on the parameter passed to the method. Passing the integer value java.util.Calendar.MONTH returns the month that the date falls in. Similarly, passing java.util.Calendar.DAY_OF_WEEK returns the day of the week represented by an integral value, 0 for Sunday, 1 for Saturday, and so on.

For determining the number of days in the month, you need to determine the current month, obtain the standard number of days by indexing into the DAYSINMONTH array, and then increment the count if the month is February and the year is a leap year as shown in Listing 2.8.

Listing 2.8   Scriptlet for Printing the Current Month's Information

```
<!-- Can be placed anywhere within the body after the JSP declarations -->
<%
        int month = cal.get(Calendar.MONTH) + 1;
        int year = cal.get(Calendar.YEAR);
        int today = cal.get(Calendar.DAY_OF_MONTH);
        // Determine the number of days in the month
        int numberOfDays = DAYSINMONTH[month];
        if (month==Calendar.FEBRUARY &&
            ((GregorianCalendar) cal).isLeapYear(year) )  {
            numberOfDays++;
        }
```

```
<!-- HTML Comment. Possibly prints
out.println("Year [" + year + "]<br>");
out.println("Month [" + month + "]<br>");
out.println("Day [" + today + "]</br>");
out.println("Number of days in month [" + numberOfDays + "]<br>"); -->
%>
```

The "Generate Cells for the Month" Scriptlet

In this part, you will generate the cells for the current month's calendar. It will display the days, listing them under their corresponding day of the week.

Because of the tabular nature of the data you are representing, you will need to use HTML table elements: table rows (<tr>) and table cells (<td>). A month usually has fewer than 32 days, but the days of a month could be stretched across six weeks. Therefore, when generating a calendar, you will need to generate 42 cells (six rows × seven columns), but not all of them will be populated with days of the month. If a cell represents a particular day of the month, the day number is displayed in it; otherwise, the cell is displayed as a blank cell with a dark gray background. The current month is displayed with a yellow background.

Table 2.5 lists the HTML snippets for the different cells that you will produce.

Table 2.5 HTML Code for Representing the Different Types of Cells

Type of Cell	HTML Snippet

Representing a day of the month	`<td valign="top">`
	`<b>day</b>`
	`</td>`

Representing the current day	`<td valign="top" bgcolor="#f1e069">`
	`<b>day</b>`
	`</td>`

Not representing a day of the current month	`<td valign="top" bgcolor="#gray">`
	` `
	`</td>`

As you can see from the code in Table 4.5, you can specify a color in HTML either by using its symbolic name or by specifying a six-letter hexadecimal value representing its RGB value.

RGB stands for *Red Green Blue*. This coloring scheme works under the premise that all colors can be derived as a combination of the three primary colors: red, blue, and green. A pure red color can be obtained by specifying the maximum value for red, ff, hexadecimal for 255, and 0 for green and blue, which is 00. Hence the color code for red in RGB format would be #ff0000. The color gray can be obtained by mixing equal amounts of red, green, and blue; its RGB format therefore is #999999. Yellow would be a combination of red and green, and a lighter shade would contain some blue as well; #f1e069 would represent one such shade.

Another format for specifying colors is *CMYK*, short for *Cyan Magenta Yellow blacK*. This scheme is used in printing houses to print color images. A color using this representation is determined by subtracting amounts from the four complementary colors: cyan, magenta, yellow, and black.

You probably have also noticed that the three types of cells have the same structure except for the additional background color and the day number in some cases. You can therefore generate all these cells within an iterative block, like a for loop. You can also add special conditions and print out the additional background colors and text.

A row describing a week has seven days, or columns. These columns must therefore be enclosed within the <tr></tr> tags to be displayed in the table. Listing 2.9 shows the source for iterating through a loop 42 times to produce the different cells for the calendar.

Listing 2.9 month.jsp: The "Generate Cells for Month" Scriptlet

```
<%
      int month = cal.get(Calendar.MONTH);
      int year = cal.get(Calendar.YEAR);
      int today = cal.get(Calendar.DAY_OF_MONTH);

Calendar beginOfMonth = Calendar.getInstance();
      beginOfMonth.set(year, month, 0);
      int startCell = beginOfMonth.get(Calendar.DAY_OF_WEEK);
      //Obtain the endCell for the month
      int endCell = DAYSINMONTH[month] + startCell - 1;
      if (month==Calendar.FEBRUARY &&
               ((GregorianCalendar) cal).isLeapYear(year) )  {
          endCell++;
      }

      /**
       * Print 42 Cells (<TD></TD>).
       * Not all of the cells represent days of the current month.
       */
      for (int cellNo = 0, day = 1; cellNo < 42; cellNo++) {
              if (cellNo%7 == 0) {
                      out.println("<tr>");
              } // end check for start of week

              out.print("<td valign=top height=57");
              // Check if the cell represents a valid day
```

```
        if (cellNo < startCell || cellNo > endCell) {
                out.print(" bgcolor=\"gray\"> ");
        } else {
                if (day == today) {
                        out.print(" bgcolor=#f1e069");
                } // end check for current day
                out.print("><b>" + day + "</b>");
                day++;
        } // end if block
        out.println("</td>");
        if (cellNo+1%7 == 0) {
                out.println("</tr>");
        } // end check for end of week
} // end for-loop
%>
```

You will need to include the scriptlet in Listing 2.9 at the location indicated by the second hidden comment, as shown in Listing 2.10. Figure 2.8 displays the output of the page in a browser.

Listing 2.10   month.jsp: Including the Scriptlet in the JSP

```
</tr>
<%-- Hidden Comment: The days go in here --%>
<%    //The 'Generate Cells for Month' Scriptlet goes here %>
</table>
```

Figure 2.8

The completed online monthly calendar version 1.0

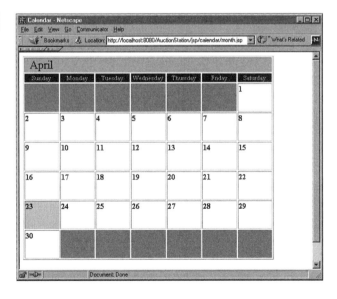

You can also internationalize the day names. You can do this by declaring the array of names of days of the week variable as follows:

```
<%! String[] dayNames = (new DateFormatSymbols()).getWeekDays(); %>
```

So far in the development of the JSP, we hard-coded the names of the days, as shown in Listing 2.11.

Listing 2.11   month.jsp: Displaying the Day Names

```
<td width="70"><font size="-1" color="ffffff">Sunday</font></td>
<td width="70"><font size="-1" color="ffffff">Monday</font></td>
<td width="70"><font size="-1" color="ffffff">Tuesday</font></td>
<td width="70"><font size="-1" color="ffffff">Wednesday</font></td>
<td width="70"><font size="-1" color="ffffff">Thursday</font></td>
<td width="70"><font size="-1" color="ffffff">Friday</font></td>
<td width="70"><font size="-1" color="ffffff">Saturday</font></td>
```

You can replace it with the scriptlet from Listing 2.12.

Listing 2.12   month.jsp: The "Generate Day Names" Scriptlet

```
<%
        for (int i = 1; i < 8; i++) {
                out.print("<td width=\"70\">");
                out.print("<font size=\"-1\" color=\"white\">");
                out.print(dayNames[i]);
                out.println("</font></td>");
        }
%>
```

The advantage of using a scriptlet over directly specifying the day names is that you can internationalize the dayNames array and thus can generate even Japanese or Spanish day names. You can initialize the monthNames and dayNames variables with Spanish names by setting them in the jspInit method as shown in Listing 2.13.

Listing 2.13   Using the Spanish Locale

```
<%! public void jspInit() {
        Locale aLocale = new Locale("ES", "ES");
        DateFormatSymbols symbols = new DateFormatSymbols(aLocale);
        monthNames = symbols.getMonths();
        dayNames = symbols.getWeekdays();
} %>
```

Figure 2.9 displays the monthly calendar for the Spanish locale

Figure 2.9

Calendar for the Spanish locale

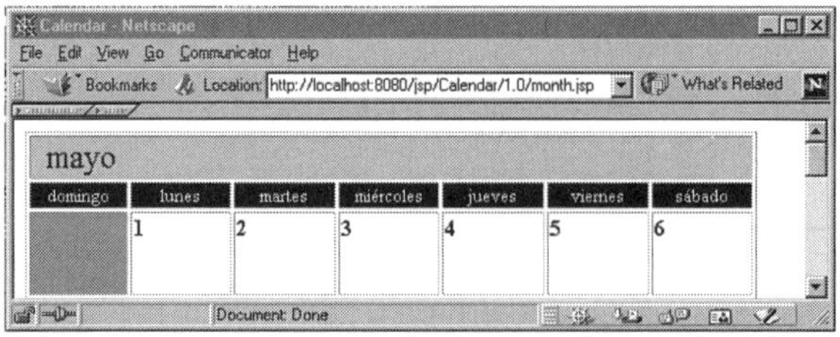

Includes Revisited

You may want to include the Calendar's output in another page. After all, the Calendar plays a supporting role in the Auction site, and you wouldn't want it to hog an entire page.

The Calendar's output can be included into another JSP's contents using the include tag introduced earlier. Before you do this, you will need to modify the JSP so that the contents can fit into a smaller area. You will need to do the following to achieve that:

- Strip all HTML tags from the JSP except the ones within the body tag. Because you will be including the JSP's content into another page, you cannot output the `<html>`, `<head>`, and `<body>` tags to a page that already has them.

- Use shortened day names, such as Sun and Mon instead of Sunday and Monday. You can shorten them even further by using only the initials: S, M, and so on.

  ```
  <%! String[] dayNames = (new DateFormatSymbols()).getShortWeekdays(); %>
  ```

- Change the width of the table and columns so that they take relative sizes instead of absolute ones. *Relative sizes* means that the sizes are proportional to the size of the window in which the HTML element is displayed. This will allow the table to be shrunk or expanded depending on the size of the display area, unlike absolute values, where the size is fixed to the specified number of pixels.

  A relative size of 100% implies that the element fits the entire display area. Likewise, a size of 14% implies that the element fits approximately 1/7th of the area if my arithmetic is still intact!

  Set these relative sizes as shown in Listing 2.13.

Listing 2.13   smallmonth.jsp: Setting Relative Table and Column Widths

```
<table width=100%>
   <tr bgcolor="pink">
   <td colspan="7"> 
      <%= monthNames[cal.get(Calendar.MONTH)]%>
   </td>
   </tr>
   <tr bgcolor="red" align="center">
     <%
        for (int i = 1; i < 8; i++) {
             out.print("<td width=\"14%\">");
             out.print("<font size=\"-1\" color=\"white\">");
             out.print(dayNames[i]);
```

Listing 2.13 smallmonth.jsp: Setting Relative Table and Column Widths

```
                out.println("</font></td>");
        }
    %>
  </tr>
<!-- End of changes from absolute to relative sizing -->
```

- Make some aesthetic changes. Go ahead and change the colors and font sizes, so people will never be able to guess that you reused the previous calendar application!

Figure 2.10 shows the output of smallmonth.jsp displayed independently.

Figure 2.10

The Small Month Calendar displayed independently

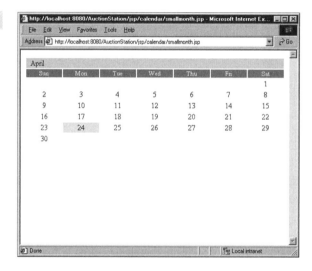

You still need to modify the home page, index.html, to include the modified calendar. Rename the home page as index.jsp because only JSPs can include content from another source. Add the page include tag for smallmonth.jsp:

```
<jsp:include page="smallmonth.jsp" />
```

Your modified home page source would look like the one in Listing 2.14.

Listing 2.14 index.jsp: The Home Page Including the Calendar

```
<html>
<head>
    <title>Auction Station</title>
</head>
<body bgcolor="white">
<img SRC="banner.gif" height=100 width=550>
<p>
<table BORDER=0 WIDTH="100%">
```

```
<tr VALIGN=TOP>
    <td>
        Welcome to <b><i>Auction Station</i></b>, the latest Person-to-Person
Auction Site. Here's where you will find everything from <i>objets d'art</i>
 to comic books... over <b>50</b> categories to choose from. <p>
Check the calendar on the right for exact dates for featured auctions.
    </td>

    <td>
        <jsp:include page="smallmonth.jsp" flush="true"/>
    </td>
</tr>
</table>

<%@ include file="footer.jsp" %>
</body>
</html>
```

Figure 2.11 displays the output of index.jsp, embedding the small monthly calendar.

Figure 2.11

The home page containing the small monthly calendar as viewed in Internet Explorer

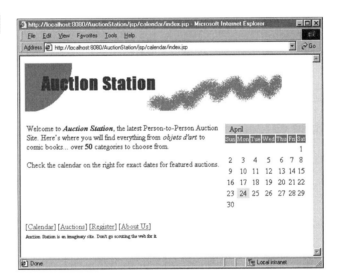

Deploying the Application

One of the advantages of using JSPs is that you can create and modify Web applications that are instantly available for usage without having to restart the server. You just need to store the JSP file in the designated directory that holds the HTML pages for your application (see Figure 2.12), and the changes are reflected immediately.

Figure 2.12

Directory structure containing Auction Station's JSP files.

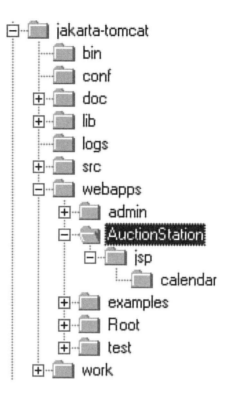

Setting a Directory as the Root in Tomcat

You may want to strip off the AuctionStation identifier in the URL. You would have a lot of redundancy on your hands if you reserve www.auction.station.net as the domain name for the Web site running Tomcat. The URL for the home page would be http://www.auction.station.net/AuctionStation/index.html, which is too long for a Web site.

You can configure the AuctionStation directory as your root directory so that the requests to documents within it can be referred to directly without specifying the directory name. You can achieve this by changing the server.xml configuration file stored in the <jakarta-tomcat>/conf directory. Add a <Context> tag within the <ContextManager> tag for the AuctionStation Web application:

```
<Context path="" docBase="webapps/AuctionStation" debug="0" reloadable="true" >
</Context>
```

Place the new <Context> tag in the document as shown in Listing 2.15.

Listing 2.15   server.xml: Modifying the server.xml Configuration to Set AuctionStation as the Root

```
<?xml version="1.0" encoding="ISO-8859-1"?>

<Server>
    <!-- Debug low-level events in XmlMapper startup -->
    <xmlmapper:debug level="0" />

    <!-- This is quite flexible; we can either have a log file per
         module in Tomcat (example: ContextManager) or we can have
         one for Servlets and one for Jasper, or we can just have
         one tomcat.log for both Servlet and Jasper.

         If you omit "path" there, then stderr should be used.

         verbosityLevel values can be:
            FATAL
            ERROR
            WARNING
INFORMATION
            DEBUG
         -->

    <Logger name="tc_log"
            path="logs/tomcat.log"
            customOutput="yes" />

    <Logger name="servlet_log"
            path="logs/servlet.log"
            customOutput="yes" />

    <Logger name="JASPER_LOG"
            path="logs/jasper.log"
            verbosityLevel = "INFORMATION" />


  <ContextManager debug="0" workDir="work" >
    <!-- ContextInterceptor
     className="org.apache.tomcat.context.LogEvents" / -->
    <ContextInterceptor
     className="org.apache.tomcat.context.AutoSetup" />
    <ContextInterceptor
     className="org.apache.tomcat.context.DefaultCMSetter" />
    <ContextInterceptor
     className="org.apache.tomcat.context.WorkDirInterceptor" />
    <ContextInterceptor
     className="org.apache.tomcat.context.WebXmlReader" />
    <ContextInterceptor
     className="org.apache.tomcat.context.LoadOnStartupInterceptor" />
        <!-- Request processing -->
    <RequestInterceptor
```

Listing 2.15   continued

```
        className="org.apache.tomcat.request.SimpleMapper" debug="0" />
    <RequestInterceptor
     className="org.apache.tomcat.request.SessionInterceptor" />
    <RequestInterceptor
     className="org.apache.tomcat.request.SecurityCheck" />
    <RequestInterceptor
     className="org.apache.tomcat.request.FixHeaders" />

    <Connector className="org.apache.tomcat.service.SimpleTcpConnector">
    <Parameter name="handler"
           value="org.apache.tomcat.service.http.HttpConnectionHandler"/>
    <Parameter name="port" value="8080"/>
    </Connector>

    <Connector className="org.apache.tomcat.service.SimpleTcpConnector">
    <Parameter name="handler"
value="org.apache.tomcat.service.connector.Ajp12ConnectionHandler"/>
    <Parameter name="port" value="8007"/>
    </Connector>

    <!-- example - how to override AutoSetup actions -->
    <Context path="/examples" docBase="webapps/examples" debug="0"
     reloadable="true" >
    </Context>
    <!-- AutoSetup for AuctionStation-->
    <Context path="" docBase="webapps/AuctionStation" debug="0"
     reloadable="true" >
    </Context>

    <Context path="/test" docBase="webapps/test" debug="0"
     reloadable="true" >
    </Context>

    </ContextManager>
</Server>
```

The text in bold represents the modified portions of the configuration file. You will
need to stop and restart the server to enforce the changes.

Debugging Your Application

There are two kinds of errors that you may encounter while developing JSP-based
Web applications:

- Translation-time errors
- Runtime errors

Translation-time errors occur because of incorrect JSP tag syntax or invalid Java code
within scriptlets, expressions, and declarations. Let's take the situation where you
might have forgotten to provide a semicolon (;) in a declaration, as in Listing 2.16.

Listing 2.16   month.jsp: An Incorrect Declaration of `monthNames` Within the JSP

```
<%@ page import="java.util.*, java.text.DateFormat, java.text.DateFormatSymbols"
%>
<%! Calendar cal = Calendar.getInstance(); %>
<%! String[] monthNames = null %>
<%! public final static int[] DAYSINMONTH = { 31, 28, 31, 30, 31, 30, 31, 31,
30, 31, 30, 31 }; %>
<%! String[] dayNames = null; %>
<%! String[] getMonthNamesForLocale(String language, String country) {
        Locale aLocale = new Locale(language, country);
        DateFormatSymbols symbols = new DateFormatSymbols(aLocale);
        return symbols.getMonths();
} %> ...
```

When you load the page generated by this JSP, you will instead be shown error information, as shown in Figure 2.13.

Figure 2.13

A translation-time error

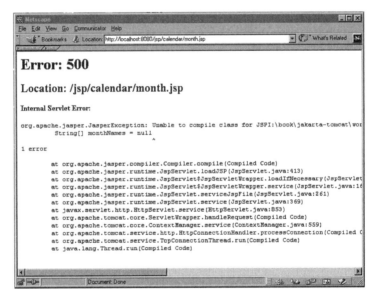

You can use the information to identify and rectify the errors. Tomcat, like any other JSP container, creates Java files from the JSP pages, compiles the Java class, and runs it to generate dynamic content. These files and classes are generated in the `<jakarta-tomcat>/work/localhost_8080` directory. You can find the filename provided with the error information displayed in the browser. A translated Java file may have a name like `_0002fjsp_0002fcalendar_0002fmonth_0002ejsp_0002fjsp_0002fcalendar_0002fmonth_jsp_0.java`.

You can also determine the Java file for a particular JSP by deleting all the files in the `<jakarta-tomcat>/work/localhost_8080` folder and requesting the page again. This way, only the Java file for the JSP will be generated, and you can easily identify it.

Runtime errors are more difficult to identify. You could print the variable values at different locations within the JSP to ensure that they are correct. This mechanism is rather laborious.

There are also some Java IDEs that allow you to debug the JSP code. IBM's VisualAge for Java Enterprise 3.0, for example, allows you to step through the content generation for a JSP as shown in Figure 2.14. However, it does not support JSP version 1.1 as yet.

Figure 2.14

Debugging JSPs using IBM's VisualAge for Java Enterprise 3.0

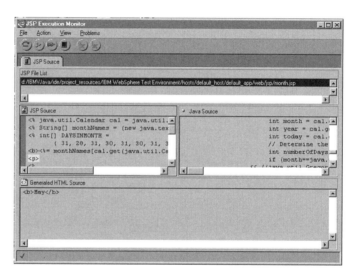

Summary

In this chapter you built your first JSP, the Calendar JSP. You also learned to use the following JSP elements:

- HTML comments
- Hidden/JSP comments
- Page directives
- Include directives
- JSP page include tag
- Declarations
- Scriptlets

Chapter 3

Adding Interactivity to the Calendar Application

In this chapter you will enhance the application to display the calendar for a user-specified month and year. This constitutes one of the really exciting parts of the Web, where users can send data across to the server and receive relevant information from that data. This type of dynamic content generation is the prequel to the bleeding edge e-business applications.

The Calendar Application Version 1.1

Version 1.0 of the application might display only the current month's calendar. Now you can enhance the application to make it display the calendar for a specified month of a specific year.

To achieve this you need to create another HTML page, input.html, that acts as an input page. The user views this page and provides values for the input fields. These values are passed using the Hypertext Transfer Protocol (HTTP) to a specified application or JSP that processes the form data and generates dynamic content, or the Calendar for the specified month in this case. The screen-flow is displayed in Figure 3.1.

Figure 3.1

Data flows between the HTML pages and JSP

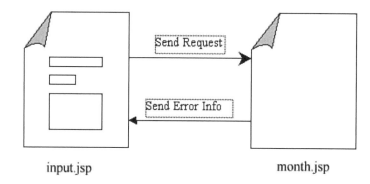

input.jsp   month.jsp

Developing the Input Page

The input page is an HTML page containing different input fields in which the user can provide data to be processed. As per the requirements, the input page should be used to specify the month and the year.

Defining the HTML Form

To create an input page containing fields, you need to add an HTML form to your HTML/JSP document. A form can be added anywhere within the body of the document like any other HTML element.

All input fields in an HTML page that need to send data to the server for processing need to be contained within a form.

A form has the following syntax:

```
<form action="FormHandlerURL" method="get|post" name="name">..</form>
```

It specifies the application on the Web server that will process the form contents using the 'action' parameter and also a request passing mechanism using the 'method' parameter. If your Web page has more than one form you will need to provide its name as well.

For our application, the enhanced month.jsp will process the requests to generate the specified month's calendar. You can specify month.jsp as the action parameter's value. You can specify either absolute or relative URLs for the action field, thus by simply specifying month.jsp you are assuming that you will be placing the HTML page/JSP in the same directory as month.jsp.

Choosing the Right Input Fields to Capture User Data

After you define the form, you will need to determine the input fields that go into the form to capture your user's data. The input fields are determined by the information you need to capture from your users. For example, to obtain your user's name, you need to provide an input text field where the user can enter the name. HTML provides a choice of input fields to choose from. Figure 3.2 displays the different input fields using the HTML interface.

Figure 3.2

An HTML page containing different types of input fields

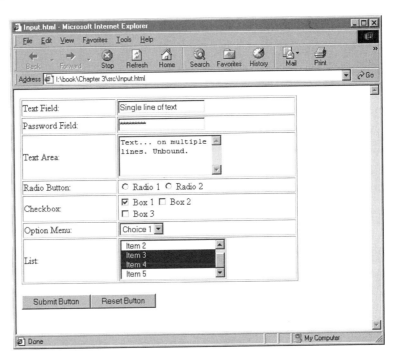

There are eight different types of input fields. The source of the input field used to obtain the result shown in Figure 3.2 is shown in the following list.

- **Text fields**—These input fields accept single-line text. This includes data such as name, age, city, email address, state, credit card number, and any similar information that can fit in one line.

  Sample:

  ```
  <input type="text" name="textinput" value="Single line of text" size="20">
  ```

- **Password fields**—Accept single-line text but mask user inputs by echoing asterisks instead of the characters typed in by the user—a must for accepting sensitive data such as passwords so that anybody who's watching over your shoulder can't determine what you just typed. Serves the purpose of shielding what you just entered and not very useful if the user is a very slow typist who punches the keyboard with a single index finger!

Sample:

```
<input size="20" type="password" value="password">
```

- **Text area**—These form fields permit free-flowing text for multiline text input. Data such as comments, descriptions, complete addresses, multiple FedEx tracking numbers or any other input that can potentially spill over to another line should be ideally captured in text areas.

Sample:

```
<textarea name="unboundtext" rows="4" cols="20">Text...on multiple lines.
Unbound</textarea>
```

- **Option buttons**—These input fields allow the user to select only one value from a set of options. For example, to identify your user's age group you could provide a set of option buttons categorizing the age groups as 15-19, 20-25, and so on.

Sample:

```
<input type="radio" name="radio" value="radio 1">
```

- **Check boxes**—If you have ever been a part of a survey, you might have checked a lot of boxes as answers to some questions. This feature has been extended to the Web in the form of check boxes. Check boxes are useful if the input required is for a yes/no or a true/false question. Some examples are smoker, married, play cricket, and so on.

Syntax:

```
<input name="smoker" type="checkbox" checked value="true">
```

- **Option menus or drop-down lists**—These fields allow a user to choose from a drop-down list of items. You might consider using this field if there are more than two choices for the input and when the display area is limited.

Listing 3.1 shows the source for a sample drop-down list containing four items with the first item selected.

Listing 3.1   Usage of the Options Menu Input Field

```
<select>
      <option value="1" selected="true">Choice 1</ option >
      <option value="2">Choice 2</ option >
      <option value="3">Choice 3</ option >
      <option value="4">Choice 4</ option >
</select>
```

- **List boxes**—These inputs are similar to Option menus, except that the visible area can be set to more than one row. They also allow the user to select more than one item.

  Listing 3.2 contains the source for a sample HTML list containing multiple selected items.

Listing 3.2   Usage of the List Input Field

```
<select size="4" multiple>
     <option value="1">Item 1</ option >
     <option value="2">Item 2</ option >
     <option value="3" selected="true">Item 3</ option >
     <option value="4" selected="true">Item 4</ option >
</select>
```

- **Buttons**—These allow the user to submit data in the HTML fields to the Web server to be processed by a specified JSP. Reset buttons, like the name suggests, reset the values in the fields within a form to their original values.

  Sample:

  ```
  <input type="submit" name="Submit" value="Submit Button">
  <input type="reset" value="Reset Button">
  ```

If you have submitted information on the Web before, you might have noticed the different approaches that Web sites have to capture user's data. In some sites, while providing your personal information, you need to specify your complete address within a multiline text area and in another you need to specify a street address, city, and zip code in different text fields and also choose from a list of states and countries.

 Note   Rule of thumb: If the input is limited to a definite set of values, allow the user to select from options rather than allowing the user to type out the values. For one, it prevents misspelled values for inputs and second it saves the user from remembering possibly abstruse values for fields. For example, you might want to save the user the trouble of finding out the numeric equivalent for the month of August and simply let the user choose the item August from the drop-down list while specifying a value for a month in the form.

To capture the user data for the Calendar application you will need to define two input-fields: the month and year. As you would typically be using the Gregorian calendar that contains twelve months, you should allow the user to choose from a list of the month names rather than type the month's name or its numeric equivalent. For capturing the year information, a text field would serve the purpose.

You will also need to add a Submit button to send the data to the server for processing. You could also specify a Reset button, but because you have only two fields it would be overkill and would waste valuable display area, as well as potentially distracting the user with the extra button to click.

Defining the HTML Fields

Now that you have identified the fields in the input page, you can add the input fields within the HTML form:

- Year

```
<input type="text" name="year" size="20" maxlength="4">
```

- Month

  Listing 3.3 displays the source for the drop-down list containing the month names.

Listing 3.3   HTML Source for the Month Options Menu Using Hard-Coded Values

```
<select name="month">
        <option value="0">January</option>
        <option value="1">February</option>
        <option value="2">March</option>
        <option value="3">April</option>
        <option value="4">May</option>
        <option value="5">June</option>
        <option value="6">July</option>
        <option value="7">August</option>
        <option value="8">September</option>
        <option value="9">October</option>
        <option value="10">November</option>
        <option value="11" selected="true">December</option>
</select>
```

The values for the field might not be the same as the text that will be displayed in the drop-down list, as you can see in the source of the previous menu.

You can also dynamically generate the options for the menu using a scriptlet like you did for obtaining the month names in month.jsp as shown in Listing 3.4.

Listing 3.4   JSP Source for Dynamically Generating the Month Options

```
<%@ page import="java.text.DateFormatSymbols" %>
<%! String[] monthNames = (new DateFormatSymbols()).getMonths(); %>

<select name="month">
<%
    int selectedMonth = 11;
    // Print all the options
```

```
    for (int i = 0; i < 12 ; i++) {
        out.print("<option value=\""+ i + "\"");
        if (i == month) {
            out.print(" selected=\"true\"");
        }
        out.println(">" + monthNames[i] + "</option>");
    } // end for-loop
%>
</select>
```

EXCURSION
HTTP Parameter Passing Methods

In the static Web world, the client requests a particular document using a URL. For dynamic Web pages, requests are specified using two main formats as defined by HTTP: GET and POST. In both, the URL of target JSP/application specified in the form constitutes a part of the request. The user-specified values are passed depending on the request method defined for the form:

- **GET**—In the GET request method, the browser rewrites the URL by including the parameters from the form as shown in the following list:

    1. The browser identifies the form which was submitted.

    2. Gathers all the name-value pairs from the input fields of the form.

    3. Encodes the spaces and other special characters in the name and values.

    4. Concatenates the pairs obtained above after separating them by ampersands (&) to create the query string.

    5. Appends the query string to the targeted JSP's URL.

    6. Sends the string obtained as above to the Web server.

       The Web server extracts the targeted JSP/application from the request and passes the query string as an environment variable to it.

- **POST**—Almost the same as GET, except the browser does not append the query string to the targeted JSP's URL but instead directs it to the standard input of the Web server. The Web server reads the content by reading a specified number of bytes from the standard input and passes on the information to the JSP/CGI application.

Each parameter passing mechanism has its own advantages. The GET protocol allows you to capture state, defined by the user values appended in the URL, so it can be bookmarked for use later or be used as another hyperlink.

The disadvantage is that some Web servers have the restriction of handling request URLs that are not more than 255 characters in length. So if you want to pass large data across you should consider using POST. Also you wouldn't like storing and passing passwords in the request URLs.

In your Web application you would use a mix of the two methods depending on your requirements: capturing state (GET) and passing large amounts of data and shielding information (POST).

Putting the Input Page Together

The input page can be an HTML or a JSP (by a mere switch of the file extension). Although the page doesn't contain any JSP tags or directives, you can still set it as a JSP. For the form, you can specify the request method as GET because the data is small and doesn't contain any sensitive information. You can add the different HTML fields within the input page, input.jsp, as shown in Listing 3.5. Figure 3.3 displays the output of the page in a browser.

Listing 3.5   input.jsp: Source of the Input Page

```
<html>
<head>
    <title>Calendar Input Page</title>
</head>
<body>
    <center><h1>Calendar Viewer</h1></center>
    <table border=0 WIDTH="500" >
        <tr>
            <td></td>
            <td width="80%"><font size=+2>Overview</font> <br>Provide the Month and
            Year andclick on the Submit button to view the Calendar for the Month.
             <p><br>
            <form method="get" action="month.jsp" name="monthform">
            <table border="0" >
                <tr>
                    <td width="40%"><b>Month:</b></td>
                    <td><select name="month">
                            <option value="0">January</option>
                            <option value="1">February</option>
                            <option value="2">March</option>
                            <option value="3">April</option>
                            <option value="4">May</option>
                            <option value="5">June</option>
                            <option value="6">July</option>
                            <option value="7">August</option>
                            <option value="8">September</option>
                            <option value="9">October</option>
                            <option value="10">November</option>
                            <option value="11" selected="true">December</option>
                        </select></td>
                </tr>
                <tr>
                    <td><b>Year:</b></td>
                    <td><input type="text" name="year" size="20" maxlength="4">
                    </td>
                </tr>
            </table>
            <br><p>
```

```
                <input TYPE="submit" NAME="Submit" ID="Submit" VALUE="Submit">
                <input TYPE="reset" NAME="Reset" ID="Reset" VALUE="Reset">
                </form></td>
        </tr>
    </table>
    </body>
    </html>
```

Fig. 3.3

The Input page rendered in Netscape Navigator

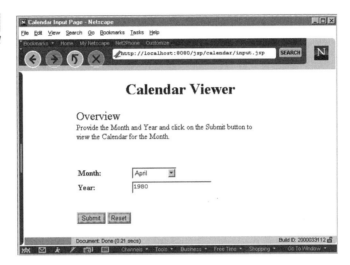

Enhancing the Monthly Calendar JSP

In this section, you will enhance the JSP you created in the previous chapter rather than reinvent one from the ground up. Most application development works that way. You always have to enhance or fix an application rather than build it again from scratch. An extra change you can make is to avoid highlighting the current day in the calendar.

Extracting User Parameters Using the Request Implicit Object

You can obtain the values specified by the user for an input field using another implicit object prepared by the JSP container, the request object, within a scriptlet as shown in the following example:

```
<% String valueAsString = request.getParameter("parameter"); %>
```

You could directly print it using an expression:

```
<%= request.getParameter("parameter") %>
```

In this case, you will need to create a scriptlet that will extract the parameters and parse them to obtain the numeric values for the month and year. After you extract these values you need to set them in the calendar instance to make it represent the specified date rather than the current one. Add a calendar initialization scriptlet in the body before the "Generate Cells for Month" scriptlet as shown in Listing 3.6. Figure 3.4 shows the output for April, 1980.

Listing 3.6   month.jsp: The Extract Parameters Scriptlet

```
<%
        int month = Integer.parseInt(request.getParameter("month"));
        int year = Integer.parseInt(request.getParameter("year"));
        cal.set(year, month, 1);
%>
```

Fig. 3.4

*The Generated
Calendar for the
specified date*

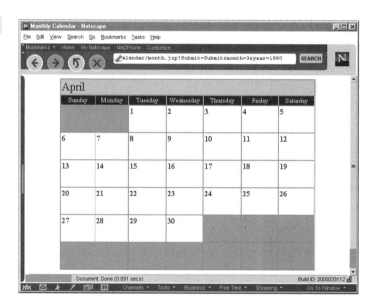

Handling Exceptional Conditions

Had the user entered an invalid year, a sight equivalent to the "blue screen of death" would flash before the user's eyes. Figure 3.5 displays the output in the browser had the user entered "aaaa" for the year:

Figure 3.5 shows an exception that occurred in the JSP indicating that the parseInt method couldn't parse the data. The exception is propagated to the user in case there are no error-handling routines. Such sights could rattle visitors to your site or users of your application, so much so that that they might never visit it again.

Figure 3.5

A Runtime Exception propagated to the browser

There are different ways to prevent and handle such exceptional conditions. You might want to use some or all of the following mechanisms:

- Using error pages
- Performing client-side validations using a scripting language
- Performing server-side validations in the JSP

Using Error Pages

In the event of an exception occurring on the server side, you might want to gracefully exit by specifying error pages for your JSPs. When exceptions occur within the JSP, the JSP container will automatically redirect to the error page. Error pages will trap arbitrary runtime exceptions and are good indications of bugs in the program.

You need to create an error page, error.jsp, that displays a generic error as shown in Listing 3.7.

Listing 3.7   error.jsp: Displaying a Generic Error Message

```
<%@ page isErrorPage="true" %>
<html>
<head>
    <title>Oops!</title>
</head>
<body>
<h1>We are sorry</h1>
The page you have just reached has some errors.
Our technical staff has been informed of the error and will fix it
```

Listing 3.7   continued

```
as soon as possible.
<p>
Error: <%= exception.getMessage() %>
<p>
Thank you for your patience
</body>
</html>
```

To specify error.jsp as the error page for JSPs, modify page directives to include the errorPage parameter:

```
<%@ page import="java.util.*, java.text.DateFormat" errorPage="error.jsp" %>
```

Figure 3.6 shows the error page as displayed in a browser when the user inputs an invalid year.

Figure 3.6

The Error Page displayed on an error

You can enhance the error JSP to send an email informing the support staff about the error as shown in the next chapter. In this way they can take corrective action to fix the bug.

Performing Client-Side Validations Using JavaScript

The second approach to preventing such an erroneous situation from occurring is to nip it at its bud. You can embed validation routines in your input page defined using a *client-side scripting language*. This way the user's data can be checked before being sent to the server, and also reduce network traffic by preventing roundtrips from the server.

Most browsers today support at least one client-side scripting language, with JavaScript being the most popular among them all. You can create routines using these scripting languages to check whether the data supplied by the user is valid, and alert the user of the mistake right away, without having to send the request with the incorrect data to the server.

JavaScript enables you to access different elements of your document using the Document Object Model and also provides some methods to operate on basic data types.

 The Document Object Model provides a programmatic access to the document. Each element of the document is a part of the hierarchy with the window containing the document as the root. In JavaScript such elements are known as *Navigator Objects*.

You can access and update each Navigator Object in the document with JavaScript by using its location within the hierarchy. For example, to retrieve the title of the document being displayed in the window, you can use `document.title`. To access the value of the month input field within the form named `monthform` you can use `document.monthform.month.value` in your JavaScript routine.

In Listing 3.8, the Submit button has been replaced with a JavaScript enhanced button. It defines a handler for the `onClick` method passing the form in which the event occurred as a parameter. The validation method extracts the value of the year field, parses it, and checks if the number obtained from that operation is a valid one. If it is not valid, determined from the return value of the `isNan()` operation, it opens an alert window displaying the error message as shown in Figure 3.7. If it is valid, it submits the form to the server. No checks need to be done for the month field because the input is constrained to the values displayed in the drop-down list.

Listing 3.8   input.jsp: Validation Routine Written in JavaScript

```
<html>
<head>
    <title>Calendar Input Page</title>
<script language="JavaScript">

<!-- Hide script from old browsers
function validate(f) {
    intValue = parseInt(f.year.value);
    if (isNaN(intValue)) {
        alert("Please enter a valid year");
        return false;
    }
    else {
        f.submit();
    }
```

Listing 3.8   continued

```
}
// End hiding -->

</script>
</head>
<body>
    <center><h1>Calendar Viewer</h1></center>
    <table border=0 WIDTH="500" >
        <tr>
            <td></td>
            <td width="80%"><font size=+2>Overview</font> <br>Provide the Month
              and Year andclick on the Submit button to view the Calendar for
              the Month. <p><br>
            <form method="get" action="month.jsp" name="monthform"
                  onSubmit="validate(this)">
            <table border="0" >
                <tr>
                    <td width="40%"><b>Month:</b></td>
                    <td><select name="month">
                            <option value="0">January</option>
                            <option value="1">February</option>
                            <option value="2">March</option>
                            <option value="3">April</option>
                            <option value="4">May</option>
                            <option value="5">June</option>
                            <option value="6">July</option>
                            <option value="7">August</option>
                            <option value="8">September</option>
                            <option value="9">October</option>
                            <option value="10">November</option>
                            <option value="11" selected="true">December</option>
                        </select></td>
                </tr>
                <tr>
                    <td><b>Year:</b></td>
                    <td><input type="text" name="year" size="20" maxlength="4">
                        </td>
                </tr>
            </table>
            <br><p>
            <input TYPE="button" NAME="Submit" VALUE="Submit"
                  onClick="validate(this.form)">
            <input TYPE="reset" NAME="Reset" VALUE="Reset">
            </form></td>
        </tr>
    </table>
    </body>
    </html>
```

> **Note**
>
> You should provide the onSubmit handler in the form tag as well. This allows the browser to validate the form data when the user submits the form by hitting the Enter button.

Figure 3.7

Alert displayed using JavaScript on an invalid input

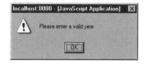

Performing Server-Side Validations

Client-side validations aren't always the recommended error-handling mechanism because of the following reasons:

- The browser might not support JavaScript. Older browsers might not support any scripting languages.
- The user might have disabled the feature.
- If the GET request method is being used, the user can set the value of the parameters by altering the URL, thus bypassing the validation routines as shown in Figure 3.8.

Figure 3.8

Manually specifying the parameters by altering the URL in the browser

You should validate the user values within the JSP and should process the values only if they have passed the validation. In the monthly calendar JSP, you should check whether the month and year provided by the user are valid integral values. You should also provide the user with feedback about the data and the mistakes in them that they provided.

Let's alter the scriptlet that reads the request parameters and initializes the java.util.Calendar instance. First, you need to create a declaration for a string representing the message you want to send across to the user when an invalid year is specified. Now enclose the potentially troublesome code within a try-catch block. In this case it's when you parse the year string to its integral equivalent.

If the operation results in an exceptional condition, forward the request to the input JSP, passing the error message as a parameter, so that the user can retry sending the information. In the JSP forward tag you need to specify the name of the JSP to which the request needs to be redirected, input.jsp in this case. You can also specify additional parameters, such as the error message for the year field, yearMsg, and the error message for the month field, monthMsg.

The JSP forward tag can not be included within the scriptlet, hence the scriptlet needs to be divided into two parts, as shown in Listing 3.9:

- For parsing the request parameters and catching the exceptions.
- For closing the if block in the previous scriptlet and for setting the values in the calendar instance.

Listing 3.9   input.jsp: Validation Routine in the JSP

```
<%! public final static String INVALID_YEAR = "Please enter a valid year," +
            " without any spaces, alphabets and special characters";
    public final static String INVALID_MONTH = "Please enter a valid month"; %>
<%
        int month = -1;
        int year = -1;
        String monthError = "";
        String yearError = "";
        try {   month = Integer.parseInt(request.getParameter("month"));
        } catch Exception exc) {
            monthError = INVALID_MONTH;
        }

        // Validate the year
        try {
            year = Integer.parseInt(request.getParameter("year"));
        } catch (Exception exc) {
            yearError = INVALID_YEAR;
        }

        if (!(monthError.length() == 0 && yearError.length() == 0)) {
%>

    <jsp:forward page="input.jsp">
        <jsp:param name="yearMsg" value="<%= yearError%>"/>
        <jsp:param name="monthMsg" value="<%= monthError%>"/>
    </jsp:forward>

<%      }
    cal.set(year, month, 1);
%>
```

You also need to alter input.jsp to allow the error message to be displayed. Input.jsp will be used for accepting the first time input as well as for the retries.

The error message that was passed as a parameter in the forward tag can be obtained just like any other request parameter from the 'request' implicit object by specifying the parameter name.

A good place to display the error message in a Web document is next to the source itself. Displaying the error message in a different color allows the user to notice the message. You can add the error message for the year next to the year label and display it with a red color to highlight the problem as shown in Listing 3.10.

Listing 3.10   input.jsp: Validation Routine in the JSP

```
<tr>
    <td><b>Year:</b><br>
        <font color="red" size="-2">
        <%
            String yearMsg = request.getParameter("yearMsg");
            out.println(((yearMsg == null) ? "": yearMsg));
        %>
        </font>
    </td>
    <td valign="top">
        <input type="text" name="year" size="20" maxlength="4">
    </td>
</tr>
```

You might also want to set the valid values within the input.jsp so the user doesn't have to enter it again. Earlier, you saw how the options for the menu could be generated dynamically by using a scriptlet. You need to enhance the scriptlet to allow the option representing the valid month to be selected in the drop-down list as shown in Listing 3.11.

Listing 3.11   input.jsp: Enhancing the Generate Month Options Scriptlet to Display Existing Selections

```
<%! String[] monthNames = (new DateFormatSymbols()).getMonths(); %>
<%
    int month = 11;
    try {
        month = Integer.parseInt(request.getParameter("month"));
    } catch (Exception exc) {
    }

    // Print all the options
    for (int i = 0; i < 12 ; i++) {
        out.print("<option value=\""+ i + "\"");
        if (i == month) {
```

Listing 3.11   continued

```
            out.print(" selected=\"true\"");
        }
        out.println(">" + monthNames[i] + "</option>");
    } // end for-loop
%>
```

Figure 3.9 shows the error message displayed in the input page when an incorrect year is specified.

Figure 3.9

The Revamped Input Page displaying error information

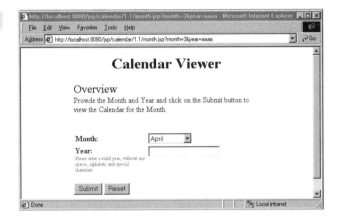

Creating a Yearly Calendar

You can create a yearly calendar by including the output of month.jsp twelve times to represent each month of the year. You can specify the month by passing the month and year parameters to the included page as shown in Listing 3.12. Figure 3.10 shows how the yearly calendar would look for the year 2000.

Listing 3.12   year.jsp: Including the Output of the `smallmonth` JSP for Displaying the Year's Calendar

```
<table>
<%
    for (int i = 0; i < 12; i++) {
        if (i%3 == 0)
            out.println("<tr>");

%>
<td>
    <jsp:include page="smallmonth.jsp" flush="true">
        <jsp:param name="month" value="<%= i %>"/>
        <jsp:param name="year" value="2000"/>
    </jsp:include>
</td>
```

```
<%
        if (i%3+1 == 0)
            out.println("</tr>");
    }
%>
</table>
```

Figure 3.10

The Year Calendar for 2000 generated using year.jsp

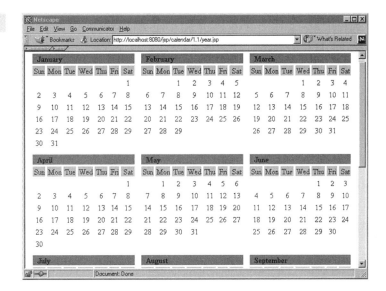

Summary

In this chapter you learned how to pass information to the Web server using HTML forms. You also discovered how to extract the request parameters and produce dynamic content using them. You also learned the different error-handling mechanisms for your Web application.

With regards to JSPs, you saw how to use implicit objects to extract request and error information. You also learned about request forwarding and parameterized inclusion of JSPs.

Next Steps

In the next chapter you will learn how to use JavaBeans in your JSPs to bring in an element of reusability and also to enhance the form validation process.

Adding JavaBeans to Implement Functionality and Send Email

As you probably noticed in the preceding two chapters, the JSP code has been well endowed with scriptlets. This has made understanding both the HTML source and the Java code interspersed in it very difficult. To add to those woes, the scriptlets cannot be tested independently of the JSP, so errors can be detected only at the content-generation stage.

So far, you have seen how to include the output of the monthly calendar into another JSP's content, but the reusability of the content-generation logic was low, and the scriptlets, declarations, and other JSP elements had to be duplicated to be used in the smallmonth JSP. In this chapter, our aim will be to create reusable components that will aid in the development process across different JSPs.

What You Are Going To Do

In this chapter, you will modify the Calendar application to incorporate components of JavaBeans to aid in content generation and to validate form data and store information for generating the calendar. You will also create a JavaBean to send email from within JSPs.

Introduction to JavaBeans

JavaBeans is the component model for Java. It is a mechanism for packaging Java classes so that they can be easily understood and used by IDEs in rapid application development.

JavaBeans can be thought of as packaged classes containing the following elements:

- **Methods**—These are public methods that can be invoked on a class.
- **Properties**—These are public methods that provide accessor and mutator methods for different attributes of the class. For example, a Java button has a property called `label` that can be used for getting and setting the text displayed in it.
- **Events**—These elements describe the notifications that a class produces. A Java button, for example, has an event called `ActionEvent` that notifies registered listeners when the button is clicked.

The main aim of encapsulating Java classes as JavaBeans by describing these elements, is to allow IDEs to build applications from them. A component providing such information can easily be "wired up" with another using its events, methods, and properties. Figure 4.1 shows how you can visually compose an application by dropping beans from a palette. The IDE *introspects* into the bean's properties, events, and methods, and provides this information to you to enable you to assemble applications. You can customize a JavaBean—for example, changing the label of a button bean—by changing its properties in its property sheet.

Figure 4.1

Visually composing an application using JavaBeans in VisualAge for Java

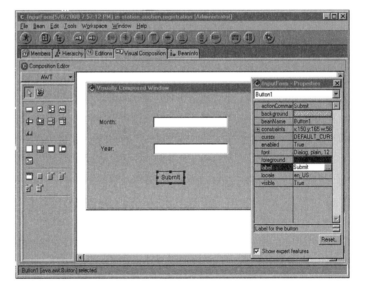

 Every public, non-abstract Java class is also a JavaBean.

Properties and events are in reality plain public methods adhering to special naming conventions and are not additions to the Java programming language.

An input property, xxx, of a bean implies that the class contains a public getter method named getXxx() that has a return type. A public setter method named setYyy() having a single input parameter becomes an output property: yyy. If both getter and setter methods, such as getZzz() and setZzz(), are defined in the class, the two methods compose the input/output property: zzz. If, for some reason, you cannot adhere to the naming conventions and want to promote the method as a property, isAAA() for example, you can create a special BeanInfo class for the bean that returns an array of property descriptors specifying the aaa property with isAAA() as the getter method.

Listing 4.1 shows the definition for an input property (month) and an output property (year).

Listing 4.1   Methods Representing the month and year Properties

```
public void setMonth(String month) {
    this.month = month;
} // the write-only month property

public String getYear() {
    return this.year;
} // the read-only year property
```

Events are generated in a bean by notifying registered listeners when they occur. Invoking callback methods on listeners performs this notification. To do this, you need to define a new interface for the event that contains the event callback methods, and make the classes that want to be notified about them implement the interface. The event-generating class keeps a collection of all these listeners and invokes the specific event method on all of them when it needs to generate an event.

To define an event for the bean, you need to define two additional methods in the class. These methods are used for registering event listeners. You also need to define a listener interface and an event object to complete the method definitions.

Table 4.1 describes an event, XxxEvent, that is generated by a class within which the two methods are defined. An interface, XxxListener, extending from java.util. EventListener, must also be created. It defines callback methods that can be invoked by the JavaBean so as to notify the registered listeners. Listing 4.2 contains the source for the definition of the XxxListener interface specifying two callback methods, xxxOccurred and startedProcessing.

Table 4.1   Event Methods

Method Signature	Description
`Public void addXxxListener(XxxListener alistener)`	Registers a listener of type `XxxListener` for receiving notifications
`Public void removeXxxListener(XxxListener alistener)`	Unregisters the listener

Listing 4.2   Defining the Event Listener

```
public interface XxxListener extends java.util.EventListener {
    public void xxxOccurred(XxxEvent event);
    public void startedProcessing();
}
```

If the JavaBean needs to pass some information to the listener, it can do so by setting it in an event object, `XxxEvent` in this case. `XxxEvent` is a class that extends from `java.util.EventObject` and can contain public fields or methods for storing and passing information. Listing 4.3 defines an event object that can be used for passing information to an `XxxListener`.

Listing 4.3   Defining the Event Object

```
public class XxxEvent extends java.util.EventObject {
    public int errCode;
    public String toString() {
        // Your code for returning the error message goes here
    }
}
```

You can package your classes within Java archives, or jar files, to easily distribute your beans. Many third-party beans are available on the Net in this format. You can find a wealth of beans in the AlphaBeans site located at `http://www.alphaWorks.ibm.com/alphabeans`.

Modifying the Calendar Application by Adding JavaBeans

Our prime aim in this section will be to reduce the scriptlets and declarations in the JSPs—month.jsp and input.jsp. You may not be able to totally do away with scriptlets (for example, while iterating through a loop to generate the cells), but you can delegate a lot of tasks to classes.

Creating the MonthBean

You will need to create a JavaBean, MonthBean, that will offtake a lot of declarations and scriptlets within month.jsp. The aim of this exercise is to provide the JSP with information that can easily be consumed by using simple expressions instead of scriptlets.

Table 4.2 shows the list of properties in MonthBean.

Table 4.2   MonthBean's Properties

Property Name	Type	Description
month	Input	Sets the month for the calendar
year	Input	Sets the year for the calendar
today	Output	Returns whether the specified date is the current one
startCell	Output	Returns the cell number in the 42-cell grid where the first day of the month lands
endCell	Output	Returns the cell number in the 42-cell grid where the last day of the month lands

The bean has two significant methods apart from the setter and getter methods:

- **update**—Sets the specified date, using the day, month, and year information, in the calendar.
- **getDayName**—Returns the day's name for the specified index.

If you have programmed in Java before, you can easily implement MonthBean using the information about its properties, events, and methods. Some information on how to implement the methods can also be obtained from the scriptlets described in month.jsp.

To get started in the process of JavaBean creation, here's what you need to do.

First, create a directory structure station\auction\calendar within your current working directory. Next, create a new Java source file, Month.java, using any text-based editor. You will need to specify the following information to create a fully working bean:

- Provide package information
- Specify packages and classes that need to be imported for use within the class
- Declare fields in the class
- Declare constructors
- Define setter and getter methods for the different properties
- Define your custom methods

The following sections explain how to accomplish each of these tasks in detail.

Provide Package Information for `MonthBean`

The first line in your source is the *package declaration*. You should specify a package name to uniquely identify your classes and to bunch related classes together. The package name should relate to the directory structure it is created in, namely `station\auction\calendar`.

A common naming scheme for package names is to reverse the URL of your company and suffix extra hierarchical information, just as you name any other URL. For example, the package names of some of Apache Software Foundation's (`http://www.apache.org/`) classes are

```
org.apache.tomcat.servlets
org.apache.tomcat.protocol.war
org.apache.jasper.compiler
```

In this case, you can use the following package declaration because the class belongs to the calendar application of Auction Station:

```
package station.auction.calendar;
```

Specify the Classes and Packages to Be Imported

Next, you need to specify the `import` statements for your class. The packages and classes to be imported are the same as the ones you specified in the page directive's `import` attribute of month.jsp version 1.1. These specify the classes you will use within your class, as shown in Listing 4.4.

Listing 4.4   MonthBean.java: Specifying the `import` Statements

```
package station.auction.calendar;

import java.text.DateFormat;
import java.text.DateFormatSymbols;
import java.util.*;
```

Declare Fields for the `MonthBean` class

After you define the `import` statements, you need to specify the class signature. The signature specifies the visibility of the class, which could be either public, signifying that any class could access it, or package-level, denoting that only classes within the same package could access it. `MonthBean` will be embedded within the JSP, so it needs to be marked public. Also, because it provides implementation, it is marked a class rather than an interface:

```
public class MonthBean {
```

Next, you will need to specify constants and variables that you will use in your class:

- Constants, as the name denotes, are fields that are immutable. In the
  MonthBean, you can specify the DAYSINMONTH integer array containing the standard number of days in the months of the year:

```
public final static int[] DAYSINMONTH =
    { 31, 28, 31, 30, 31, 30, 31, 31, 30, 31, 30, 31 };
```

  The array is marked `final` to mark it as a constant, implying that its value cannot be modified within the class. It is also declared as `static` so that the field is
  shared by all instances of the class.

For any nonstatic field declared within a class, creating a new instance of the class
would apportion additional space for the field in memory. If the field were marked as
`static`, memory would be allocated only once: when the class is loaded. This field
can be used by all instances of the class just as they would use any other field.

- Variables are fields that will change. You need to define the variables that you
  will need in your class, such as the calendar instance, month names, and day
  names as shown in Listing 4.5.

Listing 4.5   MonthBean.java: Declaring Fields for the Class

```
package station.auction.calendar;

import java.text.DateFormat;
import java.text.DateFormatSymbols;
import java.util.*;

public class MonthBean {
    public final static int[] DAYSINMONTH =
        { 31, 28, 31, 30, 31, 30, 31, 31, 30, 31, 30, 31 };

    protected Calendar cal = Calendar.getInstance();
    protected String[] monthNames = null;
    protected DateFormatSymbols symbols = null;
    protected int today = cal.get(Calendar.DAY_OF_MONTH);
```

You can specify the visibility of fields as one of the four types listed in
Table 4.3.

Table 4.3   Visibility of Fields (in Ascending Order of Accessibility)

Visibility Type	Description
private	Can be accessed only within the class it is defined in
<none>	Can be accessed by other classes within the same package as well
protected	Can be accessed by all subclasses as well
public	Can be accessed by all classes

You can mark these fields as protected to allow even subclasses to access them.

You could define month names as constants, but because we are internationalizing these names, you need to obtain that information for a specific locale at runtime.

- Property fields describe the class. For every output property of MonthBean, such as the month and year, you will need to create fields to store the information, as shown in Listing 4.6.

Listing 4.6   MonthBean.java: Declaring Fields to Store Properties

```
protected int month = cal.get(Calendar.MONTH);
protected int year = cal.get(Calendar.YEAR);
```

You can also set default values for the fields, such as the current month and year for the month and year fields respectively, to allow the bean to be used for the current date without having to specify the input properties.

Declare Constructors

A *constructor* is code invoked when a new instance of a class is created. You can initialize certain variables with parameters known at runtime.

The syntax of a constructor definition is

```
<scope/visibility> ClassName(<arguments>)
```

It has the same name as the Class it is defined in, and it can have an argument list but doesn't return any value.

You can create a constructor that doesn't take any parameters and initialize the month and day names in it, as shown in Listing 4.7.

Listing 4.7   MonthBean.java: Defining the Default Constructor

```
package station.auction.calendar;

import java.text.DateFormat;
import java.text.DateFormatSymbols;
import java.util.*;

public class MonthBean {
    public final static int[] DAYSINMONTH =
        { 31, 28, 31, 30, 31, 30, 31, 31, 30, 31, 30, 31 };

    protected String[] monthNames = null;
    protected DateFormatSymbols symbols = null;
    protected Calendar cal = Calendar.getInstance();
    protected int today = cal.get(Calendar.DAY_OF_MONTH);
```

```
    protected int month = cal.get(Calendar.MONTH);
    protected int year = cal.get(Calendar.YEAR);

    public MonthBean() {
        symbols = new DateFormatSymbols();
        monthNames = symbols.getMonths();
    }
```

You can create another constructor that takes a particular locale, specified by its language and region, as a parameter and initialize the variables, as in Listing 4.8.

Listing 4.8   MonthBean.java: The Constructor Using Locale Data as Argument

```
public MonthBean(String language, String region) {
    Locale theLocale = new Locale(language, region);
    symbols = new DateFormatSymbols(theLocale);
    monthNames = symbols.getMonths();
}
```

 Note   You can define any number of constructors taking different parameters, but you will need to define the default or no-arg constructor to allow the bean to be used in JSPs via bean tags.

The default constructor does the same operations as the second except that it uses the current locale for initializing the symbols and monthNames variables. If you needed to change the initialization process for any of the variables, you would need to modify the code in two places in the class. Object technology is all about code reuse. Code maintenance is a lot easier if you practice reuse.

You could chain the constructors to avoid this duplication by passing the default locale information as shown in Listing 4.9.

Listing 4.9   MonthBean.java: Constructor Chaining

```
public MonthBean() {
        this("EN", "US");
}
```

Declare Methods for MonthBean's Input Properties

You now need to define methods that translate into the different properties of the bean. The setter methods for the write-only or input properties are simple, and you just need to set the value of the field to the parameter passed to the method, as shown in Listing 4.10.

Listing 4.10   MonthBean.java: Specifying Setter Methods for the Input Properties

```
public void setMonth(int monthArg) {
    this.month = monthArg;
}

public void setYear(int yearArg) {
    this.year = yearArg;
}
```

You can also define additional setter methods for the properties that take a String as argument instead of int. This will allow JSP information that is text-based to be easily passed to the bean. Listing 4.11 shows how you can *overload* the setter methods with a different input type.

Listing 4.11   MonthBean.java: Overloading the Setter Methods

```
public void setMonth(java.lang.String monthArg) {
    try {
        int month = Integer.parseInt(monthArg);
        setMonth(month);
    } catch (Exception exc) {
    } // end try-catch block
}

public void setYear(java.lang.String yearArg) {
    try {
        int year = Integer.parseInt(yearArg);
        setYear(year);
    } catch (Exception exc) {
    } // end try-catch block
}
```

Declare Methods for MonthBean's Output Properties

The output or read properties, such as monthName, startCell, and endCell, are implemented using getter methods. These properties are evaluated and therefore require some extra coding, as shown in Listing 4.12.

Listing 4.12   MonthBean.java: Specifying Getter Methods for the Output Properties

```
public String getMonthName() {
    return monthNames[cal.get(Calendar.MONTH)];
}

public int getStartCell() {
    Calendar beginOfMonth = Calendar.getInstance();
    beginOfMonth.set(year, month, 0);
    return beginOfMonth.get(Calendar.DAY_OF_WEEK);
}
```

```
public int getEndCell() {
    cal.set(year, month, 1);
    int endCell = DAYSINMONTH[month] + getStartCell() - 1;
    if (month==Calendar.FEBRUARY &&
        ((GregorianCalendar) cal).isLeapYear(year) ) {
        endCell++;
    }
    return endCell;
}
```

Define Custom Methods

You will also need to define methods that do the following:

- Update the calendar instance with the latest values for the month and year
- Return the name of the day of the week by its numeric equivalent

Listing 4.13 shows how to implement these methods.

Listing 4.13   MonthBean.java: Specifying Custom Methods

```
public void update() {
    cal.set(this.year, this.month, 1);
}

public String getDayName(int day, boolean longFormat) {
    if (longFormat)
        return symbols.getWeekdays()[day];
    return symbols.getShortWeekdays()[day];
}
```

Testing the Bean

After you have finished defining the methods, you are all ready to compile your bean to create the bytecodes. Save the file and don't forget to close the braces. Run the following command in the command prompt where MonthBean.java is stored:

```
javac MonthBean.java
```

Look out for any compilation errors. If the Java source was typed correctly as per the instructions, you will find a MonthBean.class file stored in the same directory.

You can write a small test driver for MonthBean. This class uses command-line arguments to set properties of the bean and prints out the values returned by the bean. The source for the driver, TestMB.java, is shown in Listing 4.14.

Listing 4.14   TestMB.java: Testing the Bean

```
package station.auction.calendar;

public class TestMB {
```

Listing 4.14   continued

```
/**
 * Starts the application.
 * @param args an array of command-line arguments
 */
public static void main(java.lang.String[] args) {
    MonthBean mb = new MonthBean();

    mb.setMonth(args[0]);
    mb.setYear(args[1]);
    mb.update();

    System.out.println("Month Name: " + mb.getMonthName());
    System.out.println("Start Cell: " + mb.getStartCell());
    System.out.println("End Cell: " + mb.getEndCell());
}
}
```

Before you compile TestMB.java, you need to set MonthBean.class in the CLASSPATH. The CLASSPATH is an environment variable whose value specifies the directories and jar files that the Java runtime needs to search to load the class files.

You can do this in three ways:

- You can create a directory structure specified by the package name in the current directory. For a package name, station.auction.calendar, you need to create directories station, auction, and calendar within each other, as shown in Figure 4.2.

Figure 4.2

The directory structure required to set MonthBean *in the* CLASSPATH

<current working directory>

station

auction

calendar   ← place your
           class file here

- You can create the directory structure shown in Figure 4.2 within a directory other than the current working directory and make an entry for that directory in the CLASSPATH.

- You can package the classfiles retaining the directory structure as a jar file and include the jar file in the CLASSPATH.

After you set the CLASSPATH, run the test driver by providing the month and year in the command line:

```
java station.auction.calendar.TestMB <month> <year>
```

Figure 4.3 shows the output of TestMB for April 2000. You can compare the output with that of the system calendar.

Figure 4.3

Compare the outputs of MonthBean's *test driver with those of the system calendar*

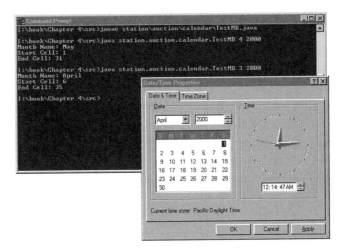

By comparing the outputs manually with a set of known values, you are unit-testing the bean. You can also automate the scripts by setting the inputs and checking the values returned by the bean in the test driver itself.

Creating the `FormValidator` Bean

In the previous chapter, you learned a rather primitive approach to validating the user's requests before processing. Now you will learn how to apply a design pattern for handling form requests and validation. I have borrowed this technique from Govind Seshadri of jGuru (`www.jGuru.com`), who wrote an excellent article titled "Advanced Form Processing Using JSP: Use the Memento Design Pattern with Java Server Pages and JavaBeans" on this topic. This article is available at `http://www.javaworld.com/javaworld/jw-03-2000/jw-0331-ssj-forms.html` (March 2000).

A design pattern is a reusable approach to solving certain problems. A compilation of such patterns or techniques is chronicled in the epic book, *Design Patterns: Elements of Reusable Object-Oriented Software* by Erich Gamma, et al., published by Addison-Wesley in 1995.

You will need to create a bean, `CalendarRequest`, that performs the following functions:

- Stores the request data, accessible as getter properties
- Validates the requests
- Stores error information, if any, associated with the input values

Create a new Java source file, CalendarRequest.java, belonging to the package `station.auction.calendar`. `CalendarRequest` will use two classes from the `java.util.*` package described in Table 4.4. These classes need to be specified in the `import` statement as well.

Table 4.4   Description of the `java.util.*` Classes Used in `CalendarRequest`

Class Name	Description
`java.util.Hashtable`	A keyed collection of objects that allows the storage and retrieval of values by passing a "key".
`java.util.ResourceBundle`	Used for accessing locale-specific information. Locale information is written in text-based property files and mapped to a particular key.

Specifying Error Data in `CalendarRequest`

`CalendarRequest` stores and validates the user-specified request parameters of input.jsp: `month` and `year`. Three errors are possible in these parameters:

- **Invalid value for `month`**—The user specifies a non-numeric value for the month.
- **Invalid value for `year`**—The user specifies a non-numeric value for the year.
- **Out of bounds value for `month`**—The user specifies a numeric value not within 0-11.

This error information will need to be passed back after validation. Because this information is largely static, it can be stored as constants within the class, as shown in Listing 4.15.

Listing 4.15   CalendarRequest.java: Specifying the Errors as Constant Fields

```
package station.auction.calendar;

import java.util.Hashtable;
import java.util.ResourceBundle;

public class CalendarRequest {
    public final static String MONTH_INVALID_BOUNDS = "MONTH_INVALID_BOUNDS";
    public final static String MONTH_INVALID_NUMBER = "MONTH_INVALID_NUMBER";
    public final static String YEAR_INVALID_NUMBER = "YEAR_INVALID_NUMBER";
```

The error constants are not very verbose because the full information is stored within localized property files keyed to these values.

To access the localized information, you will need to add a `ResourceBundle` variable that specifies the property files to be used.

```
protected static java.util.ResourceBundle bundle =
ResourceBundle.getBundle("station.auction.calendar.ErrorMessages");
```

For storing information about the current locale, you need to create a text file, ErrorMessages.properties, in the `station\auction\calendar` directory where your source files are stored. Add the complete error messages stored as key-value pairs in the property file as shown in Listing 4.16.

Listing 4.16　ErrorMessages.properties: Providing the Complete Error Information

```
MONTH_INVALID_BOUNDS=Month should be a number between 0 and 11
MONTH_INVALID_NUMBER=Month is Invalid.
            It should contain only numeric characters.
YEAR_INVALID_NUMBER=Year is Invalid. It should contain only numeric characters.
```

To localize the error information for Spanish, you need to create another file, ErrorMessages_es.properties, and store the localized information for the same keys as shown in Listing 4.17. You can do the same for a different language and region by creating more property files and naming them accordingly.

Listing 4.17　ErrorMessages_es.properties: Providing the Complete Error Information for the Spanish Locale

```
MONTH_INVALID_BOUNDS=No Comprendo-Mes - 0 y 11
MONTH_INVALID_NUMBER=No Comprendo-Mes.
YEAR_INVALID_NUMBER=No Comprendo-Ano.
```

Another advantage of using property files is that you don't need to hard-code the messages within the program. All you need to do is alter the value for the specific key and save the changes. The program picks up the new values the next time you run it without having to recompile the code.

The error information, if any, can be stored in a Hashtable against a key identifying the field in which the error occurred: `month` and `year`.

```
protected Hashtable errors = new Hashtable();
```

To extract localized information from the resource bundle, you can define a method that returns the text for a specified key: in this case one of `MONTH_INVALID_BOUNDS`, `MONTH_INVALID_NUMBER`, or `YEAR_INVALID_NUMBER` as shown in Listing 4.18.

Listing 4.18　CalendarRequest.java: `getLocalMessage()` Method That Returns the Localized Message Using Its Key

```
protected String getLocalMessage(String key) {
    return bundle.getString(key);
} // end getLocalMessage
```

Specifying Properties for `CalendarRequest`

You will need to define two input/output properties, `month` and `year`, to allow the values of the input fields to be set in and obtained from the bean. In addition to the getter and setter methods, you will also need to define fields to store information, as shown in Listing 4.19. You can also create output properties for returning the parameters as integers.

Listing 4.19 CalendarRequest.java: Creating the Month and Year Properties for CalendarRequest

```
protected String fieldMonth = null;
protected String fieldYear = null;

protected int monthAsInt = 11;
protected int yearAsInt = 0;

    public void setMonth(java.lang.String month) {
        fieldMonth = month;
    } // end setter: month

    public void setYear(java.lang.String year) {
        fieldYear = year;
    } // end setter: year

    public java.lang.String getMonth() {
        return fieldMonth;
    } // end getter: month

    public java.lang.String getYear() {
        return fieldYear;
    } // end getter: year

    public int getMonthAsInteger() {
        return monthAsInt;
    }

    public int getYearAsInteger() {
        return yearAsInt;
    }
```

The String properties represent the original values specified by the user for the month and year properties, whereas the int properties are values obtained after processing the String properties.

Adding Methods for Processing and Validating the Request

You will need to add a process method to check the correctness of the input properties, process or parse the Strings to create integer equivalents, and store any error information. Listing 4.20 shows the source for the process method. You first need to check whether the month property is valid by parsing it to create its numerical equivalent. An exceptional condition generated by this operation represents an invalid month value. You will also need to check whether the month is within bounds, between 0 and 11. Finally, you need to check the year property for validity. At the end of the method, you need to return a boolean value representing the success of the process operation. All errors are logged in the Hashtable. A non-empty Hashtable implies a failure, whereas a Hashtable without any errors denotes a success.

Note   In the process method, even if you encounter any errors while processing an input property, you should continue processing the other ones. This will allow you to inform the user about all the errors so that the user can make all the necessary changes without having to keep resending the form until all the errors are detected and fixed.

Listing 4.20   CalendarRequest.java: process() Validating and Processing the Input Properties

```java
public boolean process() {
    // Validate all the parameters
    // Validate the Month
    try {
        monthAsInt = Integer.parseInt(getMonth());
        if (monthAsInt < 0 || monthAsInt > 11) {
            errors.put("month", getLocalMessage(MONTH_INVALID_BOUNDS));
        }
    } catch (NumberFormatException exc) {
        errors.put("month", getLocalMessage(MONTH_INVALID_NUMBER));
    }
    // Validate the year
    try {
        yearAsInt = Integer.parseInt(getYear());
    } catch (NumberFormatException exc) {
        errors.put("year", getLocalMessage(YEAR_INVALID_NUMBER));
    }
    return errors.isEmpty();
} // end method: process
```

Extracting Error Information from CalendarRequest

After you invoke the process method on CalendarRequest, you need to make the error information available for access, to be displayed in the retry page.

Create a new method, getError, that accepts the field name and returns the error associated with it, if any. The Hashtable that stores the errors returns a null value if no errors were found for the particular field. A null should not be displayed on the retry page as it will indicate null in the retry information. Listing 4.21 shows how you can return the error information for a particular field.

Listing 4.21 CalendarRequest.java: getError() Returning the Error Information for a Specific Field

```
public String getError(String field) {
    String errInfo = (String) errors.get(field);
    if (errInfo == null) {
        return "";
    }
    return errInfo;
} // end method: getError
```

Testing the CalendarRequest Bean

Create a test driver, TestCR, that tests the bean with values passed in the command line. It first sets the values obtained from the command line as properties of the bean, invokes the process method on it, and checks for errors. It displays the resultant values of the processed fields as well as the error information, as shown in Listing 4.22.

Listing 4.22 TestCR.java: Test Driver for the CalendarRequest Bean

```
package station.auction.calendar;

public class TestCR {
    public static void main(java.lang.String[] args) {
        CalendarRequest cr = new CalendarRequest();
        cr.setMonth(args[0]);
        cr.setYear(args[1]);

        System.out.println("Month : " + cr.getMonth());
        System.out.println("Year : " + cr.getYear());

        if (!cr.process()) {
            System.out.println(cr.getError("month"));
            System.out.println(cr.getError("year"));
        }

        System.out.println("INT Month : " + cr.getMonthAsInteger());
        System.out.println("INT Year : " + cr.getYearAsInteger());
    }
}
```

Copy the Java source and property files into the calendar directory. You can use the same directory structure as the one for storing MonthBean.java. Compile the source files and run the test driver. Pass different values for the month and year, and test for compliance. Outputs of some test cases are shown in Figure 4.4.

Figure 4.4

Results of testing
`CalendarRequest` *by*
passing different argu-
ments to TestCR

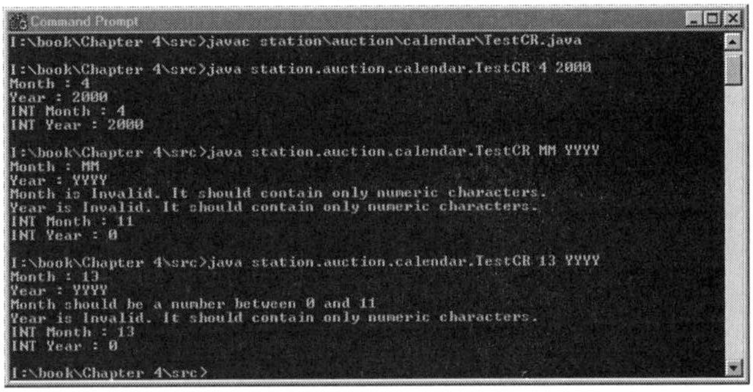

Providing Reusability Using Inheritance

As you might have noticed, some methods and fields of the `CalendarRequest` bean are generic. They include the `errors Hashtable`, the `getError` method, and a constant for an empty string, `EMPTY_STRING`. Any similar form-handling bean can use these elements as well. You can provide some reusability by moving the generic elements to another class and inheriting these features from it in the specific form-handling class, such as `CalendarRequest`.

Create a text file named FormValidator.java defining the `FormValidator` class containing the generic elements, as shown in Listing 4.23.

Listing 4.23   FormValidator.java: Moving the Generic Elements to a Parent Class,
FormValidator

```
package station.auction;
import java.util.Hashtable;

public abstract class FormValidator {
      public final static String EMPTY_STRING = "";
      protected Hashtable errors = new Hashtable();
public void setError(String name, String value) {
        errors.put(name, value);
}
public String getError(String spec) {
    String errInfo = (String) errors.get(spec);
    if (errInfo == null) {
        return EMPTY_STRING;
    }
    return errInfo;
}
}
```

To enforce the design pattern for a form handler and validator bean, you can add an abstract method, `process()`, in the parent class.

```
public abstract boolean process();
```

An *abstract method* is one with no implementation, and an abstract class is one containing at least one abstract method. A subclass of an abstract class must provide concrete implementation for the abstract methods defined in it, unless it is marked abstract itself. Not implementing these methods in the subclass will result in compilation errors.

You will need to make the following modifications to the `CalendarRequest` class:

- Make the `CalendarRequest` class extend from `FormValidator`:

  ```
  public class CalendarRequest extends station.auction.FormValidator
  ```

- Delete the `errors` field and the `getError` method from the class.

Compile the `FormValidator` and `CalendarRequest` source files and run the test cases again.

Create a JavaScript Routine to Generate Code for the Form-Handling Bean

You might have noticed that the technique used in creating the bean for handling the form is simple. You need to follow some steps to create the form-validating bean:

- For a form in the HTML page, <*form-name*>, create a Java source file named <*form-Name*>Request.java. Add the specific package and `import` statements.

- For the form, define the handler and validator class named <*form-Name*>Request extending from `FormValidator`.

- For each field in the form that is not a button, add fields named `field`<*Form-field-Name*> as well as getter and setter methods representing input/output properties having the same name as the form field.

- Add code for methods of the bean, such as `process()`.

You can automate the process of creating JavaBeans that validate a form by creating a JavaScript routine that implements the technique just described. I briefly introduced JavaScript in Chapter 3 while discussing creating client-side scripts to validate HTML forms. An extremely powerful feature of JavaScript is *reflection*, with which you can programmatically traverse the HTML document using its in-memory document model containing different navigator objects. You can use this reflection feature to generate code for any form by traversing through the form elements (input fields, choices except buttons) and appending code associated with them to a string variable. To generate the code, you just need to write the string variable to the browser, as shown in Listing 4.24.

Listing 4.24 CreateBean.js: JavaScript Routine for Generating a Form Validator Bean for a Specified Form

```
function generate(f) {
    beanSource = "<PRE>";
    <!-- Add the import statements and the class definition -->
    beanSource += "import station.auction.FormValidator;\n";
    beanSource += "import java.util.ResourceBundle;\n\n" +
            "public class " + properCase(f.name) +
            "Request extends FormValidator { \n";
    <!-- Iterate through all the fields in the form -->
    for (i = 0; i < f.elements.length; i++) {
        type = f.elements[i].type;
        <!-- Do not process button fields -->
        if (type == "button" || type == "reset" || type == "submit" )
          continue;
        <!-- Define fields for storing each form-field's value -->
        beanSource += "\tprotected String field" +
                properCase(f.elements[i].name) + " = null;\n";
    }
    <!-- Add the resource bundle field -->
    beanSource += "\tprotected ResourceBundle bundle = \n" +
                "\t\tResourceBundle.getBundle(\"ErrorMessages\");\n\n";

    fName = "";
    <!-- Iterate through the fields again to generate
        the getter and setter methods -->
    for (i =0; i < f.elements.length; i++) {
        type = f.elements[i].type;
        if (type == "button" || type == "reset" || type == "submit" )
          continue;

        fName = properCase(f.elements[i].name);

        beanSource += "\tpublic String get" + fName + "() {\n";
        beanSource += "\t\treturn field" + fName + ";\n";
        beanSource += "\t}\n\n";

        beanSource += "\tpublic void set" + fName + "(String arg1) {\n";
        beanSource += "\t\tfield" + fName + " = arg1;\n";
        beanSource += "\t}\n\n";
    }
    <!-- Generate skeleton code for the process method -->
    beanSource +=
        "\tpublic boolean process() {\n\t\treturn errors.isEmpty();\n\t}\n";

    beanSource += "}</PRE>";
    this.document.write(beanSource);
    beanSource = "";
}
```

The properCase function returns a string with its first letter capitalized.

```
function properCase(str) {
    str1 = str.substr(0, 1);
    str2 = str.substr(1, str.length - 1);
    return (str1.toUpperCase() + str2);
}
```

You can incorporate the JavaScript routine in the HTML/JSP pages by adding a <script> tag specifying the file in the head of the HTML/JSP page.

```
<script language="JavaScript" src="CreateBean.js"></script>
```

Note

The <script> tag with the src attribute is supported only by JavaScript 1.2 compliant browsers like Netscape and IE 4+. For browsers supporting earlier versions of JavaScript, you can include the contents of CreateBean.js directly within the <script> tag.

Add an extra button in the form to invoke the generate method for generating the source for the bean, as shown in Listing 4.25.

Listing 4.25   Form.html: Adding a "Generate Source" Button to Invoke the JavaScript Routine

```
<form method="get" action="month.jsp" name="Calendar">
    <table border="0" >
        <tr>
            <td width="40%"><b>Month:</b></td>
            <td><select name="month">
                </select></td>
        </tr>
        <tr>
            <td><b>Year:</b></td>
            <td valign="top"><input type="text" name="year"
                size="20" maxlength="4"></td>
        </tr>
    </table>
    <br><p>
        <input TYPE="Submit" NAME="Submit" VALUE="Submit">
        <input TYPE="reset" NAME="Reset" VALUE="Reset">
        <input TYPE="button" VALUE="Generate Source"
            onClick="generate(this.form)">
</form><
```

Figure 4.5 shows the generated code displayed in the browser for the Calendar form used in input.jsp.

Figure 4.5

Code generated by the JavaScript routine for the Calendar form

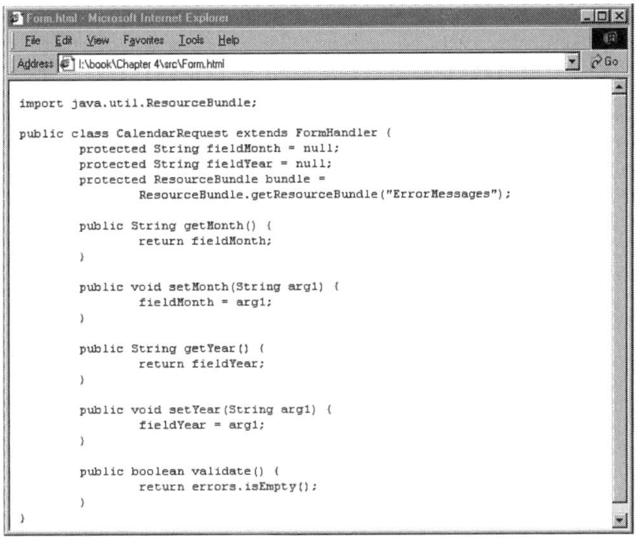

```
import java.util.ResourceBundle;

public class CalendarRequest extends FormHandler {
        protected String fieldMonth = null;
        protected String fieldYear = null;
        protected ResourceBundle bundle =
                ResourceBundle.getResourceBundle("ErrorMessages");

        public String getMonth() {
                return fieldMonth;
        }

        public void setMonth(String arg1) {
                fieldMonth = arg1;
        }

        public String getYear() {
                return fieldYear;
        }

        public void setYear(String arg1) {
                fieldYear = arg1;
        }

        public boolean validate() {
                return errors.isEmpty();
        }
}
```

Composing the JSPs Using JavaBeans

Now that you have created and tested the `MonthBean` and `CalendarRequest` JavaBeans, you will need to integrate them into the JSPs using simple JSP `useBean` tags.

The syntax for the `useBean` tag is

```
<jsp:useBean id="beanInstanceName" scope="page|request|session|application"
{ class=" package.class " [ type="package.class" ] | type="package.class"|
beanName="{ package.class | <%= expression %>}" type="package.class "}
{ /> | other elements </jsp:useBean> }
```

The tag translates into a field in a Java class as

```
package.class beanInstanceName = null;
```

The scope defines the lifetime of the bean instance or object reference. The different scope attributes are described in Table 4.5.

Table 4.5   Description of the Scope Parameters in Ascending Order of Accessibility

Class Name	Description
page	The bean instance is accessible only within the JSP. The reference to the object is discarded after the current request to the JSP is completed.
request	The bean instance can be accessible across different JSPs that are connected by the same client request. This implies that JSPs chained by forward requests can access the same JavaBean. The reference to the object is discarded after the client request is completed.

Table 4.5 continued

Class Name	Description
session	The reference to the bean instance remains until the invalidation of the current session using `session.removeValue("beanInstanceName")`.
application	The object reference remains until the server is shut down.

Any form-based application can be divided into three collaborating components:

- Input
- Output
- Controller to moderate the input and output

The different components in the JSP can collaborate by passing object references or bean instances. This can be easily achieved by setting the scope of the bean to request or session.

HTTP is by design a stateless protocol. There is no way that the Web server can directly distinguish between different requests from clients. To build state onto this protocol, various application-specific mechanisms can be used:

- **URL rewriting**—In this technique, the JSP appends the URL path with additional data, such as a session-tracking ID associated with the particular client. On the next request from the client, the session ID can be extracted from the URL path and the state maintained. This is very similar to the way data is passed using the GET parameter-passing mechanism of HTTP. Sensitive information can also be passed after encrypting it suitably.

- **Hidden form fields**—Session data can also be passed within hidden form fields. These fields are like any other HTML form fields, which are passed to the server when the form is submitted. These fields, as the name denotes, are not displayed on the browser for manipulation. The biggest problem with the technique is that the URLs cannot be bookmarked for later use because the data stored within the form fields will not be captured.

- **Cookies and session data**—This is a popular technique used for session tracking. Using this technique, the JSP container sends a cookie or session data containing objects to the client. The browser on the client's part stores this data in text files (cookies) or in memory (session data). It returns this data on each subsequent request to the server, thereby associating the request with a session.

For the HTTPS protocol, the Secure Sockets Layer provides a built-in session-tracking mechanism allowing multiple requests from the client to be directly associated with a session.

For the Calendar application, you can create another JSP, validator.jsp, that creates the form-handling bean, `CalendarRequest`, and forwards it to the appropriate JSP based on the success of the process operation. Until now, month.jsp both validated and generated the calendar. The use of the validator will increase the modularity in the program. The flows between the various JSPs and the beans used in them are shown in Figure 4.6.

Figure 4.6

Data flows and bean usage in the different JSPs

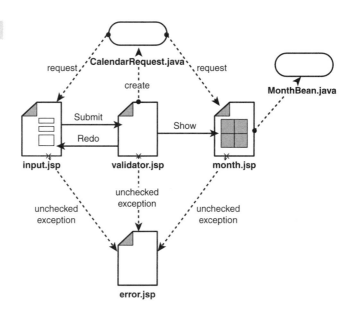

The Validator JSP

In the Calendar application, input.jsp is the input component, month.jsp the output, and validator.jsp the controller that passes the validated inputs received from input.jsp to month.jsp. If the validator cannot process the inputs due to incomplete or incorrect values, it sends the request back to input.jsp for a retry.

The Validator JSP creates an instance of the `CalendarRequest` bean and sets the different user-specified parameters on it. It passes this information to the output, month.jsp, and to the input for the retry. You can set the bean's scope as `request` because you only require the instance to be available until the current client request terminates. Alternatively, you could set the scope as `session`, but that would require you to remove the instance in the JSP after the client requests.

```
<jsp:useBean id="validator" class="station.auction.calendar.CalendarRequest"
  scope="request">
```

After you create the bean, you need to set the different properties on it from the request parameters by using a scriptlet as follows:

```
<% validator.setMonth(request.getParameter("month"));
   validator.setYear(request.getParameter("year")); %>
```

You can also set the property from the request parameters using `<jsp:setProperty>` tags:

```
<jsp:setProperty name="validator" property="month" param="month"/>
<jsp:setProperty name="validator" property="year" param="year"/>
```

JSP 1.1 provides a useful technique for setting the properties from requests using introspection. By specifying the property name as *, the JSP container automatically sets all the request parameters on the bean having the same property names as the parameters.

```
<jsp:setProperty name="validator" property="*"/>
```

After setting the request parameters on the bean, you need to invoke the `process()` method on the instance. A `true` return value indicates that no errors were encountered, and the request can be forwarded to month.jsp for displaying the calendar. A `false` return value indicates errors, and the request should be forwarded to input.jsp for retry. The complete source for validator.jsp is shown in Listing 4.26.

Listing 4.26   **validator.jsp: Controlling the Request Sequence Using the `CalendarRequest` Bean**

```
<jsp:useBean id="validator" class="station.auction.calendar.CalendarRequest"
    scope="request">
  <jsp:setProperty name="validator" property="*"/>
</jsp:useBean>
<%-- Notice that this JSP doesn't generate any output --%>
<%
    if (!validator.process()) {
       // Errors occurred. Retry
%>
       <jsp:forward page="input.jsp"/>
<% }
   else {
       // Display Calendar
%>
       <jsp:forward page="month.jsp"/>
<%
   } // end if-else block
%>
```

The Output JSP—month.jsp

The output-generating component, month.jsp, uses two JavaBeans for generating the monthly Calendar:

- The `CalendarRequest` instance created by validator.jsp and obtained from the request scope:

```
<jsp:useBean id="validator"
➡class="station.auction.calendar.CalendarRequest"
    scope="request"/>
```

Note   Specifying a `useBean` tag in the JSP doesn't always imply the creation of a new instance. If the bean's scope was marked as `request`, `session`, or `application`, the JSP container checks whether the object's reference with the specific id already exists within the scope. If a reference already exists, a new instance is not created, but the reference is extracted from the specified scope.

- `MonthBean` for generating the different elements of the calendar that is created within the JSP. A new instance needs to be created with the input properties. This instance does not need to be visible outside the JSP, hence its scope is set to `page`, which is also the default scope:

```
<jsp:useBean id="cal" class="station.auction.calendar.MonthBean"
 scope="page"/>
```

To set the input of the properties for the bean, you can specify them just as you did for `CalendarRequest` in validator.jsp. However, the conversion from string to integer for the request parameter has to be repeated. To prevent this repetition, you can obtain the processed integer values from the `CalendarRequest` bean instead. You will need to update the calendar instance with the newly set properties:

```
<%     cal.setMonth(validator.getMonthAsInteger());
       cal.setYear(validator.getYearAsInteger());
       cal.update(); %>
```

The `MonthBean` instance, `cal`, can be used like any other Java variable in expressions and scriptlets within the JSP, as shown in the bold sections of Listing 4.27.

Listing 4.27   month.jsp: Using the `MonthBean` Instance Within Expressions and Scriptlets

```
<jsp:useBean id="validator" class="station.auction.calendar.CalendarRequest"
     scope="request"/>
<jsp:useBean id="cal" class="station.auction.calendar.MonthBean"/>
<%     cal.setMonth(validator.getMonthAsInteger());
       cal.setYear(validator.getYearAsInteger());
       cal.update(); %>
```

Listing 4.27 continued

```
<html>
<head>
<title>Calendar</title>
</head>
<body>
        <table border="1">
        <tr bgcolor="silver">
                <td colspan="7"> <font size="+2">
                <%= cal.getMonthName()%></font>
                </td>
        </tr>
        <tr bgcolor="black" align="center">
        <%
                for (int i = 1; i < 8; i++) {
                        out.print("<td width=\"70\">");
                        out.print("<font size=\"-1\" color=\"white\">");
                        out.print(cal.getDayName(i, true));
                        out.println("</font></td>");
                }
        %>
        </tr>
<%
        int startCell = cal.getStartCell();
        int endCell = cal.getEndCell();
        for (int cellNo = 0, day = 1; cellNo < 42; cellNo++) {
                if (cellNo%7 == 0) {
                        out.println("<TR>");
                } // end check for start of row
                out.print("<TD VALIGN=TOP HEIGHT=57");
                if (cellNo < startCell || cellNo > endCell) {
                        out.print(" BGCOLOR=\"#999999\"> ");
                } else {
                        out.print("><B>" + day + "</B>");
                        day++;
                } // end if block
                out.println("</TD>");
                if (cellNo+1%7 == 0) {
                        out.println("</TR>");
                } // end check for end of row
        } // end for-loop
%>
        </table>
</body>
</html>
```

The Input JSP

The input component in our application, input.jsp, needs to be altered to use the
CalendarRequest instance passed by the validator:

```
<jsp:useBean id="validator" class="station.auction.calendar.CalendarRequest"
 scope="request"/>
```

You should use this bean instance to provide error information, if any, and the default values for the form fields, as shown in the following list:

- To generate the error message for the month field, use the following expression:

  ```
  <%= validator.getError("month")%>
  ```

- To generate the default value for the month field, use the following expression:

  ```
  <select>
  <%
      // Print all the options
      for (int i = 0; i < 12 ; i++) {
          out.print("<option value=\""+ i + "\"");
          if (i == validator.getMonthAsInteger()) {
                  out.print(" selected=\"true\"");
          }
              out.println(">" + monthNames[i] + "</option>");
      } // end for-loop
  %>
  </select>
  ```

- To generate the error message for the year field, use the following expression:

  ```
  <%= validator.getError("year")%>
  ```

- To generate the default value for the year field, use the following expression:

  ```
  <input type="text" name="year" size="20" maxlength="4"
                  value="<%= validator.getYearAsInteger()%>">
  ```

Deploying and Running the Application

In order to run your application, you need to copy your JSPs to the designated application folder within the webapps directory of your Tomcat installation. You could use the same directory structure you created: webapps/AuctionStation/jsp/calendar/1.11.

You also need to set the JavaBeans you created in the CLASSPATH. There are two ways you can do this:

1. Make an entry in the CLASSPATH variable for the CalendarRequest and MonthBean beans. Again, you can do this in two ways: Add the directory containing the station/auction/calendar directory structure in the CLASSPATH or package all the classes in a jar file and set the jar file in the CLASSPATH.

2. Create a directory structure WEB-INF/classes in the AuctionStation directory. Store the classes for the beans in the classes folder according to the package structure (station/auction/calendar) in that directory. Tomcat automatically sets these classes in the CLASSPATH, so you don't need to manually alter the CLASSPATH variable.

Restart the Tomcat server to make the changes take effect, and test the JSPs by pointing your browser to `http://localhost:8080/jsp/calendar/1.11/input.jsp`.

Sending Email from Within JSPs

In the previous chapter, you learned to trap unchecked exceptions using error pages. Error pages allowed you to exit gracefully from such situations. You should inform the technical staff about an error when it occurs.

There are numerous ways you can send email from within your Java application or JSP:

- Invoking an external program, such as sendmail, and passing the email information as command-line arguments. This is not a 100% pure Java solution for sending email and will not necessarily work on another platform. It also requires that you have the sendmail application configured on your host:

```
try {
    String args[] = { "sendmail", "from@auction.station.net",
        "to@auction.station.net",
        "\"Send Message using Native sendmail application\"",
"\"Body...\""};
    java.lang.Process process = java.lang.Runtime.getRuntime().exec(args);
        Process.waitFor();
} catch (Exception exc) {
    exc.printStackTrace();
}
```

- Using a 100% pure Java solution using Sun's JavaMail and Java Activation Framework classes.

Using JavaMail and Java Activation Framework for Handling Email

JavaMail provides a framework for building mail and messaging services so application components can send and receive mail. The JavaMail API defines classes that handle mail-related protocols such as SMTP and POP3. The Java Activation Framework, JAF, provides concrete implementation for handling different MIME types used in the JavaMail program.

SMTP—SMTP stands for Simple Mail Transfer Protocol, a protocol for sending email on the net. It's very similar to the way postal letters or snail-mail is sent in the real world. A user posts the letter in a post box or a post office, and the postal department delivers the message to the addressed location.

POP—POP stands for Post Office Protocol, a protocol that allows users to download email from their mailing system. It is again analogous to the real-world scenario, where a user has to go to the post office to pick up mail from a registered post box.

MIME—Short for Multipurpose Internet Mail Extensions. It allows rich data such as images, audio, and video to be sent in email. The original mail applications used only plain text messages; MIME provides for sending richer content.

how tōō prō nouns′ it	SMTP: as it is spelled
	POP: pop (as in soda pop)
	MIME: rhymes with rhyme!

You can create a generic `SendMail` JavaBean that handles requests from different clients, not just for sending mail to the support staff. The bean accepts input parameters such as the following

- Name of the sender
- Address of the sender
- Name of the recipient(s)
- Address of the recipient(s)
- Subject
- Body of the message

To send the email, you will also need an SMTP host to configure your JavaMail applications with. On the Net, several SMTP hosts are available that you can use for sending mail. You could also set up an SMTP host within your organization using one of several mail server implementations, for example the Java Apache Mail Enterprise Server, a.k.a. Apache JAMES (`http://java.apache.org/james/`), a 100% pure JavaMail server.

Table 4.6 lists some of the JavaMail classes that you can use for sending email within your JSP.

Table 4.6   JavaMail Classes That You Will Need for the Email Bean

JavaMail Class	Description
`javax.mail.Session`	Represents a mail session. It stores defaults and collects properties such as the mail host's name, user name and password necessary for sending and receiving mail from a mail server.

Table 4.6 continued

JavaMail Class	Description
`javax.mail.internet.InternetAddress`	Stores information about the "from," "to," "cc," and "bcc" fields of an email. It stores the mandatory address plus an optional personal name.
`javax.mail.Message`	Models email messages and is used to store information such as the addresses, subject, body, and MIME body parts.
`javax.mail.intenet.MimeMessage`	Provides implementation for the `javax.mail.Message` interface to represent MIME style messages.
`javax.mail.Transport`	Models a message transport so that you can send and receive messages from SMTP/POP3 hosts.

Creating the SendMail JSP to Send Email

You can create a JSP to send email. The JSP does not produce an output, and for all practical purposes is a Java class. It sets the email elements—from, to, subject, and body fields—from the request parameters. The classes listed in Table 4.6 can be connected to form the sendmail JSP, as shown in Listing 4.28.

Listing 4.28 sendmail.jsp: JSP That Builds and Sends an Email Based on Request Parameters

```
<%@ page import="java.util.Properties, javax.mail.*, javax.mail.internet.*" %>
<%
    // Collect all the information required for the email
    String fromAddr = request.getParameter("fromAddr");
    String fromName = request.getParameter("fromName");
    String toAddr = request.getParameter("toAddr");
    String toName = request.getParameter("toName");
    String subject = request.getParameter("subject");
    String body = request.getParameter("body");

    // Specify the SMTP Host, replace mail.auction.station.net
    // with your SMTP host
    Properties props = new Properties();
    props.put("mail.smtp.host", "mail.auction.station.net");

    // Create a mail session, turn on the debug flag
    Session ssn = Session.getDefaultInstance(props, null);
    ssn.setDebug(true);

    try {
        // set the from information
        InternetAddress from = new InternetAddress(fromAddr, fromName);
```

```
    // Set the to information
    InternetAddress to = new InternetAddress(toAddr, toName);

    // Create the message
    Message msg = new MimeMessage(ssn);
    msg.setFrom(from);
    msg.addRecipient(Message.RecipientType.TO, to);
    msg.setSubject(subject);
    msg.setContent(body, "text/plain");

    // Send the message across
    Transport.send(msg);
} catch (MessagingException mex) {
    mex.printStackTrace();
}
%>
```

In your Error JSP, you might want to send an email to the support staff informing them of the error and also provide them with enough information so that they can fix the problem. You can include the Email JSP within the Error JSP to send emails regarding the errors. In the previous chapter, you included the outputs of the Calendar JSP within the home page. Here, you will include the Email JSP that doesn't produce any output.

Within the Error JSP, you need to set the different request parameters while including the Email JSP:

- **From Name**—A symbolic name like "Error Reporter."
- **From Address**—A symbolic address for Error Reporter. Some SMTP hosts do not allow addresses that are not from the same domain. You can specify a nonexistent email address—the same way that spammers operate!
- **To Name**—Name of the support staff member.
- **To Address**—Valid address of the support staff member.
- **Subject**—Abstract of the error that occurred. This can be obtained from the exception implicit object provided in the JSP.
- **Body**—The stack trace of the exception along with the query string used in the JSP.

  Obtaining the stack trace is a bit tricky. Exceptions allow you to write directly to the standard output using the `exception.printStackTrace()` method. In this case you need to extract the stack trace, store it as a `String`, and send it with the message.

  The `Throwable` interface, from which every Exception subclasses, overloads the `printStackTrace` method to accept a parameter of type `java.io.PrintWriter`. You will need to encapsulate an instance of `java.io.StringWriter` within a

PrintWriter and pass it as the parameter to the method. Invoking the toString method on the StringWriter object then returns the string containing the stack trace. The source for this is shown in the bold portion of Listing 4.29.

Listing 4.29 error.jsp: Sending the Error Information to sendmail.jsp

```
<%@ page isErrorPage="true" %>
<html>
<head>
    <title>Oops!</title>
</head>
<body>
<h1>We are sorry</h1>
The page you have just reached has some errors.
Our technical staff have been informed of the error and will fix
it as soon as possible.
<p>

<% // Create the body passing the exception trace and the query string
    String body = null;
    java.io.StringWriter sw = new java.io.StringWriter();
    java.io.PrintWriter pw = new java.io.PrintWriter(sw);
    exception.printStackTrace(pw);
    body = sw.toString() + request.getQueryString();
%>
<%-- Include the Email JSP and set the different parameters --%>
<jsp:include page="sendmail.jsp" flush="true">
    <jsp:param name="fromName" value="Error Reporter"/>
    <jsp:param name="fromAddr" value="error@auction.station.net"/>
    <jsp:param name="toName" value="Web Integrator"/>
    <jsp:param name="toAddr" value="maneesh@auction.station.net"/>
    <jsp:param name="subject" value="<%= exception %>"/>
    <jsp:param name="body" value="<%= body %>"/>
</jsp:include>

<p>
Thank you for your patience
</body>
</html>
```

Setup for Running the Application

Store the JSPs within the <tomcat-root>/WebApps/AuctionStation/jsp folder.

To run the JavaMail application, sendmail.jsp, you need to set the JavaMail and JAF classes in the CLASSPATH. You can download the latest packages of these two libraries from Sun's Java site.

- JavaMail: http://java.sun.com/products/javamail/
- JAF: http://java.sun.com/beans/glasgow/jaf.html

Instructions for installing the JavaMail and JAF classes are provided in their respective packages.

Stop and restart Tomcat to make the changes in the CLASSPATH take effect.

Running the application causes a mail containing the error stack trace to be sent out. The recipient can read the email using a standard email client. An email sent out to me from the error.jsp for an error that I forced in month.jsp is shown in Figure 4.7.

Figure 4.7

Email detailing the error trapped in error.jsp

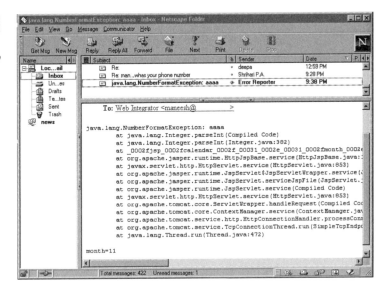

Using a JavaBean for Sending Email

As you saw in the previous section, you can write Java code, such as a send email routine, within JSPs using scriptlets. A problem with this technique is that someone could directly invoke sendmail.jsp and use your site for bulk mailing, a.k.a spam. JSPs should not be used for purposes apart from generating Web content. You should use JavaBeans if you need to write Java code.

You can easily convert the sendmail JSP, shown in Listing 4.30, into a JavaBean by promoting the setters on the `javax.mail.Message` instance as input properties.

Listing 4.30   SendMail.java: Input Properties for the `SendMail` JavaBean

```
package station.auction.beans;

import java.util.*;

import javax.mail.*;
import javax.mail.internet.*;
```

Listing 4.30 continued

```java
public class SendMail {
    private javax.mail.Message mail = null;
public SendMail() {
        this("mail.auction.station.net");
}
public SendMail(String hostName) {
        Properties props = new Properties();
        props.put("mail.smtp.host", hostName);

        // Create a mail session
        Session session = Session.getDefaultInstance(props, null);
        session.setDebug(true);

        mail = new MimeMessage(session);
}
public void setFromAddress(String fromName, String fromAddress) {
    try {
        InternetAddress from = new InternetAddress(fromAddress, fromName);

        mail.setFrom(from);
    } catch (Exception exc) {
        // Suppress all exceptions
    }
}
public void setToAddress(String toName, String toAddress) {
    try {
        InternetAddress to = new InternetAddress(toAddress, toName);

        mail.addRecipient(Message.RecipientType.TO, to);
    } catch (Exception exc) {
        // suppress all exceptions
    }
}
public void setSubject(String subject) {
    try {
        mail.setSubject(subject);
    } catch (Exception exc) {
        // suppress exceptions
    }
}
public void setBody(String body) {
    try {
        mail.setContent(body, "text/plain");
    } catch (Exception exc) {
    }
}
}
```

After you composed the email message by setting the input properties for the bean, you need to send the message to the recipients. To do this, you need to define a send method that sends the message, as shown in Listing 4.31.

Listing 4.31   SendMail.java: Sending the Message Synchronously Using the send Method

```
public void send() {
    try {
        Transport.send(mail);
    } catch (javax.mail.MessagingException mexc) {
        //oops
    }
}
```

You can send the message immediately or asynchronously. Sending it immediately or asynchronously means that the method blocks until the message is sent out. This implies that the JSP's output is not generated until the email is sent out, something you may not want. Asynchronous transmission means that the method completes and returns without waiting for the email to be sent.

You can implement asynchronous transmission by doing some multithreaded programming. All you need to do is make the SendMail class implement the Runnable interface and define the public run() method (part of the Runnable interface) that sends out the message, as shown in Listing 4.32.

Listing 4.32   SendMail.java: Sending the Message Asynchronously

```
public void send() {
    // Send the message asychronously
    (new Thread(this)).start();
    // To send it Synchronously uncomment the next line
    // Transport.send(mail);
    return;
}
public void run() {
    try {
        Transport.send(mail);
    } catch (javax.mail.MessagingException mexc) {
    }
}
```

Altering Error.jsp to Use the SendMail JavaBean

You can use the useBean tag to create an instance of the SendMail JavaBean, set the input properties, and send the message in a scriptlet. You can use the scriptlet shown in Listing 4.33 to replace the include tags that we used earlier.

Listing 4.33   error.jsp: Sending the Error Message Using the SendMessage JavaBean

```
<jsp:useBean id="message" class="station.auction.beans.SendMail"/>
<%
    message.setFromAddress("Auction Station Error",
                            "error@auction.station.net");
    message.setToAddress("Web Integrator", "maneesh@auction.station.net");
    message.setSubject(exception);
    message.setBody(body);
    message.send();
%>
```

Testing and Running the Application

Copy the SendMail class to the web-inf/classes/station/auctions/beans directory. Set the JavaMail and JAF classes in the CLASSPATH and restart the Tomcat server.

Next Steps

In this chapter, you learned how to streamline the JSP Web application development process using JavaBeans. You also learned how to use a design pattern for developing form-based applications. Finally, you created a JavaBean to send email.

In the next chapter, you will learn to create and use custom tag libraries for facilitating greater reusability and maintainability in your JSPs.

Chapter 5

Creating a Custom Tag Library for Displaying Errors and Sending Email

In the preceding chapters, you saw how to provide reusability in your JSPs using include mechanisms and JavaBeans. In this chapter, you will learn about a new mechanism for generating dynamic content in JSP 1.1 called *tag libraries*. The tag library feature allows you to invent your own custom HTML-like tags for your JSPs. You then need to back your tags with Java code that is executed when the JSP container encounters the custom tag. In this way, your JSP generates content using simple custom tags instead of Java code interspersed in scriptlets. Custom tags also fully demarcate the responsibilities of the developers, who create the tag libraries describing custom tags, from those of the Web integrators, who use the custom tags.

Custom tags encapsulate functionality to provide a reusable, maintainable, and portable content generation solution for JSPs. The tags are easy to write, and you can even develop macros or tools to manipulate them within the JSP.

What You Are Going To Do

In this chapter, you will create a custom tag library that provides custom tags for the following:

- Generating the current date
- Generating formatted error information
- Sending email

Incorporating Custom Tags

Before you get started with creating a custom tag library, it's important that you become familiar with its operation. Within a JSP, you can add custom tags—HTML-like tags but with a specific name and prefix. In our application, we will create custom tags such as the following:

```
<as:today/>
<as:error color="blue">The Month is invalid</as:error>
<as:loop n="5">
   <td><as:insertCount/></td>
</as:loop>
<as:email smtpHost="mail.auction.station.net">
   <as:from address="maneesh@auction.station.net">Maneesh Sahu</as:from>
   <as:to address="errors@auction.station.net">Error Reporter</as:to>
   <as:subject>Stop the press</as:subject>
   <as:body>An Error occurred </as:body>
</as:email>
```

The name of the custom tag has a prefix, in this case as, and a descriptive name such as today, error, and email.

Custom tags can be broadly classified into four types:

- Simple action tags such as `<as:today/>`. As the name suggests, the tag is easy to incorporate into a JSP. It can also take an attribute. The tag performs an action or generates some content when the JSP container encounters it.
- Simple action tags with body such as `<as:error color="blue">..</as:error>` and the email tags. These tags allow you to include a body or nest other custom tags in the tag.
- Nested action tags. A custom tag nested within another co-operates to provide a specific action. In the case of the email custom tag, from, to, subject, and body tags are nested within it to compose the email message.
- Co-operating action tags. Two or more custom tags that are not nested within the other but interact with each other to pass parameters and results.
- Iterative action tags such as `<as:loop n="5">..</as:loop>` are a little more complex and allow you to iterate more than a single time on the body. An iterative tag looks like a simple action tag, but its handler describes its iterative operation.

These simple tags make the JSP source cleaner and more readable. The task of creating the tags before they can be used in a JSP is a little more complex. For each custom tag that you use in your JSP, you need to provide three components:

- JSP pages for including the custom tags. The JSP container activates custom tags only when you specify a *taglib directive* in the JSP:

  ```
  <%@ taglib uri="identifier" prefix="prefix" %>
  ```

The taglib directive specifies the location of the tag library descriptor. It also defines a prefix that you must use with your custom tag names.

- A tag library descriptor is an XML document that defines the custom tags that can be used in JSPs and associates these tags with their *tag handler* or action classes. The descriptor also provides information such as the valid attributes for the tag and whether the tag is a simple or nested one, as well as the class name and location of the tag handler.

XML, short for *eXtensible Markup Language*, is a way of defining new markup languages. At first glance, it looks like any other HTML document. However, it allows you to define your own tags and structure for your documents. The tag library descriptor is one example of an XML document. The source of one such descriptor is shown in Listing 5.1.

Listing 5.1   A Sample Tag Library Description: An Example of an XML Document

```
<?xml version="1.0" encoding="ISO-8859-1" ?>
<!DOCTYPE taglib
        PUBLIC "-//Sun Microsystems, Inc.//DTD JSP Tag Library 1.1//EN"
        "http://java.sun.com/j2ee/dtds/web-jsptaglibrary_1_1.dtd">
<taglib>
  <tlibversion>1.0</tlibversion>
  <jspversion>1.1</jspversion>
  <shortname>as</shortname>
  <uri>http://localhost:8080/AuctionStation/jsp/mytags.jar</uri>
  <info>Auction Station's Tag Library</info>

  <tag>
    <name>today</name>
    <tagclass>station.auction.taglib.DateTagHandler</tagclass>
    <bodycontent>empty</bodycontent>
    <info>Prints the Current Date</info>
  </tag>
</taglib>
```

All XML documents usually begin with the optional XML header `<?xml version="1.0"?>`. They also specify the location of the *Document Type Definition*, or the DTD, using the `DOCTYPE` directive. The DTD defines the structure of the document as well as its tags and attributes. In the case of the taglib XML document, the DTD defines a *root element* or tag, `taglib`. This root element nests other elements such as the `tlibversion`, `jspversion`, `shortname`, `uri`, and `info` tags. It also defines one or more tag elements for each custom tag that you want to use in your JSP. The tag element in turn contains other elements such as the `name`, `tagclass`, `bodycontent`, and `info` that define the tag, its attributes, and its handler.

- A tag handler is a Java class that, as the name denotes, specifies how the tag is handled when it is encountered by the JSP container. For example, the `today` tag prints the current date in the generated page at the location it is defined in.

You will see the three components as we build the custom tags, beginning with our today tag.

Developing a Simple Action Tag—today

The first custom tag that you will build is the today tag. It embeds the current date in the long format into the generated page at the location it is defined in. The tag is a simple action tag, having no attributes and no body. You can use it in your JSP by including `<as:today/>` anywhere in the body of the HTML structure. The prefix as used in the custom tag is used to differentiate tags, similar to the way package names differentiate Java classes with the same names.

 A tag with no body is known as an *empty element*. It can be defined with the open and close tag style as `<emptytag></emptytag>` or using the shorthand notation `<emptytag/>`.

Creating the today Tag Handler

After you have decided on the structure of your custom tag, you need to specify the operations associated with it. In this case you have an empty tag without any attributes, and the operation associated with it is the print date.

Create a new class, `TodayTagHandler`, having a package name `station.auction.taglib`. Import the Java classes, `java.util.Date` and `java.text.DateFormat`, and the JSP classes that you require in your class:

```
package station.auction.taglib;

import java.util.Date;
import java.text.DateFormat;
import javax.servlet.jsp.*;
import javax.servlet.jsp.tagext.*;
```

Next, you need to make the `TodayTagHandler` class implement the `Tag` interface:

```
public class TodayTagHandler implements javax.servlet.jsp.tagext.Tag {
```

The `Tag` interface marks the class as a request-time server-side object that is invoked by the JSP container when its associated custom tag is encountered. A tag handler supports a runtime protocol that facilitates passing information from the JSP page to the handler. It defines six significant methods, as described in Table 5.1.

Table 5.1 Methods of the `Tag` Interface, Listed in the Order of Execution by the JSP Container

Method	Description
`public void setPageContext (PageContext ctx)`	The JSP container invokes this method when the tag is encountered. The tag handler can use the `pageContext` to access and set scoped variables or attributes and also include content for the page.
`public void setParent (Tag parent)`	This method sets the tag handler for the custom tag that this tag is immediately nested in.

Method	Description
public int doStartTag() throws JspException	This method is invoked when the JSP container encounters the start tag. You can perform the necessary actions within this method.
public int doEndTag() throws JspException	This method is called after returning from doStartTag(). You may want to define your actions in this method if you haven't already done so in doStartTag().
public Tag getParent()	Method for accessing the parent tag handler. This method can be used to obtain the parent tag any time during its lifetime.
public void release()	This method indicates that the JSP container is releasing the tag instance. You can do any necessary cleanup within this method.

To keep a reference to the attributes set by the JSP container, such as the pageContext and the parent tag handler, you should define local variables for your class:

```
protected PageContext pageContext;
protected Tag parent;
```

You will need to initialize these variables within their respective callback methods as shown in Listing 5.2.

Listing 5.2   TodayTagHandler.java: Implementing the Setter and Getter Methods for the Tag Interface

```
public void setPageContext(PageContext pageContext) {
    this.pageContext=pageContext;
}

public void setParent(Tag parent) {
    this.parent=parent;
}

public Tag getParent() {
    return parent;
}
```

Now you can implement the method that gets invoked when the start tag is encountered. Within this method, you will obtain a String variable representing the current date. You can obtain this using the Date and DateFormat classes. To embed this String in the generated page's output, you can use the PageContext variable. The PageContext allows you to access the different scoped variables as well as write text into the page's content as shown in Listing 5.3. At the end of the method, you must return an integer value, one of Tag.EVALUATE_BODY_INCLUDE or Tag.SKIP_BODY, indicating whether the body of the tag must be evaluated (EVALUATE_BODY_INCLUDE) or the body must be ignored (SKIP_BODY). In this case, today is an empty tag, and you can therefore skip the body.

Listing 5.3   TodayTagHandler.java: The `doStartTag` Method Defining the Action, Embedding a Long Format of the Current Date into the Generated Page

```
public int doStartTag() throws JspException {
    try {
        Date today = new Date();
        DateFormat formatter = DateFormat.getDateInstance(DateFormat.LONG);

        // Write the formatted date into the generated page
        this.pageContext.getOut().write(formatter.format(today));
    }
    catch(java.io.IOException e) {
        throw new JspException("IO Error: " + e.getMessage());
    }
    return SKIP_BODY;
}
```

Because today is an empty tag, you need not define any special action in doEndTag(); however, you do need to return the integer value EVAL_PAGE if you want to evaluate the rest of the page, or SKIP_PAGE if the request should be completed without evaluating the remaining part of the page:

```
public int doEndTag() {
    return EVAL_PAGE;
}
```

The release() method releases some resources to make the references, such as the parent tag handler, available for *garbage collection*:

```
public void release() {
    parent = null;
}
```

 In Java you do not have to do any memory management within your program, such as deallocating memory locations. Java has a garbage collector that runs in a separate background thread determining unreferenced objects (those that will not be used in the program) and recycling the memory used by those objects.

An object becomes unreferenced when it goes out of the current scope; for example, a variable defined within a method or block goes out of scope when the method returns or the block is executed. These objects are garbage collected to reclaim the memory used by them. If an object is referenced by another object, for instance when you pass the object as an argument to another object within the block, its lifetime goes beyond the life of the scope it is declared in. The object is therefore not available for garbage collection even when it goes out of scope. It is therefore the responsibility of the programmer to remove unused references by setting the field holding its reference to null to enable reclamation of memory.

Many methods of your `TagHandler` class are generic:

- Setting the `Parent` tag handler
- Setting the `PageContext` attribute
- Obtaining the `Parent` tag handler
- Release

You can define all these methods in a class and make your custom tag handlers extend from this class to obtain reusability. The JSP tag extension library provides one such prebuilt class, `javax.servlet.jsp.tagext.TagSupport`, that defines and implements these methods. It also defines the fields for storing the attributes set by the JSP container: `pageContext` and `parent`. In addition to the generic fields and methods, it also provides default implementation for the `doStartTag()` to simply return `SKIP_BODY` and `doEndTag()` to return `EVAL_PAGE`.

You could alter `TodayTagHandler` by extending the `TagSupport` class instead of implementing all the methods of the `Tag` interface, as shown in Listing 5.4.

5

Listing 5.4   TodayTagHandler.java: Inheriting the Method and Fields from `TagSupport` in `TodayTagHandler`

```java
package station.auction.taglib;
import java.text.DateFormat;
import java.util.Date;
import javax.servlet.jsp.*;
import javax.servlet.jsp.tagext.*;

public class TodayTagHandler extends TagSupport {
    public int doStartTag() throws JspException {
        try {
            Date today = new Date();
            DateFormat formatter = DateFormat.getDateInstance(DateFormat.LONG);

            // Write the formatted date into the generated page
            this.pageContext.getOut().write(formatter.format(today));
        } catch(java.io.IOException e) {
            throw new JspException("IO Error: " + e.getMessage());
        }
        return SKIP_BODY;
    }
}
```

Save the Java source file, TodayTagHandler.java, in the `AuctionStation/web-inf/classes/station/auction/taglib` directory of the `<tomcat-root>/webapps` folder.

Open a command prompt. Set servlet.jar found in `<tomcat-root>/lib` in the `CLASSPATH`. Compile the Java source from the `AuctionStation/web-inf/classes` directory to produce the class file- TodayTagHandler.class, using

```
javac station/auction/taglib/TodayTagHandler.java
```

Describing the today Tag Using a Tag Library Descriptor

After you have compiled your tag handler, you need to write its descriptor to enable it to be used within a JSP. Create a new text file called as-taglib.tld. The as in the filename stands for Auction Station!

Specify the XML header information and specify the tag lib DTD:

```
<?xml version="1.0" encoding="ISO-8859-1" ?>
<!DOCTYPE taglib PUBLIC "-//Sun Microsystems, Inc.//DTD JSP Tag Library 1.1//EN"
➥"web-jsptaglib_1_1.dtd">
```

Provide information about your tag library within the taglib element:

```
<taglib>
  <tlibversion>1.0</tlibversion>
  <jspversion>1.1</jspversion>
  <shortname>as</shortname>
  <info>Auction Station's Tag Library</info>
```

The shortname tag is a name that the JSP can use to reference the tag library.

You can make entries for each tag that you created by defining tag elements as shown in Listing 5.5.

Listing 5.5   as-taglib.tld: Describing the today Tag Within the Tag Element Structure

```
<tag>
    <name>today</name>
    <tagclass>station.auction.taglib.TodayTagHandler</tagclass>
    <bodycontent>empty</bodycontent>
    <info>Prints the Current Date</info>
</tag>
```

The tag element defines a set of elements nested within it as described in Table 5.2.

Table 5.2   Description of the Subelements of the tag Element

Subelement	Description
name	The custom tag name, in this case today.
tagclass	The fully qualified tag handler class name. In this case station.auction.taglib.TodayTagHandler.
bodycontent	Specifies the type of content the body has. Takes one of three values—empty, JSP, and tagdependent. The value empty implies that the tag doesn't have a body; JSP implies that it has a body; and tagdependent implies that the TagHandler determines the type of body content within the action. In this case it is the bodycontent that is marked empty because it is a simple action tag with no body.
info	Description of the tag.

End your `taglib` with the end element `</taglib>`.

You can store your .tld file anywhere within your `webapps` folder. For now, save it in the `<tomcat>/webapps/AuctionStation/jsp` directory.

Using the `today` Tag in a JSP

After you have defined your taglib descriptor file, you can use the custom tags defined in it in any of your JSPs. Let's create a simple JSP, customtags.jsp, that prints out the date in bold using the `today` tag.

Create a new JSP in the `<tomcat>/webapps/AuctionStation/jsp` directory and name it customtags.jsp. Provide a `taglib` directive specifying the JSP to use the as-taglib.tld file to extract information for all tags with the prefix "as":

```
<%@ taglib uri="as-taglib.tld" prefix="as" %>
```

The URI refers to the location of the .tld file. Because it is in the same directory as the JSP it will be used in, you need to specify the relative URI containing only the filename.

You can use the `today` tag anywhere in the body of the JSP. Add the tag along with its prefix anywhere in the JSP after the `taglib` directive:

```
Today is: <b><as:today/></b>
```

Using Proxy URIs

By putting the tag library descriptor within the webapps folder, it is accessible via HTTP from any client. To prevent the descriptor file from being accessed directly you should store the file in the WEB-INF directory. A file in the WEB-INF directory is inaccessible via HTTP even though it is contained in the webapps folder. This folder therefore should ideally contain JavaBeans, configuration files, and tag lib descriptors that you don't want to expose to the clients.

To allow the JSP to access this file you have to make an entry for the descriptor in web.xml file stored in the WEB-INF directory. This specifies a "proxy" URI to be used for identifying the .tld file in the JSP, such as `http://www.auction.station.net/as-taglib`. This URI refers to the .tld file stored in the WEB-INF folder as shown below:

```
<taglib>
    <taglib-uri>
        http://www.auction.station.net/as-taglib
    </taglib-uri>
    <taglib-location>
        /WEB-INF/as-taglib.tld
    </taglib-location>
</taglib>
```

You can now use the proxy URI specified in web.xml as the URI for the .tld file in the JSP:

```
<%@ taglib uri="http://www.auction.station.net/as-taglib" prefix="as" %>
```

Running and Testing the JSP

Restart the Tomcat server to make the changes take effect. Launch your browser and point it to the location `http://localhost:8080/jsp/customtags.jsp`. If the current day were May 23, 2000, your browser would display the information shown in Figure 5.1. (It's unlikely that you will get the same output unless you set your system date back to May 23, 2000!)

Figure 5.1

Output of the custom-tags.jsp page in the browser

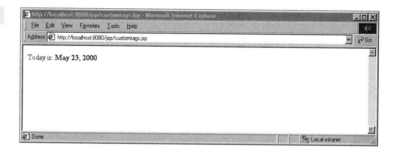

You can debug the actions of tag handlers by printing information in the system console using `System.out.println(...)`. During page generation, the messages will be displayed in the command window you started Tomcat in.

Developing a Simple Body Action Tag—`error`

In this section you will build a tag to display error messages. In the previous chapter, you displayed error messages with a red foreground color and a font one size smaller than the normal. For example, in input.jsp, you used the following HTML code to display error messages for an incorrect month and year:

```
<font color="red" size="-2">Error Message</font>
```

Now you will replace the HTML tags used in the preceding example with a simple `error` tag:

```
<as:error>Error Message</as:error>
```

Using the `error` tag also allows you to provide a consistent, site-wide approach for displaying error messages. The tag will also allow you to customize the display of the error message using a template-based approach. For displaying the error message, all you need to do is to set the parameters in the template. You could customize the template to match your requirements:

```
<font color=\"{1}\" size=\"-1\"> {0} </font>
```

The `error` tag takes an optional attribute, `color`, that specifies the foreground color for displaying the error message. The default color is red, and you can override it by passing a hexadecimal or symbolic color:

```
<as:error color="blue">Warning Message</as:error>
```

Creating the `error` Tag Handler

You might have inferred from the structure of the tag that it is a simple action with a body. The tag extension framework provides another interface, `BodyTag`, that extends the `Tag` interface to manipulate the body of an action. The extra methods act on a `BodyContent` object that represents the generated body content within the tags. The body of the tag could be plain text, HTML tags, JSP expressions and scriptlets, custom tags, or a combination of these elements. The `BodyContent` interface makes the evaluated body available for usage. Table 5.3 describes the additional methods in the `BodyTag` interface that are not present in `Tag`.

Table 5.3   Additional Methods of the `BodyTag` Interface, Listed in the Order of Execution by the JSP Container

Method	Description
`void setBodyContent (BodyContent b);`	The JSP container invokes this method to pass the body content. This method will not be called if there is no body.
`void doInitBody() throws JspException;`	Prepares for evaluation of the body. This method is invoked once per action invocation after a new body content has been obtained and set on the tag handler. Not used in simple actions.
`int doAfterBody() throws JspException;`	This is the post-evaluation callback method invoked by the container.

The procedure for creating the `ErrorTagHandler` is similar to the one used for creating the `TodayTagHandler` class. Create a new Java source file, ErrorTagHandler.java, and define the `ErrorTagHandler` class in it that implements the `BodyTag` interface.

```
package station.auction.taglib;

import java.text.MessageFormat;
import java.util.ResourceBundle;

import javax.servlet.jsp.*;
import javax.servlet.jsp.tagext.*;
public class ErrorTagHandler implements BodyTag {
```

You need to import two extra classes for generating the error messages:

- **`java.util.ResourceBundle`**—Used for extracting the values from a property file.

- **`java.text.MessageFormat`**—This class is useful in constructing and formatting messages using a template-based approach. For example, the template for displaying the error could be

```
<font color="{1}">{0}</font>
```

The numbered "variables" {0} and {1} can be substituted at runtime with the real values, `"blue"` and `"The Month is invalid"`, using the `MessageFormat` class.

```
MessageFormat formatter = new MessageFormat("<font
color=\"{1}\">{0}</font>");
Object[] msgArgs = { "The Month is invalid", "blue" };
String message = formatter.format(msgArgs);
```

After the template has been "formatted," the resultant message would be

```
<font color="blue">The Month is Invalid</font>
```

Add a field of type `ResourceBundle` to obtain the error message template from a property file:

```
protected static ResourceBundle bundle =
    ResourceBundle.getBundle("station.auction.taglib.ErrMsg");
```

Create another field, `formatter`, of type `MessageFormat` that uses the template obtained from the `ResourceBundle` instance:

```
protected static MessageFormat formatter =
    new MessageFormat(bundle.getString("message"));
```

For every attribute, xxx, defined in the tag, you need to provide a public setter method, `setXxx(String arg)` and a field to store it within the tag handler. To store the `color` attribute passed in the tag, you also need to define a setter method, `setColor`, and a `String` field to store it in the class:

```
public String fieldColor = "red";
public void setColor(String color) {
    fieldColor = color;
}
```

Add additional fields for storing the parent tag, page context, and body content attributes set by the JSP container:

```
protected Tag parent = null;
protected BodyContent bodyContent = null;
protected PageContext pageContext = null;
```

Implement the methods defined by the `BodyTag` interface as shown in Listing 5.6.

Listing 5.6 ErrorTagHandler.java: Implementing Methods of the `BodyTag` Interface

```
public void setPageContext(PageContext arg1) {
    pageContext = arg1;
}
public void setParent(Tag arg1) {
    parent = arg1;
}
public void setBodyContent(BodyContent arg1) {
    bodyContent = arg1;
}
public Tag getParent() {
    return parent;
}
public void release() {
    parent = null;
    pageContext = null;
    bodyContent = null;
}
```

In addition to the setter and getter methods for the properties set by the JSP container, you need to implement the callback methods specified by `BodyTag`.

During the lifecycle of a simple body tag handler, the JSP invokes the callback methods in the following sequence:

1. `setPageContext`.

2. `setParent`.

3. Methods to set attributes, for example, `setColor`.

4. `doStartTag`. For a body tag, it can return `SKIP_BODY` if the body should not be evaluated or `EVAL_BODY_TAG` if evaluation is required.

5. `setBodyContent`. This sets the `bodyContent` property if a body evaluation is required, that is, if `doStartTag` returns `EVAL_BODY_TAG`.

6. `doInitBody`. Invoked before the first time a body is evaluated only if `doStartTag` returned `EVAL_BODY_TAG`.

7. `doAfterBody`. Invoked after every body evaluation. For simple body actions, you should return `SKIP_BODY`. If you need a new evaluation of the body, you should return `EVAL_BODY_TAG`.

8. `doEndTag`. You can safely use the body content and the other attributes set by the JSP container to generate the required content. At the end of the method you should return `EVAL_PAGE` or `SKIP_PAGE` depending on whether you want to evaluate the rest of the page.

9. `release`. You can release any unused resources you used in the class in this method.

The implementation of the remaining callback methods of the BodyTag interface is shown in Listing 5.7. Within the doEndTag method, you need to pass the error message and the color as parameters to format the message.

Listing 5.7 ErrorTagHandler.java: Implementing the Remaining Callback Methods of the BodyTag Interface

```
public void doInitBody() throws JspException {
}

public int doStartTag() throws JspException {
    return EVAL_BODY_TAG;
}

public int doAfterBody() throws JspException {
    return SKIP_BODY;
}

public int doEndTag() throws JspException {
    try {
        String msg = "";
        if (bodyContent != null) {
            msg = bodyContent.getString();
        }
        Object[] msgArgs = { msg, fieldColor };
        String errMessage = formatter.format(msgArgs);
        this.pageContext.getOut().write(errMessage);
    }
    catch(java.io.IOException e) {
        throw new javax.servlet.jsp.JspException("IO Error: " + e.getMessage());
    }

    return EVAL_PAGE;
}
```

Note

Instead of implementing all the methods defined in the BodyTag interface, you could inherit from the BodyTagSupport class defined in the tag extension framework. In the BodyTagSupport implementation of the BodyTag interface, the doStartTag method returns EVAL_BODY_TAG, the doAfterBody returns SKIP_BODY, and doEndTag returns EVAL_PAGE.

You could easily redefine ErrorTagHandler to extend from BodyTagSupport by only providing the setter method for the color attribute and implementing the doEndTag method as shown in Listing 5.8.

Listing 5.8   ErrorTagHandler.java: Redefining `ErrorTagHandler` by Extending from `BodyTagSupport`

```java
package station.auction.taglib;

import java.text.MessageFormat;
import java.util.ResourceBundle;
import javax.servlet.jsp.*;
import javax.servlet.jsp.tagext.*;

public class ErrorTagHandler implements BodyTag {
    protected static ResourceBundle bundle =
        ResourceBundle.getBundle("station.auction.taglib.ErrMsg");
    protected static MessageFormat formatter =
        new MessageFormat(bundle.getString("message"));

    protected String fieldColor = "red";

    public void setColor(String newColor) {
        fieldColor = newColor;
    }

    public int doEndTag() throws JspException {
        try
        {
            String msg = "";
            if (bodyContent != null) {
                msg = bodyContent.getString();
            }
            Object[] msgArgs = { msg, fieldColor };
            this.pageContext.getOut().write(formatter.format(msgArgs));
            System.out.println(formatter.format(msgArgs));
        }
        catch(java.io.IOException e)
        {
            throw new javax.servlet.jsp.JspException("IO Error: " +
                                                     e.getMessage());
        }

        return EVAL_PAGE;
    }
}
```

Save the Java source file, ErrorTagHandler.java, in the `AuctionStation/web-inf/classes/station/auction/taglib` directory of the `<tomcat-root>/webapps` folder.

Open a command prompt. Set servlet.jar found in `<tomcat-root>/lib` in the CLASSPATH. Compile the Java source from the `AuctionStation/web-inf/classes` directory to produce the class file- ErrorTagHandler.class, using

```
javac station/auction/taglib/ErrorTagHandler.java
```

Create a properties file, ErrMsg.properties, in the same directory where you save your Java file. Make an entry for the message name-value pair. The value specifies the template to be used for generating the error messages. Make sure you escape any quotation symbol (") by prefixing it with the backward slash (\) to prevent an error at runtime. Also provide the two "variables," {0} for the error message and {1} for the color:

```
message=<font color=\"{1}\" size=\"-1\">{0}</font>
```

Describing the `error` Tag in the Taglib Descriptor

You need to make an entry of the `error` tag in a taglib descriptor before you can use it. You can use the as-taglib.tld file that you created earlier to store the `error` tag description.

The only difference between the description of the error tag from the `today` tag is the bodycontent element for the `error` tag. The element specifies that the bodycontent type is JSP implying that the tag can contain JSP tags and other custom tags in its body. Also notice the extra attribute element in the `tag` element to describe the optional `color` attribute as shown in Listing 5.9

Listing 5.9   as-taglib.tld: Adding an Entry in the `taglib` Descriptor for the `error` Tag

```
<?xml version="1.0" encoding="ISO-8859-1" ?>
<!DOCTYPE taglib
        PUBLIC "-//Sun Microsystems, Inc.//DTD JSP Tag Library 1.1//EN"
        "http://java.sun.com/j2ee/dtds/web-jsptaglibrary_1_1.dtd">
<taglib>
    <tlibversion>1.0</tlibversion>
    <jspversion>1.1</jspversion>
    <shortname>as</shortname>
    <uri>http://localhost:8080/AuctionStation/jsp/mytags.jar</uri>
    <info>Auction Station's Tag Library</info>

    <tag>
        <name>today</name>
        <tagclass>station.auction.taglib.TodayTagHandler</tagclass>
        <bodycontent>empty</bodycontent>
        <info>Prints the Current Date</info>
    </tag>

    <tag>
        <name>error</name>
        <tagclass>station.auction.taglib.ErrorTagHandler</tagclass>
        <bodycontent>JSP</bodycontent>
        <info>Prints Error Messages</info>
        <attribute>
            <name>color</name>
            <required>false</required>
        </attribute>
    </tag>
</taglib>
```

Using the `error` Tag in a JSP

You can use the error tag to display error messages in the input JSPs used for the form-based calendar application developed earlier. For simplicity, just add the error tag to the customtags.jsp you built earlier. Because the JSP already includes the `taglib` directive for the tag lib descriptor, you can use the `error` tag right away.

Modify the JSP to include the `error` tag, one for displaying the "invalid month" error message and the other to display the date on which the error occurred.

```
<as:error>The Month is Invalid<as:error> <p>
<as:error color="blue">The error occurred on <b><as:today/><b></as:error>
```

Running and Testing the JSP

Restart the Tomcat server to make the changes take effect. Launch your browser and point it to the location `http://localhost:8080/jsp/customtags.jsp`. If the current day were May 24, 2000, your browser would display the information shown in Figure 5.2.

Figure 5.2

Output of the custom-tags.jsp page in the browser

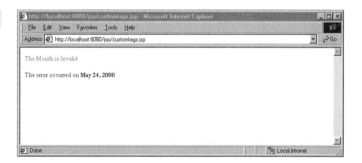

Developing a Nested Body Action Tag—email

You now graduate to the next higher level of complexity of the custom tag actions-nested tags within the body. In this section you will build an email tag structure to send email messages using the `SendMail` JavaBean that you built in the previous chapter.

```
<as:email smtpHost="SMTP Host Name">
    <as:from address="Sender's Email Address">Sender's Name</as:from>
    <as:to address="Recipient's Email Address">Recipient's Name</as:to>
<as:subject>Subject of the Message</as:subject>
    <as:body>Body of the Message</as:body>
</as:email>
```

The nested email action has a tag structure beginning with the root `email` tag that contains an `smtpHost` attribute specifying which SMTP server is to be used for sending the message. The `email` tag contains four nested tags:

- `from` tag for specifying the sender's information. The sender's address is passed in the `address` attribute and the name in the body of the tag.

- to tag for specifying the recipient's information. The recipient's address and name are passed within the address attribute and body as in the from tag.

- subject tag for specifying the subject of the message within the body.

- body tag for specifying the message's content.

The email tag structure is another potential family of XML documents because it is structured and has a well-defined tag set. You can formally document the email tag structure using a DTD, or Document Type Definition, as shown in Listing 5.10.

Listing 5.10   Describing the Email Tags and Structure Using a DTD

```
<!-- DTD defining the email tag structure.
     Neither the JSP container nor the taglib will use it. -->

<!-- Declare the email tag and define its structure  -->
<!ELEMENT email (from, to+, subject, body) >
<!ATTLIST email smtpHost     CDATA    #IMPLIED>

<!-- Declare the from tag -->
<!ELEMENT from (#PCDATA) >
<!ATTLIST from address     CDATA #REQUIRED>

<!-- The to tag -->
<!ELEMENT to (#PCDATA) >
<!ATTLIST to address     CDATA #REQUIRED>

<!-- The subject tag -->
<!ELEMENT subject (#PCDATA) >

<!-- The body tag -->
<!ELEMENT body (#PCDATA) >
```

An ELEMENT declaration introduces a tag and specifies a structure in its body. The first ELEMENT declaration specifies that an email tag has a from tag, followed by one or more to tags, a subject tag, and a body tag. If the tag has no nested structure within it and only has a body of text, you can specify its *content model* as #PCDATA, a mnemonic for character data, as in the case of the from, to, subject and body element declarations. An ATTLIST declaration specifies the attributes of a tag. For the email tag, it specifies an optional (#IMPLIED), character-based (CDATA) smtpHost attribute.

You now need to create tag handlers for every tag that you defined in the structure. Because the tags have a body, either a nested structure or a text body, you need to define BodyTag handlers for each of them. You can extend from BodyTagSupport to reuse the default implementation of the BodyTag interface.

Creating the `EmailTagHandler` Class

The `email` tag nests the other tags; therefore, the tag handler for this tag, `EmailTagHandler`, needs to implement the `BodyTag` interface (or extend the `BodyTagSupport` class). The `EmailTagHandler` reuses the `SendMail` JavaBean, created in the previous chapter, for composing the email message and sending it out. The strategy for handling the email structure is as follows:

1. Create an instance of the `SendMail` when the start tag is encountered, within the `doStartTag` method. Set the SMTP host in the JavaBean using the value obtained from the `smtpHost` property obtained using the `setSmtpHost` callback method.

2. Set the instance as a page attribute using the `pageContext` obtained from the `setPageContext` callback method. The handlers of the nested handlers will use this page attribute for composing the message.

3. Send the message when the end of the tag is encountered. This works on the premise that the nested tags have done the necessary actions of setting the different properties of the `SendMail` JavaBean instance.

To implement the handler, create a Java source file, EmailTagHandler.java, and provide the `import` statements as well as the declaration that the class extends from `BodyTagSupport`:

```
package station.auction.taglib;

import javax.servlet.jsp.*;
import javax.servlet.jsp.tagext.*;
import station.auction.beans.SendMail;

public class EmailTagHandler extends BodyTagSupport {
```

Provide fields for storing the `SendMail` bean instance as well as the `smtpHost` property:

```
protected station.auction.beans.SendMail message = null;
protected java.lang.String smtpHost = "mail.auction.station.net";
```

You can set your SMTP host as the default value that will be used when the `email` tag doesn't have the `smtpHost` attribute.

Provide the public setter method for the `smtpHost` attribute as well as a protected accessor:

```
public void setSmtpHost(String newSmtpHost) {
    smtpHost = newSmtpHost;
}
protected String getSmtpHost() {
    return smtpHost;
}
```

Override the default implementation of the doStartTag method to create the message and set it in the page context as shown in Listing 5.11. The method returns EVAL_BODY_TAG because the nested action tags have to be evaluated.

Listing 5.11   EmailTagHandler.java: Overriding the doStartTag Method for Creating the Email Message

```java
public int doStartTag() {
    System.out.println("[EmailTagHandler] Creating the message");

    message = new SendMail(getSmtpHost());
    pageContext.setAttribute("message", message,
        javax.servlet.jsp.PageContext.PAGE_SCOPE);

    return EVAL_BODY_TAG;
}
```

You can expose beans created in the tag handlers to the remainder JSP elements of the page or to other tag handlers by setting the bean instances as attributes in the page context. These beans can be used just like any other beans in the page that were created or referenced using the <jsp:useBean> tag. You can also set the lifetime of the attribute by specifying its scope as one of PAGE_SCOPE, SESSION_SCOPE, REQUEST_SCOPE, and APPLICATION_SCOPE, which are constants for page, session, request, and application defined on the PageContext class.

Create the doEndTag method for sending the message. Return EVAL_PAGE at the end of the method to indicate that the remainder page should be evaluated. Release the message instance created in the tag handler in the release method, by removing it from the page context and setting it to null as shown in Listing 5.12.

Listing 5.12   EmailTagHandler.java: Overriding the doEndTag and release Methods for Sending the Email and Cleaning Up

```java
public int doEndTag() {
    System.out.println("[EmailTagHandler] Sending the message");
    message.send();

    return EVAL_PAGE;
}

public void release() {
    pageContext.removeAttribute("message");
    message = null;
    super.release();
}
```

Creating the Nested Tag Handler Classes

Create tag handlers `FromTagHandler`, `ToTagHandler`, `SubjectTagHandler` and `BodyTagHandler` (all extending from `BodyTagSupport`) for the `from`, `to`, `subject`, and body nested tags. They have similar actions wherein they set information obtained from attributes and the body on the `message` bean obtained from the page context.

You need to define a `setAddress` method and a field to store the address attributes in the `FromTagHandler` and `ToTagHandler`.

```
public class FromTagHandler extends BodyTagSupport {
    protected String address = null;

protected String getAddress() {
    return address;
}
public void setAddress(String newAddress) {
    address = newAddress;
}
```

For all the nested tag handlers, you need to override the `doAfterBody` method, to use the email information obtained from the `address` attribute (if available) and the body and set it on the `SendMail` instance obtained from the page context to compose the message. Listing 5.13 shows the source for the `doAfterBody` method of the `FromTagHandler`.

Listing 5.13   FromTagHandler.java: Overriding the `doAfterBody` to Set the `from` Attribute of the Email Message

```
public int doAfterBody() {
    System.out.println("[FromTagHandler] Setting the From Attributes");

    SendMail message = (SendMail) pageContext.getAttribute("message");
    String name = "";
    if (bodyContent != null) {
        name = bodyContent.getString();
    }
    message.setFromAddress( name, getAddress());

    return SKIP_BODY;
}
```

You can use the same code for the other nested tag handlers, replacing `message.setFromAddress( name, getAddress());` with the necessary setter method as the case may be. For `SubjectTagHandler`, you need to replace it with `message.setSubject(name);`.

Save the Java source files for the different handlers in the `AuctionStation/web-inf/classes/station/auction/taglib` directory of the `<tomcat-root>/webapps` folder.

Open a command prompt. Set servlet.jar found in `<tomcat-root>/lib` in the CLASS-PATH. Compile the Java sources from the `AuctionStation/web-inf/classes` directory to produce the classfiles.

```
javac station/auction/taglib/*.java
```

Describing the Email Tags in the Taglib Descriptor

You need to make an entry of the email tags in the `taglib` descriptor before you can use it. You can use the as-taglib.tld file that you created earlier for the `today` and `error` tags.

Specify the tag name, its associated tag handler class, bodycontent as `JSP`, descriptive information, and attributes as shown in Listing 5.14.

Listing 5.14   as-taglib.tld: **Adding Entries for the Email Tags in the taglib Descriptor**

```
<tag>
    <name>email</name>
    <tagclass>station.auction.taglib.EmailTagHandler</tagclass>
    <bodycontent>JSP</bodycontent>
    <info>Creates an Email Message and sends it</info>
    <attribute>
        <name>smtpHost</name>
        <required>false</required>
    </attribute>
</tag>

<tag>
    <name>from</name>
    <tagclass>station.auction.taglib.FromTagHandler</tagclass>
    <bodycontent>JSP</bodycontent>
    <info>Sets the Senders information in the message</info>
    <attribute>
        <name>address</name>
        <required>true</required>
    </attribute>
</tag>

<tag>
    <name>to</name>
    <tagclass>station.auction.taglib.ToTagHandler</tagclass>
    <bodycontent>JSP</bodycontent>
    <info>Sets the Recepients information in the message</info>
    <attribute>
        <name>address</name>
        <required>true</required>
    </attribute>
</tag>

<tag>
```

```
   <name>subject</name>
   <tagclass>station.auction.taglib.SubjectTagHandler</tagclass>
   <bodycontent>JSP</bodycontent>
   <info>Sets the Subject of the message</info>
</tag>

<tag>
   <name>body</name>
   <tagclass>station.auction.taglib.BodyTagHandler</tagclass>
   <bodycontent>JSP</bodycontent>
   <info>Sets the Body of the message</info>
</tag>
```

Using the Email Tag Structure in a JSP

You can use the email tag structure in any JSP that needs to send email messages. For a simple usage, you can use it in customtags.jsp as shown in Listing 5.15.

Listing 5.15   customtags.jsp: Including the Email Tags for Sending Email

```
<%@ taglib uri="http://www.auction.station.net/as-taglib" prefix="as" %>

<as:error>The Month is Invalid<as:error> <p>
<as:error color="blue">The error occurred on <b><as:today/><b></as:error>

<as:email>
    <as:from address="error@auction.station.net">Auction Station Error</as:from>
    <as:to address="yourname@auction.station.net">Your Name</as:to>
    <as:subject>Simple Subject</as:subject>
    <as:body>Simple body, you could place expressions and scriptlets to generate
        the body as well.
    </as:body>
</as:email>
```

You could also use it in error.jsp created in the previous chapter for sending error details to the developer, as shown in Listing 5.16.

Listing 5.16   error.jsp: Modifying error.jsp to Use the Email Custom Tags for Sending Email

```
<%@ page isErrorPage="true" %>
<%@ taglib uri="as-taglib.tld" prefix="as" %>

<html>
<head>
    <title>Oops!</title>
</head>
<body>
<h1>We are sorry</h1>
The page you have just reached has some errors.
Our technical staff have been informed of the error and will
fix it as soon as possible.
<p>
```

Listing 5.16   continued

```
<% // Create the body passing the exception trace and the query string
   String body = null;
   java.io.StringWriter sw = new java.io.StringWriter();
   java.io.PrintWriter pw = new java.io.PrintWriter(sw);
   exception.printStackTrace(pw);
   body = sw.toString() + request.getQueryString();
%>

<as:email>
    <as:from address="error@auction.station.net">Auction Station Error</as:from>
    <as:to address="yourname@auction.station.net">Your Name</as:to>
    <as:subject><%= exception%></as:subject>
    <as:body><%= body%></as:body>
</as:email>

<p>
Thank you for your patience
</body>
</html>
```

Running and Testing the JSP

Restart the Tomcat server to make the changes take effect. Ensure that the JavaMail and JAF jar files are set in the CLASSPATH. Launch your browser and point it to the location http://localhost:8080/jsp/customtags.jsp. Because the tag does not generate any output, the only way you can check whether the handlers are operating properly is to look at the recipient's inbox for new messages. You can also print messages to the console for debugging, as shown in Figure 5.3.

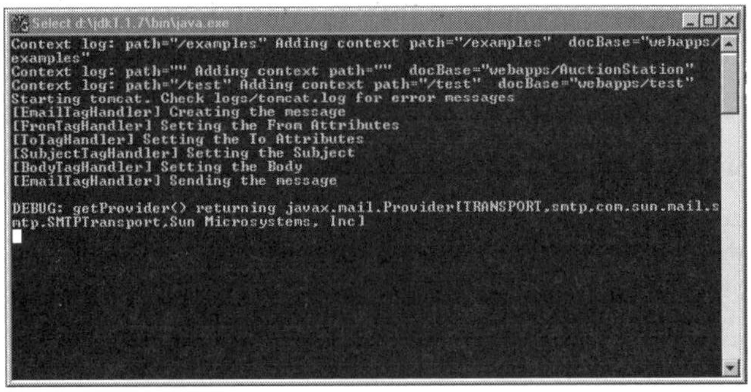

Figure 5.3

Debugging messages of the email tag handler printed in the command window

Next Steps

In this chapter you learned how to provide extra reusability and maintainability in your JSPs using the tag library feature. Custom tags are to JSPs what JavaBeans are to the Java programming language. I expect that soon vendors will be providing off-the-shelf custom tag libraries that you can use in your JSPs.

So far you learned to use simple actions—actions with body and nested actions. In the next chapter, you will learn how to use databases in your application to build a user registration and extend the monthly calendar to show events as well. You will also build co-operating and iterative action tags for database access.

In This Chapter

- *Getting Started with Using a Relational Database*
- *Adding Events to the Calendar*
- *Developing a Custom Tag Library for Database Handling*
- *Creating the Registration Module*
- *Performing Database Connection Pooling*
- *Next Steps*

Chapter 6

Accessing Databases to Create the Calendar of Events and Registration Module

Now that you are well versed in JSP syntax, it's time to get down to doing the real stuff. Most of the dynamic content on the Web is generated from data stored in databases, mostly in its most common form: relational databases.

Getting Started with Using a Relational Database

At the heart of relational databases lies the relational model, developed through the pioneering efforts of Dr. E. F. Codd at IBM. He developed the model to simplify his data storage, retrieval, and updating mechanism, which until then was cumbersome and data-dependent.

The relational model is built on the concept of a table in which data is stored. Each table contains rows of data containing different columns or fields. Each record, or *tuple*, corresponds to a unique row in the table, and each tuple's attributes correspond to columns in the row. To store information about users in a relational database, for example, you create a table containing columns for different attributes of the user, such as name, email, and user ID. For each user, you will need to create a row in the table and provide appropriate values for the different columns. Figure 6.1 shows the table structure for storing information about users.

The table contains four columns (attributes): first name, last name, email, and user ID. These are basic character data. You can also use richer data formats, such as numbers, dates, floating-point numbers, and even graphical images for your column types. For each user—Jim, Deepa, David, Kenneth, and Maneesh—you would insert a row in the table to provide the values for the different columns.

Figure 6.1

The Users table, containing the rows and columns

First Name	Last Name	Email	User ID
Jim	Moore	jimoore@..	jimoore
Deepa	Jivan	dj@auction..	dj
David	Gaertner	gaertner@..	gaertner
Kenneth	Serrao	ken@aucti..	ken
Maneesh	Sahu	msahu@a..	msahu

The Database Manager System (DBMS) handles complex operations, such as storing and retrieving data from the file system. It also provides indexing facilities that optimize searches and queries for data, and data integrity checks such as testing the validity of column values with respect to the column types and constraints.

All you need to do in your application is connect to the database and execute Structured Query Language (SQL) statements. SQL is an English-like language for querying and manipulating databases.

how tōō prō nouns' it

SQL: Some people pronounce it *sequel* (that was the original name for the language), and others pronounce it as it is spelled, *ess-que-el*.

SQL is now an industry standard established by the American National Standards Institute (ANSI). Most of the relational DBMSs support SQL at some level with SQL-92 being the fully compliant level. SQL provides an exhaustive set of commands to do the following tasks:

- Query or find data
- Insert, update, and delete data
- Create, modify, and delete database objects, such as tables
- Administer and control data and database objects

The advantage of using SQL is that it is simple and can be used interchangeably with any SQL-compliant database. All the database examples in this book have been developed and run on DB2—Universal Database. DB2 is IBM's award-winning database, which has been ported to run on virtually every major platform including Palm OS devices.

Note A trial version of DB2 for Windows is included on the companion CD-ROM. If you are developing the JSPs on Linux, Solaris, or any other platform, you can download an evaluation copy from `http://www.ibm.com/db2`.

You can also use any other ODBC-compliant database, such as Sybase, Oracle, Informix, or mSQL, to develop and run the JSP applications. *ODBC*, short for *Open Database Connectivity*, is a standard database access-mechanism that was jointly developed by Microsoft and IBM to address the tight coupling between an application and a DBMS. In ODBC access, an extra layer, referred to as the *driver*, is inserted between the application and the DBMS. It translates the queries and updates specified by the application, mostly SQL statements, into commands that can be understood by the DBMS. The underlying DBMS responds to the commands and then translates them back to the application. This translation mechanism is transparent to the application, and hence the database configured for ODBC access can be replaced by another ODBC-compliant database.

Defining the Database and the Users Table Using SQL

The first step toward developing database-backed JSP applications is to create a database. A *database* is a collection of database objects, such as tables, views, and aliases. You need to create a connection with a database before creating, accessing, or manipulating tables.

You can create and define a database using the command-line (text-based) interface or a graphical user interface provided by the DBMS. DB2 provides both these interfaces, a command-line processor for the SQL-savvy users and the Control Center for a user who isn't conversant with SQL or for users who have been pampered with the convenience it provides!

Most databases have a command-line processor to enter and execute SQL statements. You can use the DB2 command-line processor by invoking the following statements on the command line:

```
db2cmd
db2
```

This would launch a new window, initialize the DB2 environment, and start the command-line processor as shown in Figure 6.2.

Your first step will be to create a new database, AUCTION. You can do this using the SQL Data Definition Language command:

```
CREATE DATABASE auction
```

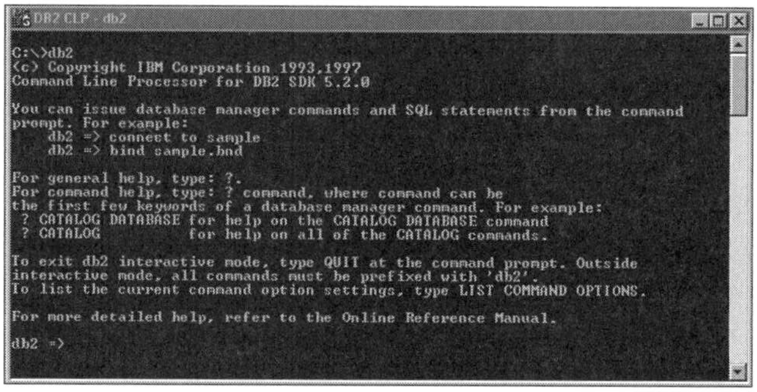

Figure 6.2

The DB2 command-line processor

You need to create a database connection before you create, modify, or query tables in the database. This is done using the CONNECT TO command:

```
CONNECT TO auction
```

You can now issue data definition, manipulation, and query commands against database objects in the Auction database. Your first exercise is to store user information in the database. On analysis, the user information consists of personal information, such as name, date of birth, address, and password details. A user can specify different addresses, such as home, office, and mailing addresses. This information cannot be stored in a single row because of the unknown multiplicity of the addresses: You cannot define specific fields to store the data when you don't know how many addresses there will be. You will therefore need to normalize the table and create another table, Address, for storing the addresses.

Normalization is a mechanism for refining your data model. It prescribes a set of rules of thumb that should be applied to the model before creating the physical tables.

- Store atomic data. When storing the username in the database, often you would like to retrieve only the last name. If you stored the username consisting of the first, last, and middle name, you would be unable to return users sorted by last names as well as first names. This is not applicable for data types, such as DATE, TIME, and TIMESTAMP, because the DBMS provides built-in SQL functions for extracting the month, year, and day from the fields.

- Remove fields that are derived from another. You should not store fields such as Full Name because the full name can be derived by concatenating the first name, initial, and last name.

- If the multiplicity of the fields is unknown (not present or more than one), create a new table, move the fields to the table, and copy the primary key field as a foreign key. In the case of Users, an address may be available for a user or more than one address (home, office, and mailing) can be provided. You can provide individual fields for each type of address, but that would result in a lot of empty spaces or holes in the table if the information were not provided. The normalization process is to move the address fields to another table, Address, along with the user ID. An inner join can obtain the addresses for a particular user.

Note You can find more information about normalization at `http://www.` `troubleshooters.com/littstip/ltnorm.html`.

You can formally define associations between tables and provide referential integrity using a FOREIGN KEY relationship in the Address table for the Users table. The data model for storing user information is shown in Figure 6.3.

Figure 6.3

Data model for storing user information

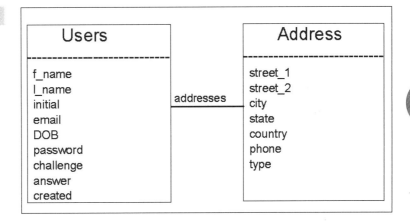

The data model can be translated into physical tables in the database using SQL CREATE TABLE statements. The CREATE TABLE statement has the following structure:

```
CREATE TABLE <name> (
    <column_name_1> <type_1> <constraint>
…
);
```

The data-definition statements for the user information are shown in Listing 6.1.

Listing 6.1 database.ddl: Creating the Users and Address Tables for Storing User Information

```
CREATE TABLE Users  (
    user_id VARCHAR(15) NOT NULL,
    f_name VARCHAR(30),
    l_name VARCHAR(30),
    initial CHAR(1),
    email VARCHAR(30),
```

Listing 6.1 continued

```
    dob DATE,
    type  SMALLINT,
    password VARCHAR(10),
    challenge VARCHAR(50),
    answer VARCHAR(40),
    created TIMESTAMP,
    PRIMARY KEY (user_id)
);

CREATE TABLE Address (
    user_id VARCHAR(15) NOT NULL,
    type CHAR(1) NOT NULL,
    street_1 VARCHAR(40),
    street_2 VARCHAR(40),
    city VARCHAR(20),
    state CHAR(2),
    country VARCHAR(25),
    phone VARCHAR(20),
    PRIMARY KEY (user_id, type),
    FOREIGN KEY (user_id) REFERENCES Users(user_id)
);
```

The relationship between the Users and Address tables is enforced using the FOREIGN KEY relationship defined in the Address table. This implies that a row cannot be inserted in the Address table without a row in the Users table having a matching user_id field.

You can also create the table using DB2's Control Center. It saves you the trouble of having to remember the database field types. Figure 6.4 shows how you can visually create the Users table.

Figure 6.4

Creating the Users table using the Control Center

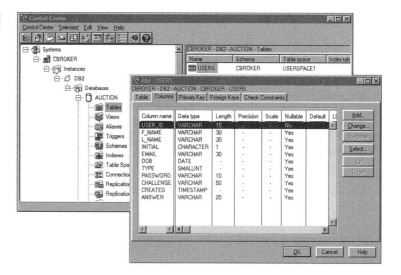

Other data-definition commands include

- ALTER for modifying a table
- DROP for deleting a table from the database

Inserting Users Using SQL Data Manipulation Commands

You can populate the table with users using data manipulation commands. There are three commands of importance:

- INSERT for inserting rows into the table
- UPDATE for updating existing rows
- DELETE for deleting rows from the table

The INSERT statement inserts one or more rows into the table using the provided values as shown for the Users table in Listing 6.2.

Listing 6.2   populateUsers.sql: Populating the User Table with Sample Data

```sql
INSERT INTO USERS(USER_ID, F_NAME, L_NAME, INITIAL, EMAIL, TYPE, CREATED)
➥VALUES
  ('jimoore', 'Jim', 'Moore', '', 'jimoore@auction.station.net', 1,
➥ CURRENT TIMESTAMP),
  ('dj', 'Deepa', 'Jivan', '', 'dj@auction.station.net', 2,
➥CURRENT TIMESTAMP),
('david', 'David', 'Gaertner', '','gaertner@auction.station.net', 1,
➥CURRENT TIMESTAMP),
   ('ken', 'Kenneth', 'Serrao', '','ken@auction.station.net', 1,
➥CURRENT TIMESTAMP),
   ('asar', 'Arun', 'Sar', 'K', 'asar@auction.station.net', 1,
➥CURRENT TIMESTAMP);
```

You can invoke similar commands to insert addresses in the Address table. Remember to provide a user ID that exists in the Users table while doing so.

Querying Users

You can get data from the database and impose ordering upon it using the data query command, SELECT. The SELECT statement returns all the rows in the table. The query SELECT * FROM Users returns the attributes of all the users (rows) in the Users table.

You can constrain the result set by appending a WHERE clause to the query. To return all users in the Users table whose TYPE is 2, you can use the query SELECT * FROM Users WHERE TYPE=2.

If you need only a subset of the column values, you can specify the columns to be returned. For example, you can return only the first and last names of all the users in the Users table by specifying only the f_name and l_name fields as SELECT f_name, l_name FROM Users.

You can sort the results according to the values of a particular column using the ORDER BY clause. To sort the Users according to the last name, you can use the query SELECT * from Users ORDER BY l_name.

You can also return result sets consisting of data from two or more tables using inner joins. To return all the addresses of users whose TYPE is 2, you can create an inner join by specifying two or more databases in the SELECT FROM clause, and a WHERE clause for constraining the result set to rows matching a specified condition. The column names can be qualified by a name to differentiate common field names in the tables.

```
SELECT addr.street_1, addr.street_2, addr.city from Address addr, Users user
➥ WHERE addr.user_id = user.user_id AND user.type = 2.
```

After you are done operating on the database, you must disconnect from it using the CONNECT RESET statement.

Database Access by Java Applications

You have a set of options for connecting to databases from Java applications. SQL remains the most popular way to issue commands to the database. Some of the popular Java database access mechanisms include

- Java Database Connectivity (JDBC)
- SQL Java (SQLJ)

JDBC

Java Database Connectivity (JDBC) is the most common mechanism for accessing databases from Java applications. The JDK in fact contains the JDBC classes contained in the java.sql.* package. The JDBC classes connect to the database using one of the following drivers:

- **JDBC-ODBC Bridge driver**—The JDK provides a driver to allow Java applications to access ODBC-configured data sources.
- **Native drivers**—DBMSs provide drivers that can be used to directly connect to the database.
- **JDBC Net drivers**—This driver connects to databases on remote machines using a network protocol.
- **All-Java driver**—This driver is entirely written in Java to allow portability of database access across platforms.

JDBC provides a set of classes to allow Java applications to access databases, issue commands, and execute queries as described in Table 6.1.

Table 6.1   JDBC Classes for Accessing Databases and Executing Commands

Class Name	Description
DriverManager	This class is responsible for loading a specific JDBC driver.
Connection	This class is used to establish a database connection.
Statement	This class is used for issuing commands (using static SQL statements) to the database for data definition, querying, and manipulation.
PreparedStatement	This class provides support for creating dynamic queries by parameterizing the variables in the SQL statement.
ResultSet	This class returns the matching rows returned by the DBMS for the query.

The java.sql.* package also provides classes to allow Java applications to directly operate on SQL data types, such as DATE, TIME, and TIMESTAMP.

SQLJ

SQL Java (SQLJ) is a new standard for embedding SQL statements directly into Java programs. This application is then translated into all-Java source and compiled into Java bytecode for execution by the Java Virtual Machine. This can be performed without using any additional classes. The translator in fact generates JDBC code that performs the operations specified using the SQL statement, such as making the connection, creating the statement, executing the SQL command, and returning the result set. This simplifies writing and maintaining Java database applications. Listing 6.3 shows the source for an application that prints the user information of a particular user.

Listing 6.3   UserInfo.sqlj: Specifying a SQL Query for Retrieving User Information Using SQLJ

```
String firstName = null;
String lastName = null;
String userId = "koshy";
#sql { SELECT f_name INTO :firstName, l_name INTO :lastName WHERE user_id =
:userId;
System.out.println("First Name: " + firstName + " Last Name: " + lastName);
```

SQLJ cannot be directly used in JSPs because the JSPs themselves need to be translated into Java source and compiled into bytecode. You could, however, use them for database access within JavaBeans.

Adding Events to the Calendar

You will now enhance the Calendar Application to display events for a particular day. This can be achieved by hyperlinking the days displayed in the monthly calendar.

When the user clicks on any of the links, a window is opened, displaying the events for the day.

The information about the events is stored in the Events table. You can enter the information in the table using simple SQL INSERT statements as shown in Listing 6.4.

Listing 6.4   PopulateCalendar.sql: Inserting Events into the Events Table

```
CONNECT TO AUCTION;

INSERT INTO EVENTS ( EVENT_ID, NAME, DESCRIPTION, START_DATE) VALUES
  ('1', 'Anniversary Sale', 'Our first Anniversary auctions...special dutch
➥ auctions', '2000-05-05-00.00.00.000000'),
  ('2', 'Douglas Adams Special', 'Auction of personally autographed books by
➥Douglas Adams', '2000-05-08-00.00.00.000000')
,
  ('3', 'Indian Antiques', 'Handicrafts, fabrics, Jewellery...the best of India',
➥ '2000-05-13-00.00.00.000000')
  ('4', 'Fleetwood Mac Special', 'Exchange fleetwood mac albums,
➥memorabilia and waive shipping fees', '2000-05-21-09.45.00.000000'),
  ('5', 'Digital Cameras', 'Exchange your film-based cameras for digital
➥cameras', '2000-05-29-16.00.00.000000'),
  ('6', 'MAD Comics', 'Special Edition of MAD comics, cheap!',
➥'2000-05-21-12.30.00.000000'));

CONNECT RESET;
```

Setting Up a Connection to the Database

Provide declarations for the driver, URL, user ID, and password to make a database connection from your JSP. Some JDBC drivers are shipped along with specific DBMSs. DB2 ships two JDBC drivers—a native JDBC driver for accessing local databases (COM.ibm.db2.jdbc.app.DB2Driver) and another for accessing remote databases (COM.ibm.db2.jdbc.net.DB2Driver). You can use these drivers directly without doing any configurations other than setting the archive containing these classes in the CLASSPATH.

The URL for connecting to a database using the Native DB2 driver is jdbc:db2:<databasename> where *databasename* is a database on your local machine or an alias to a remote database. To access the local database, Auction, the URL would be jdbc:db2:auction. You may also need to provide a user ID and password to connect to the database if you specified extra security for your database.

You can also use the JDBC-ODBC Bridge driver (sun.jdbc.odbc.JdbcOdbcDriver) that is shipped along with the JDK. You would need to configure the database for ODBC access. In Windows 95/98/NT, you can do this in the ODBC Data Source

Administrator (Start Menu | Settings | Control Panel | ODBC). In the System DSN tab, add a system data source by clicking on the Add button. This launches the Create New Data Source dialog that lists the drivers registered with it. Figure 6.5 shows two registered drivers.

Figure 6.5

Creating a new DB2 data source

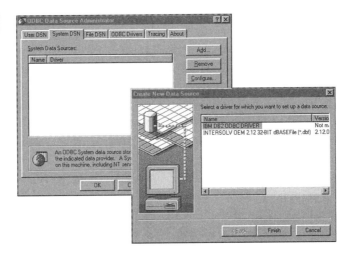

To access a DB2 database, select the IBM DB2 ODBC Driver option from the list and click on the Submit button. This launches the IBM ODBC Driver-Add dialog displaying the local databases in the Data Source Name drop-down menu as shown in Figure 6.6.

Figure 6.6

Registering the Auction database for ODBC access

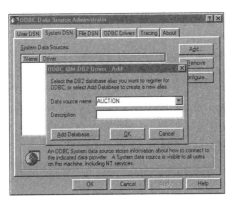

If you have already created the Auction database, select Auction and click OK. This will configure the database as a system data source and list it as one of the sources, as shown in Figure 6.7.

Figure 6.7

The Auction database configured as a system data source

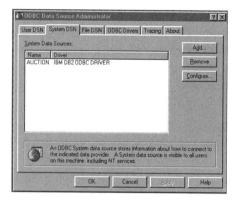

The URL for making a connection to a database using the JDBC-ODBC bridge is `jdbc:odbc:<databasename>`—in this case, `jdbc:odbc:auction`.

Use a Native JDBC driver if you have a choice between using it and the JDBC-ODBC driver. The Native JDBC driver performs better because the database connection is direct without having to pass through the intermediate ODBC Bridge.

Create a JSP for Printing a Day's Events

Create a JSP, dayevents.jsp, that prints the events for a particular day. The day is specified using request information representing the day, month, and year. This implies that the request information must be appended to the JSP's URL. To display the events for May 28, 2000, the request information `month=5&&day=28&&year=2000` must be appended to pass the values.

Provide the Page Directive

Add the page directive to the page. Provide information to import the `java.sql.*` package and to specify the error page:

```
<%@ page import="java.sql.*" errorPage="error.jsp" %>
```

Declare Variables for the Page

Declare variables for specifyin the driver, URL, user ID, and password:

```
<%! protected String driver="sun.jdbc.odbc.JdbcOdbcDriver";
protected String url="jdbc:odbc:Auction";
protected String userid = null;
protected String password = null; %>
```

Create a constant specifying the SQL query string. This returns a set of rows containing the event's name, description, and start date for a specific day. Without a WHERE clause, the SELECT statement would return all the rows in the table containing the specified columns. To constrain the result to those for a particular day, you need to specify the WHERE clause specifying a condition. The condition checks the column values with another. In this case you also need to use the MONTH, YEAR, and DAY SQL functions to compare the event's start date with the specified elements of the date. You can sort the rows based on the values of a particular column using the ORDER BY clause.

```
<%! public static String GET_DAYS_EVENTS_QUERY =
"SELECT name, description, start_date FROM Events " +
"WHERE MONTH(start_date) = ? AND YEAR(start_date) =? AND DAY(start_date) = ?"+
"ORDER BY HOUR(start_date), MINUTE(start_date)"; %>
```

Add a field to store the different month names.

```
<%! protected String[] monthNames =
➡ (new java.text.DateFormatSymbols()).getMonths(); %>
```

Store the different request parameters in String variables so that the information can be used easily within expressions and scriptlets.

```
<%
    // Get the request parameters and do checks
    String month = request.getParameter("month");
    String year = request.getParameter("year");
    String day = request.getParameter("day");
%>
```

Provide the title and heading for the page using the date information.

```
<html>
<title>Events for <%= month%>, <%= day%>, <%= year%></title>
<body>
    <center><FONT SIZE="+3">Events for <%= month%>-<%= day%>-<%=
year%></font></center>
    <p>
```

Load the Drivers and Create a Connection

Create a scriptlet to load the JDBC driver and create a database connection. The JDBC drivers are dynamically loaded at runtime using the Class.forName() method. After the driver has been loaded, you can create a connection using the java.sql.DriverManager class by passing the URL of the database as well as the user ID and password necessary to make the connection.

```
<%
    // Load the driver
    Class.forName(driver);

    // Obtain a connection to the database
    Connection conn = DriverManager.getConnection(url, userid, password);
```

Execute SQL Statements Using JDBC

After you obtain the java.sql.Connection instance from the getConnection method invoked on DriverManager, you can execute SQL statements (queries and updates) on the database. You can use either a java.sql.Statement or a java.sql. PreparedStatement instance to send your SQL queries and updates to the database using JDBC.

If you are using a Statement instance, all you need to do is execute the query or update after passing the necessary SQL statement. You can also use the PreparedStatement if you need to optimize a large number of queries and updates. You can "prepare" an SQL statement and set the values for the different parameters, identified by the question (?) symbol using setter methods. For retrieving the days, you can prepare the SQL statement by passing the GET_DAYS_EVENTS_QUERY representing the SELECT query for retrieving rows for a specific day. Set the different values for the different parameters using setter methods. Because all the parameters are string values, you need to invoke setString methods on the PreparedStatement and pass the variable number *n*, identified by the *n*th question mark in the statement and the actual value.

```
// Prepare the query statement
PreparedStatement stmt = conn.prepareStatement(GET_DAYS_EVENTS_QUERY);
stmt.setString(1, month);
stmt.setString(2, year);
stmt.setString(3, day);
```

Execute the SELECT statement by invoking executeQuery on the PreparedStatement. This returns a ResultSet instance that you can store within a temporary variable, rs.

```
ResultSet rs = stmt.executeQuery();
```

Note If you were modifying the database by inserting, updating, or deleting rows in the table or by creating, deleting, or modifying tables, you need to invoke executeUpdate on the PreparedStatement instead of executeQuery.

Retrieve Values from the ResultSet Instance

To obtain the matching rows returned, you need to iterate the ResultSet instance. You can retrieve the different rows by invoking the next method on rs. You can use the getter methods on rs to return the values of the different columns. The getter methods, getXXX, specify the column type (XXX) and return type for the column's value. You can specify a column by passing the column name or by passing the column number in the result set.

Note Specifying a column using a column number gives you faster retrieval than using its column name. However, this technique results in difficulty maintaining the SQL code, akin to naming variables in your code, such as month as 1 and so on. Your column identification decision can be based on trade-offs that are based on performance versus maintainability. You can ease the trade-off by using symbolic constants for the column numbers.

In this case the column 1 represents the event's name, column 2 represents the event's description, which is another `String` value, and column 3 represents the start date of the event, which is a Timestamp. The column numbers correspond to the order of appearance of the column names in the SQL query statement.

```
static final int NAME_COL = 1;     //should be declared as page variable
static final int DESCRIPTION_COL = 2;     //should be declared as page variable
static final int STARTDATE_COL = 3;     /should be declared as page variable
String eventName = rs.getString(NAME_COL);
String description = rs.getString(DESCRIPTION_COL);
java.sql.Timestamp aDate = rs.getTimestamp(STARTDATE_COL);
```

You can iterate through the different events using the scriptlet, and generate the body by embedding expressions in the HTML code. Display the event name, month name, year, time, and description for each event within the loop.

```
<%     Timestamp aDate = null;
       // Iterate through the results
       while (rs.next()) {
           aDate = rs.getTimestamp(STARTDATE_COL);
%>

<p> <font size="+2"><%= rs.getString(NAME_COL)%></font>
<br><font size="+1"><%= monthNames[aDate.getMonth()]%> <%= day%>
<%= aDate.getHours()%>:<%= aDate.getMinutes()%> <br></font><font size="-1"><%=
rs.getString(DESCRIPTION_COL)%></font>

<%
       }
%>

</body>
</html>
```

Modifying the Monthly Calendar JSP to Display Events

You can modify the monthly calendar JSPs, month.jsp and smallmonth.jsp, to display the events when the hyperlink specified for a day is clicked. Instead of displaying the events in the same page as the monthly calendar, you can open a new browser window and display the events in it.

You can do this using JavaScript and the Document Object Model. You can create a new window and specify the URL (location) of the page in it in a JavaScript function, openWindow. Add the JavaScript function within the HEAD tag of the monthly calendar JSP.

```
<script LANGUAGE="Javascript">

  <!--
    function openWindow(url) {
    width = 600;
    height = 400;
    Win = open(url, 'as_events', 'toolbar=0, location=0, directories=0,
➥status=0, menubar=0,
                    resizable=1 ,width=' + width + ',height=' + height +
➥',scrollbars=yes');
    Win.focus();
    }
  //-->
</script>
```

To open a link in a new window, you need to define an anchor tag passing the URL in the JavaScript function for defining the href attribute. To open the events page for the date May 28, 2000, you will need to provide a link to the JavaScript function, passing the URL in your page as follows:

```
<a href="javascript:openWindow('daysevents.jsp?month=5&&day=28&&year=2000');">
➥28 May 2000
</a>
```

In the "Generate Days for Month" scriptlet, add a JavaScript hyperlink for the daysevents.jsp, passing the request information as shown in Listing 6.5.

Listing 6.5   month.jsp: Hyperlinking the Days in the "Generate Days for Month" Scriptlet

```
<%
    int startCell = cal.getStartCell();
    int endCell = cal.getEndCell();
    for (int cellNo = 0, day = 1; cellNo < 42; cellNo++) {
        if (cellNo%7 == 0) {
            out.println("<TR>");
        } // end check for start of row

        out.print("<TD VALIGN=TOP HEIGHT=57");
        if (cellNo < startCell || cellNo > endCell) {
            out.print(" BGCOLOR=\"#999999\"> ");
        } else {
        out.print("><A HREF=\"javascript:openWindow('daysevents.jsp?month=" );
        out.print((validator.getMonthAsInteger() + 1) +
➥"&&year=" + validator.getYear() );
        out.print("&&day=" + day + "');\"><B>" + day + "</B></A>");
        day++;
```

```
        } // end if block

        out.println("</TD>");

        if (cellNo+1%7 == 0) {
            out.println("</TR>");
        } // end check for end of row
    } // end for-loop
%>

} else {
    out.print(">"); //I'll close that table cell here so I don't confuse my
html.
%>
<A HREF="javascript:openWindow('daysevents.jsp?month=<%=
➥ (validator.getMonthAsInteger() + 1) %>&year=<%=
➥ validator.getYear() %>&day=<%= day %>');"><B><%= day %></B></A>
<%
            day++;
        } // end if block
```

Running the Calendar of Events Application

Populate the Events table with information. If you populated the table using
PopulateCalendar.sql, your table would be as shown in Figure 6.8.

6

Figure 6.8

Snapshot of the Events table

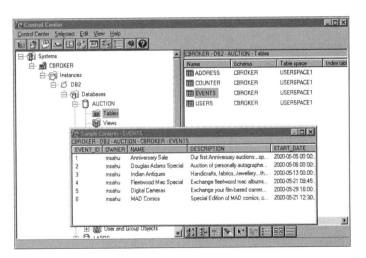

Launch your browser and specify input.jsp in the location. Display the calendar for
May 2000 in your browser. (You can specify any other month and year, but because
you inserted rows only for May, you will get empty pages for any other month.)
Click on any day in the calendar, such as 21, to see the events for the particular day,
as shown in Figure 6.9.

Figure 6.9

Events for 21 May, 2000 displayed in the pop-up window launched by clicking on the hyperlink in the calendar

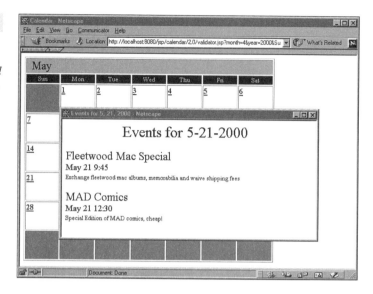

Note

If you look at the HTML source produced by the monthly calendar JSP, you will notice a lot of long URLs for hyperlinking the days to the events.

```
<TD VALIGN=TOP HEIGHT=57>
<A HREF="javascript:openWindow('daysevents.jsp?month=5&&year=
➥2000&&day=1');">
å<B>1</B></A></TD>
<TD VALIGN=TOP HEIGHT=57><A HREF="javascript:openWindow
➥('daysevents.jsp?month=5&&year=2000&&day=2');">
å<B>2</B></A></TD>
<TD VALIGN=TOP HEIGHT=57><A HREF="javascript:openWindow
➥('daysevents.jsp?month=5&&year=2000&&day=3');">
å<B>3</B></A></TD>
<TD VALIGN=TOP HEIGHT=57><A
HREF="javascript:openWindow('daysevents.jsp?month=5&&year=
➥2000&&day=4');">
å<B>4</B></A></TD>
```

This is because you are constructing the entire URL and passing it to the JavaScript openWindow function. You can reduce the size of the URLs, and thereby the size of the generated page, by passing only the day number to the function as shown in Listing 6.6.

Listing 6.6   month.jsp: Modifying the JavaScript openWindow Function to Construct the URL Within Its Body

```
<script LANGUAGE="Javascript">

  <!--
    function openWindow(day) {
      width = 600;
      height = 400;
      url='daysevents.jsp\?month=<%= (validator.getMonthAsInteger() + 1)%>' +
          '&&year=<%= validator.getYear()%>&&day=' + day;
      Win = open(url, 'as_events', 'toolbar=0,location=0,directories=0,status=0,
  menubar=0,resizable=1,width=' + width + ',height=' + height +
',scrollbars=yes');
      Win.focus();
    }
  //-->
</script>
```

 Note

Within the "Generate Days" scriptlet, you only need to pass the day to the openWindow function.

```
out.print(">A HREF=\"javascript:openWindow
('" + day + "');\"><B>" +
åday + "</B></A>");
```

The generated HTML source containing the links would now look like this:

```
<TD VALIGN=TOP HEIGHT=57>
<A HREF="javascript:openWindow('1');">
å<B>1</B></A></TD>
<TD VALIGN=TOP HEIGHT=57>
<A HREF="javascript:openWindow('2');">
å<B>2</B></A></TD>
<TD VALIGN=TOP HEIGHT=57>
<A HREF="javascript:openWindow('3');">
å<B>3</B></A></TD>
```

As you might also notice, the formatting information for the table cell is printed for every day. In Chapter 9, you will learn about using Cascading Style Sheets to remove this redundancy.

6

Developing a Custom Tag Library for Database Handling

In the preceding chapter, you learned how to create and use simple and nested actions. In this section, you will create a set of co-operating and iterative tags that you can use for database queries and manipulation instead of using JDBC directly.

Connection, User Id, and Password Tags

The connection tag creates a database connection using information such as the URL, name, and password. The user Id and password can be provided as subelements of the connection tag.

```
<db:connection id="conn" url="jdbc:odbc:auction">
    <db:userId><%= userId%></db:userId>
    <db:password><%= password%></db:password>
</db:connection>
```

The nested tags set the user ID and password information to create the connection. At the end of the connection tag, a SQL connection object is made available to the pageContext, accessible using the value provided in the id attribute.

The connection tag's structure can be understood from its definition in the tag description library, shown in Listing 6.7. By now I assume you are able to extrapolate the connection structure from its description in the .tld file. The only new entry is the teiclass that specifies the TagExtraInfo class for the tag handler. You will learn more about the teiclass when you create the ConnectionTagExtraInfo class.

Listing 6.7 db-taglib.tld: Tag Descriptors for the connection, userid, and password Actions

```
<tag>
    <name>connection</name>
    <tagclass>station.auction.db.taglib.ConnectionTagHandler</tagclass>
    <teiclass>station.auction.db.taglib.ConnectionTagExtraInfo</teiclass>
    <bodycontent>JSP</bodycontent>
    <info>Creates a connection to a database using its URL and driver</info>
    <attribute>
        <name>id</name>
        <required>true</required>
    </attribute>
    <attribute>
        <name>url</name>
        <required>true</required>
    </attribute>
    <attribute>
        <name>driver</name>
        <required>false</required>
    </attribute>
</tag>

<tag>
    <name>userId</name>
    <tagclass>station.auction.db.taglib.UserIdTagHandler</tagclass>
    <bodycontent>JSP</bodycontent>
    <info>Specifies the user ID for making the connection</info>
</tag>
```

```
<tag>
    <name>password</name>
    <tagclass>station.auction.db.taglib.PasswordTagHandler</tagclass>
    <bodycontent>JSP</bodycontent>
    <info>Specifies the password for making the connection</info>
</tag>
```

Creating the `ConnectionTagHandler`

The class and method definitions for `ConnectionTagHandler` can be understood from its descriptor. Because this class nests other actions, it has a body and therefore needs to implement `BodyTag` or extend `BodyTagSupport`. You can provide the class with the package name—`station.auction.db.taglib`—and you need to provide import statements for the JDBC and tag extension classes that you will use in the class.

This class has two attributes defined on it—`url` and `driver`; therefore, it requires the definition of two setter methods for the two attributes, as well as fields for them, as shown in Listing 6.8.

Listing 6.8   ConnectionTagHandler.java: Class Definition and Attributes

```
package station.auction.db.taglib;

import java.sql.Connection;
import java.sql.DriverManager;

import javax.servlet.jsp.*;
import javax.servlet.jsp.tagext.*;

public class ConnectionTagHandler extends BodyTagSupport {
        protected String url = null;
        protected String driver = "sun.jdbc.odbc.JdbcOdbcDriver";

public void setDriver(String newDriver) {
    driver = newDriver;
}
public void setUrl(String newUrl) {
    url = newUrl;
}

protected String getDriver() {
    return driver;
}
protected String getUserId() {
    return userId;
}
```

6

You also need to provide fields and setter and getter methods for the user ID and password information that the nested tag handlers will set on their parent tag handler .

```
protected String userId = null;
protected String password = null;

public void setPassword(String newPassword) {
    password = newPassword;
}
public void setUserId(String newName) {
    userId = newName;
}
protected String getPassword() {
    return password;
}
protected String getUserId() {
    return userId;
}
```

The `TagHandler` creates a connection object using the information set on it and makes it available to the rest of the page by setting it on the `pageContext`. You can create the connection object in the `doEndTag` method when you can safely assume that all the information has been set, as shown in Listing 6.9.

Listing 6.9 ConnectionTagHandler.java: Overriding the `doEndTag` Method to Create the Connection Object

```
public int doEndTag() throws JspException {
    try {
        System.out.println("[ConnectionTagHandler] doEndTag, url[" + getUrl() +
          "], user id[" + getUserId() + "], password[" + getPassword() + "]");
        // Load the driver and create the connection
        Class.forName(driver);
        Connection con = DriverManager.getConnection(getUrl(), getUserId(),
➥ getPassword());

        System.out.println("[ConnectionTagHandler] conn " + con);

        // Set as a page context attribute
        this.pageContext.setAttribute(getId(), con, PageContext.PAGE_SCOPE);
    } catch (Exception exc1) {
        new JspException(exc1.getMessage());
```

```
    }
    return EVAL_PAGE;
}
```

Creating the `ConnectionTagExtraInfo` for Specifying Return Values

You can formally specify the variables created and set in the page context by the tag handler by creating a `TagExtraInfo` class for the specific action. The JSP container also uses this information for introspecting into the action's return values.

Create a class, `ConnectionTagExtraInfo`, that extends from `TagExtraInfo`. Provide a method, `getVariableInfo`, that returns a list of variables created within the action as an array of `VariableInfo`. It takes a `TagData` parameter that you can use to determine the tag attribute values.

Within the method, define the connection object created within the action and set in the page context by specifying its information:

 Tip It's a good practice to specify the variable names using one of the tag's attribute's values. If you were to hard-code the names instead, they could potentially clash with the definition of other variables in the JSP. Using the former naming scheme, on such a clash you only need to change the attribute value within the tag without the need for any change and recompilation in the `TagExtraInfo` class.

- **Name of the object (variable) reference**—You can either hard-code the name of the object or set it to a value obtained from the tag attributes, in this case the `id` attribute.
- **Type or class name of the object**—In this case `connection` is of type `java.sql.Connection`.
- **Validity of the object**—In this case the connection object is returned in all cases; therefore, it is valid (`true`).
- **Availability of the object**—Specifies when the object is available for use, one of `VariableInfo.AT_BEGIN` (at the beginning of the tag), `VariableInfo.NESTED` (available within the body only), or `VariableInfo.AT_END` (available at the end of the tag). In this case the connection object is created at the end of the tag, so its availability is `VariableInfo.AT_END`.

You need to create as many `VariableInfo` entries as the object references you need to make available from your tag handler. In this case, only the connection information is returned, so the array of `VariableInfo` contains only one member, as shown in Listing 6.10.

Listing 6.10   ConnectionTagExtraInfo.java: Defining the Variables Created by the Connection Tag Handler

```
import javax.servlet.jsp.*;
import javax.servlet.jsp.tagext.*;

public class ConnectionTagExtraInfo extends TagExtraInfo {
public VariableInfo[] getVariableInfo(TagData data) {
    return new VariableInfo[]  {
        new VariableInfo((String) data.getAttribute("id"),
            "java.sql.Connection",
            true,
            VariableInfo.AT_END)
    };
}
}
```

Creating the `UserIdTagHandler`

The `UserIdTagHandler` extracts the user ID from the body of the `userId` tag and sets the information on the `ConnectionTagHandler`. Because the information is provided within the body, you can extend `UserIdTagHandler` from `BodyTagSupport`. You can obtain the body content in the `doAfterBody` callback method. You can also obtain the `ConnectionTagHandler` to set the information on, from the `getParent` method defined in the `Tag` interface, as shown in Listing 6.11.

Listing 6.11   UserIdTagHandler.java: Setting the User ID on the Parent `ConnectionTagHandler`

```
package station.auction.db.taglib;

import javax.servlet.jsp.*;
import javax.servlet.jsp.tagext.*;

public class UserIdTagHandler extends BodyTagSupport {
public int doAfterBody() {
    System.out.println("[UserIdTagHandler] doAfterBody, User ID Body-> " +
➥getBodyContent().getString());

    ConnectionTagHandler connxn = (ConnectionTagHandler) getParent();
    connxn.setUserId(getBodyContent().getString());
    return SKIP_BODY;
}
}
```

Note The doAfterBody method returns SKIP_BODY, which implies that the tag doesn't iterate after the body is evaluated. However, if the method returned EVAL_BODY_TAG, the doAfterBody method would be invoked repeatedly until a SKIP_BODY is returned. You will see how this technique is used for iteration when you create the ForeachTagHandler.

Creating the `PasswordTagHandler`

The PasswordTagHandler can be created similarly to UserIdTagHandler because it only obtains the password from the body content and sets it on the parent ConnectionTagHandler. You only need to modify the doAfterBody method to pass the body content to the parent tag by invoking the setPassword method on it.

Query and Modify Tags

You can use the connection created from the connection tag structure to make queries or perform data manipulation.

```
<db:connection id="conn" url="jdbc:odbc:auction">
    <db:userId><%= userId%></db:userId>
    <db:password><%= password%></db:password>
</db:connection>

<db:query id="getAllRows" connection="conn">
SELECT * FROM <Table>
</db:query>
<db:modify id="insertRow" connection="conn">
INSERT INTO <Table> VALUES <%= values%>
</db:modify>
```

The sets of tags seem unrelated, as they aren't nested within one another. The only relation between the two is the value of the connection attribute in the query and modify tags. It takes the same value as the id parameter of the connection tag. To make the connection and query/modify tags co-operate, you need to do the following:

1. Specify an id attribute in the source tag, in this case, the connection tag.

2. Set an object reference in the pageContext using the id attribute. For example, the connection tag sets a connection object in the pageContext so that it can be used by the query and modify tag handlers.

3. Specify an attribute in the tags that need to use the object created by the source. While using the tag, you need to pass the same value as the one used in the id attribute. For example, the query and modify tags have the connection attribute, which should ideally take the same value as the id attribute in the preceding connection tag.

4. Extract the object reference within the setter method of the tag handler using the value passed as the parameter.

The tag definition for the query and modify tags is as shown in Listing 6.12.

Listing 6.12   db-taglib.tld: Tag Descriptors for the Query and Modify Tags

```
<tag>
    <name>query</name>
    <tagclass>station.auction.db.taglib.QueryTagHandler</tagclass>
    <teiclass>station.auction.db.taglib.QueryTagExtraInfo</teiclass>
    <bodycontent>JSP</bodycontent>
    <info>Specifies a SQL query</info>
    <attribute>
        <name>id</name>
        <required>true</required>
    </attribute>
    <attribute>
        <name>connection</name>
        <required>true</required>
    </attribute>
</tag>

<tag>
    <name>modify</name>
    <tagclass>station.auction.db.taglib.ModifyTagHandler</tagclass>
    <teiclass>station.auction.db.taglib.ModifyTagExtraInfo</teiclass>
    <bodycontent>JSP</bodycontent>
    <info>Specifies a SQL modify statement- Create/Insert/Update/Delete</info>
    <attribute>
        <name>id</name>
        <required>true</required>
    </attribute>
    <attribute>
        <name>connection</name>
        <required>true</required>
    </attribute>
</tag>
```

The bodies of the query and modify tags take an SQL statement—a SELECT statement for the query tag and a CREATE, INSERT, UPDATE, or DELETE SQL statement for the modify tag. The query action sets a ResultSet object in the page context for iterating through the returned rows. In fact, we will create an action tag, foreach, later in this chapter, that will iterate throughout the result set. The modify tag returns an integer result representing the success or failure of the execution of the modify statement .

Creating the `QueryTagHandler`

Create a tag handler, `QueryTagHandler`, for defining the action. The handler extracts the connection object from `pageContext` using the connection attribute value within the `setConnection` method of the `QueryTagHandler`, as shown in Listing 6.13.

Listing 6.13   QueryTagHandler.java: Extracting the Connection Object Reference from the Page Context

```
public void setConnection(String newConnection) throws JspException{
    try {
        System.out.println("[QueryTagHandler] setConnection, Attribute-> "
 + newConnection);
        con = (Connection) pageContext.findAttribute(newConnection);
        System.out.println("[QueryTagHandler] Connection : " + con);
    } catch (Exception exc) {
        throw new JspException(exc.getMessage());
    }
}
```

You will also need to define a field and accessor method for the connection object.

```
package station.auction.db.taglib;

import java.sql.Connection;
import java.sql.ResultSet;
import java.sql.Statement;

import javax.servlet.jsp.*;
import javax.servlet.jsp.tagext.*;

public class QueryTagHandler extends BodyTagSupport {
    protected Connection con = null;
public Connection getConnection() {
    return con;
}
```

You need to override the `doAfterBody` method to create the SQL statement obtained from the body of the tag and execute it using the connection object. Set the `ResultSet` obtained on executing the statement in the page context to enable it to be used in the page. The object reference is identified in the page context by the `id` attribute. The source for the method is shown in Listing 6.14.

Listing 6.14   QueryTagHandler.java: Overriding the `doAfterBody` Method to Execute the Statement and Set the `ResultSet`

```
public int doAfterBody() throws JspException {
    try {
        String query = getBodyContent().getString();
        System.out.println("[QueryTagHandler] doAfterBody, Query Body-> " +
getBodyContent().getString());
```

6

Listing 6.14 continued

```
        // Create the statement and execute the query
        Statement stmt = getConnection().createStatement();
        ResultSet rs = stmt.executeQuery(query);

        // Set the ResultSet in the page context
        this.pageContext.setAttribute(getId(), rs, pageContext.PAGE_SCOPE);

    } catch (Exception exc) {
        throw new JspException(exc.getMessage());
    }
    return SKIP_BODY;
}
```

Creating the `QueryTagExtraInfo` Class

Specify the variable information for the `ResultSet` created by the `QueryTagHandler` in the `QueryTagExtraInfo` class.

```
public VariableInfo[] getVariableInfo(TagData data) {
    return new VariableInfo[] {
new VariableInfo((String) data.getId(),
            "java.sql.ResultSet",
            true,
            VariableInfo.AT_END)
    };
}
```

Creating the `ModifyTagHandler`

The `ModifyTagHandler` is similar to the `QueryTagHandler` except that it performs an `executeUpdate` instead of an `executeQuery` on the `Statement` object. It has the same attributes and therefore the same fields and setter and accessor methods. To provide reusability, you can make the `ModifyTagHandler` class inherit from `QueryTagHandler` and override the `doAfterBody` method with the specific implementation. The method also sets the success flag returned from the execute operation, as shown in Listing 6.15.

```
public int doAfterBody() throws JspException {
    try {
        String modify = getBodyContent().getString();
        System.out.println("[ModifyTagHandler] doAfterBody, Query Body-> " +
➥getBodyContent().getString());

        Statement stmt = getConnection().createStatement();

        int result = stmt.executeUpdate(modify);
```

```
        pageContext.setAttribute(getId(), new Integer(result),
➥PageContext.PAGE_SCOPE);
    } catch (Exception exc) {
        throw new JspException(exc.getMessage());
    }
    return SKIP_BODY;
}
```

Create the `TagExtraInfo` class specifying the integer variable that is created within the handler.

```
public VariableInfo[] getVariableInfo(TagData data) {
    return new VariableInfo[] {
        new VariableInfo((String) data.getAttribute("id"),
            "Integer",
            true,
            VariableInfo.AT_END)
        };
    }
}
```

The `Foreach` Iterative Tag

You will now create the `foreach` tag that iterates through the `ResultSet` created by the query tag. It has the following tag description:

```
<tag>
    <name>foreach</name>
    <tagclass>station.auction.db.taglib.ForeachTagHandler</tagclass>
    <bodycontent>JSP</bodycontent>
    <info>Iterates through the result set of a query</info>
    <attribute>
        <name>query</name>
        <required>true</required>
    </attribute>
</tag>
```

Creating the `ForeachTagHandler`

Create a class, `ForeachTagHandler`, that extends from `BodyTagSupport`. Add the `setQuery` method for setting the query attribute, and define a local field and accessor method for it.

Implement the `BodyTag`'s callback methods as shown in Table 6.2.

Table 6.2   Overridden Methods of the `ForeachTagHandler` Class

Method	*Description*
doStartTag()	Obtain the `ResultSet` from the page context identified by the query attribute's value. Initialize the local variable with this value. Check whether the `ResultSet` is empty. If it is empty, return `SKIP_BODY`, else return `EVAL_BODY_TAG`.

Table 6.2 continued

Method	Description
doAfterBody()	Check whether the result set has been iterated completely. If it has been iterated, return SKIP_BODY, else replace the old row in the page context with the new value and return EVAL_BODY_TAG so that the doAfterBody method is invoked again.
doEndTag()	Write the body content to the page context's output stream.

The source for these methods is as shown in Listing 6.16.

Listing 6.16 ForeachTagHandler.java: Overriding Methods of the BodyTag Interface to Make It Iterate

```
public int doStartTag() throws JspException {
    try {
        rs = (ResultSet) pageContext.findAttribute(getQuery());
        System.out.println("[ForeachTagHandler] doStartTag " + rs);

        if (rs.next()) {
            return EVAL_BODY_TAG;
        }
    } catch (Exception exc) {
    }
    return SKIP_BODY;
}

public int doAfterBody() throws JspException {
    System.out.println("[ForeachTagHandler] in doAfterBody: " + rs);
    try {
        if (rs.next()) {
            // Set the next row
            pageContext.setAttribute(getQuery(), rs, PageContext.PAGE_SCOPE);
            return EVAL_BODY_TAG;
        }
    } catch (Exception exc) {
        throw new JspException(exc.getMessage());
    }
    return SKIP_BODY;
}

public int doEndTag() {
    try {
        System.out.println("[ForeachTagHandler] doEndTag" +
➥getBodyContent().getString());

        pageContext.getOut().write(getBodyContent().getString());
    } catch (Exception exc) {
    }
    return EVAL_PAGE;
}
```

Setting Up the Tag Library

Save the Java source files for the tag handlers and extra information in the `<tomcat>/`
`webapps/AuctionStation/web-inf/classes/station/auction/db/taglib` directory.
Compile all the Java files to generate the class files. Consolidate all the database tag
descriptors into one tag library file, db-taglib.tld. Provide the extra tag library information.

```
<?xml version="1.0" encoding="ISO-8859-1" ?>
<!DOCTYPE taglib
        PUBLIC "-//Sun Microsystems, Inc.//DTD JSP Tag Library 1.1//EN"
        "http://java.sun.com/j2ee/dtds/web-jsptaglibrary_1_1.dtd">
<taglib>
  <tlibversion>1.0</tlibversion>
  <jspversion>1.1</jspversion>
  <shortname>db</shortname>
  <uri>http://localhost:8080/AuctionStation/jsp/mytags.jar</uri>
  <info>Database Tag Library</info>
```

Modifying the Calendar of Events JSP Using the Database Tags

You can use the database tag library within daysevents.jsp or any other JSP where
you need to perform database queries or modifications.

Provide the taglib declaration in daysevents.jsp. Provide the tags in the taglib with a
db prefix.

```
<%@ page import="java.sql.*" errorPage="error.jsp" %>
<%@ taglib uri="db-taglib.tld" prefix="db" %>
```

The declaration also assumes that db-taglib.tld is stored in the same directory as day-
sevents.jsp. You can also set up a proxy URL as shown in the preceding chapter.

Remove all the declarations except for `monthNames`.

```
<%! protected String[] monthNames =
➡ (new java.text.DateFormatSymbols()).getMonths(); %>
```

Extract the request information and print the page header just as in the previous version of the JSP.

```
<%
    // Get the request parameters and do checks
    String month = request.getParameter("month");
    String year = request.getParameter("year");
    String day = request.getParameter("day");
%>
<html>
<title>Events for <%= month%>, <%= day%>, <%= year%></title>
<body>
    <center><font size="+3">Events for <%= month%>-<%= day%>-<%= year%>
➡</font></center>
    <p>
```

Add the connection tag for accessing the auction database by specifying its URL, jdbc:odbc:auction, and the connection ID, conn.

```
<db:connection id="conn" url="jdbc:odbc:auction"/>
```

> **Note**
> In the taglib file, we described the connection tag as a simple action tag. Because we are not passing any name and password information for making the connection, we can omit nesting the userid and password tags implying that the connection tag has no body. You can therefore use the shortcut empty tag notation for the connection tag.

Add the query tag for finding the events for a specific day. Specify the connection, conn, and the id parameter identifying the variable to store the ResultSet.

```
<db:query id="eventsForDay" connection="conn">
    SELECT name, description, start_date FROM Events
        WHERE MONTH(start_date) = <%= month%>
            AND YEAR(start_date) = <%= year%>
            AND DAY(start_date) = <%= day%>
        ORDER BY HOUR(start_date), MINUTE(start_date)
</db:query>
```

Add a foreach tag to iterate through the eventsForDay ResultSet. In the body of the tag, add the JSP source that will be evaluated for each iteration.

```
<db:foreach query="eventsForDay">
    <% Timestamp aDate = eventsForDay.getTimestamp(3); %>
    <p> <font size="+2"><%= eventsForDay.getString(1)%></font>
    <br><font size="+1"><%= monthNames[aDate.getMonth()]%> <%= day%>
    <%= aDate.getHours()%>:<%= aDate.getMinutes()%> <br></font>
    <font size="-1"><%= eventsForDay.getString(2)%></font>
</db:foreach>
```

Finish the page by adding the closing body and html tags.

```
</body>
</html>
```

Save the changes and reload the calendar application so that the changes take effect. You will not notice any change in the output of daysevents.jsp, but you will notice the simplicity of the JSP page itself!

Creating the Registration Module

Now you will create the registration module that allows new users to register themselves and registered users to log in. Users who have forgotten their passwords can get the information mailed to them at their registered email ID or answer a hint question.

Registering New Users

Registration is a two-step process. First the user chooses an ID and specifies personal information such as the name and email address. The submitted data is validated and the database updated to insert the user information. In the next step, the user provides address information and a password and challenge combination. On submission, the address information is inserted into the database and an email sent out, informing the user of the completion of his registration.

Registering a New User: Step 1

The registration process begins when the user visits Step1.jsp and submits registration information using the form in it. The request is sent to the validator JSP, which validates the inputs and forwards the request to either AddUser.JSP for inserting the information or Step1.jsp for a retry. The flows between the different JSPs are as shown in Figure 6.10.

Figure 6.10

Flow of data in the first step of the registration process

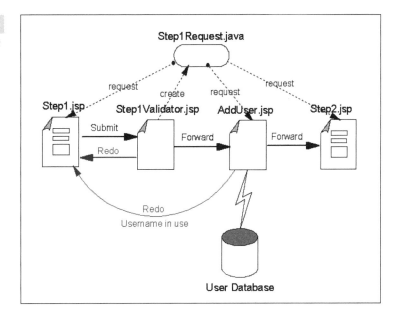

User Database

Step1.jsp contains different fields for accepting user information as described in Table 6.3.

Table 6.3   Form Fields in Step1.jsp

Field	Description
firstName	Text field that accepts the user's first name
lastName	Text field that accepts the user's last name

Table 6.3   continued

Field	Description
midInitial	Text field that accepts the user's middle initial
email	Text field that accepts the user's email address
userId	Text field that accepts the user's choice of user ID

You can set the size and maxlength for the different fields according to the size of the respective columns in the database. For example, you can set maxlength of the firstName field to 30, which is the size of the corresponding F_NAME column in the Users table.

We will be adopting the form-handling technique described in Chapter 4. To do that, you need to create a request bean, Step1Request, that stores the values passed in the form, validates the values, and creates error messages. You can use the bean to print error information and the default values for the fields. Listing 6.17 shows the source for the input page, embedding the form handler JavaBean for displaying the error information and the default values.

Listing 6.17   Step1.jsp: Creating the Form for Accepting User Information for the First Step in the Registration Process

```
<%@ taglib uri="../as-taglib.tld" prefix="as" %>
<jsp:useBean id="validator"
class="station.auction.registration.Step1Request" scope="request"/>

<html>
<head>
    <title>Auction Station Registration - Step 1</title>
</head>
<body>

<form name="registration" method="post" action="Step1Validator.jsp">
<font size="+2">Auction Station Registration<br>Step 1 of 2</font>

<table width="80%" border="0">
  <tr><td colspan="2" bgcolor="lightblue">
      <b>User Registration</b><br>All field names marked in <b>bold</b>
      are required.
  </td></tr>
  <tr><td><b>First Name</b><br><as:error><%= validator.getError("firstName")%>
                    </as:error></td>
      <td><input type="text" name="firstName" size="30"
              value="<%= validator.getFirstName()%>"/></td>
  </tr>
  <tr><td>Middle Initial<br><as:error><%= validator.getError("midInitial")%>
                    </as:error></td>
```

```
        <td><input type="text" name="midInitial" size="5" maxlength="1"
            value="<%= validator.getMidInitial()%>"/></td>
   </tr>
   <tr><td><b>Last Name</b><br><as:error><%= validator.getError("lastName")%>
                        </as:error></td>
     <td><input type="text" name="lastName" size="30"
              value="<%= validator.getLastName()%>"/></td>
   </tr>
   <tr><td><b>Email</b><br><as:error><%= validator.getError("email")%>
                        </as:error></td>
     <td><input type="text" name="email" size="30"
              value="<%= validator.getEmail()%>"/></td>
   </tr>
  <tr><td><b>Choose User id</b><br><as:error><%= validator.getError("userId")%>
                        </as:error></td>
     <td><input type="text" name="userId" size="15"
              value="<%= validator.getUserId()%>"/></td>
   </tr>
   <tr bgcolor="lightblue">
     <td><center><input type="Submit" value="Next &gt;&gt;"></center></td>
     <td><center><input type="Reset" name="Reset" value="Reset"></center></td>
   </tr>
</table></form>
</body>
<html>
```

Create the `Step1Request` bean with the package name `station.auction.registra-tion`. Provide the bean with the input and output properties for the different fields.

You can use the `CreateBean` JavaScript routine that you created in Chapter 4 to generate the bean class from the form. If you prefer to code the class by hand, you need to create a new class, `Step1Request`, that extends from `station.auction.FormValidator`. Create getter and setter methods for every field defined in the form. Essentially, create input and output properties with the same names as the input fields. Provide a `ResourceBundle` instance for extracting the error information from Step1ErrorMessages.properties. Flesh out the `process` method by validating the field values and setting the error information, if any, in the errors Hashtable, as shown in Listing 6.18.

Listing 6.18   Step1Request.java: Fleshing Out the Process Method to Validate the Input Field Values

```
protected String getLocalMessage(String key) {
    return bundle.getString(key);
} // end getLocalMessage

public boolean process() {
    // Validate all the parameters
    if (fieldFirstName == null || fieldFirstName.trim().length() == 0) {
        errors.put("firstName", getLocalMessage("INVALID_FIRST_NAME"));
    }
```

Listing 6.18   continued

```
    if (fieldLastName == null || fieldLastName.trim().length() == 0) {
        errors.put("lastName", getLocalMessage("INVALID_LAST_NAME"));
    }
    if (fieldMidInitial != null) {
        if (fieldMidInitial.length() > 1) {
          errors.put("midInitial", getLocalMessage("INVALID_MID_INITIAL"));
    }
    }
    if (fieldEmail == null || fieldEmail.trim().length() == 0 ||
➥fieldEmail.indexOf("@") == -1) {
        errors.put("email", getLocalMessage("INVALID_EMAIL"));
    }
    if (fieldUserId == null || fieldUserId.trim().length() == 0) {
        errors.put("userId", getLocalMessage("INVALID_USER_ID"));
    }
    return errors.isEmpty();
}
```

The basic validation checks you should perform for the field values are

- Check whether a required field is NULL.
- Check whether a field is of the expected type. If the field is all numeric, you should check whether there are non-numeric characters in it. If the field is for an email, you should check whether it adheres to the email naming scheme.
- Check the other constraints specified by the database. This includes checks for the length of the string, precision of the decimal values, and so on.

Figure 6.11 shows the output of Step1.jsp displaying the different fields. The error information and default values are empty strings and hence are not visible in the page.

If you look at the source of Step1.jsp (refer to Listing 6.17), you will notice that we used Next >> for the submit buttons label instead of just plain 'Next >>'. Characters such as the greater than sign (>), less than sign (<), space, and others cannot be directly embedded in the HTML/JSP source because they are used to identify markup tags and other elements. HTML provides built-in *entities* that you should use when you need to display such characters: > for >, < for <,   for the nonbreaking space, and more.

A complete list of the HTML entities can be found at http://www.w3.org/MarkUp/html-spec/html-spec_13.html.

Figure 6.11

Output of Step1.jsp displayed in the browser

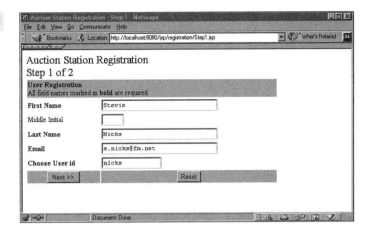

After the form data is submitted, the field values are set into the Step1Request bean using the introspective setProperty tag. Step1Validator.jsp validates the parameters by invoking the process method. On successful validation, it passes the request to AddUser.jsp for insertion into the Users table of the database. If the fields are incomplete or incorrect, the request is returned to Step1.jsp for a retry. The source for the Step1Validator JSP is as shown in Listing 6.19.

Listing 6.19   Step1Validator.java: Forwarding the Request Based on the Success of the Validation

```
<jsp:useBean id="validator"
    class="station.auction.registration.Step1Request" scope="session">
    <jsp:setProperty name="validator" property="*"/>
</jsp:useBean>
<%
    if (!validator.process()) {
        // Errors occurred. Retry
%>
        <jsp:forward page="Step1.jsp"/>
<% }
    else {
        // Display AddUser Page
%>
        <jsp:forward page="AddUser.jsp"/>
<%
    } // end if-else block
%>
```

The AddUser JSP inserts the user information, stored as properties in the Step1Request bean, as a new row in the Users table. It will be inserting only a part of the user information in the table because the other part that makes up the password-challenge word combination will be obtained from step 2 of the registration process.

6

You can use the database taglib, the modify tag in particular, to perform the database inserts. The SQL insert operation will throw an exception if a row with the same user ID already exists in the table. This exceptional condition is produced as a result of the database constraint where the USER_ID field was specified as a primary key. Other constraints such as NOT NULL on a field imply that a value has to be specified for the field while inserting or updating the row. You can handle the exception by placing the modify tag within a try-catch block. If an exception is thrown, implying that the user ID already exists, you need to add the error message for the same into the Step1Request instance and forward the request back to Step1.jsp. Listing 6.20 contains the source for Step1Validator.jsp, and Figure 6.12 shows the output of the registration process when the user chooses a user ID already in use.

Listing 6.20   AddUser.jsp: Inserting the User Information into the Users Table

```
<%@ taglib uri="../db-taglib.tld" prefix="db" %>
<jsp:useBean id="validator"
    class="station.auction.registration.Step1Request" scope="session"/>
<db:connection id="conn" url="jdbc:odbc:auction"/>
<%
    try {
%>

    <db:modify id="insertUser" connection="conn">
        INSERT INTO Users (user_id, f_name, l_name, initial,
➥email, password) VALUES
            ( '<%= validator.getUserId()%>',
              '<%= validator.getFirstName()%>',
              '<%= validator.getLastName()%>',
              '<%= validator.getMidInitial()%>',
              '<%= validator.getEmail()%>',
              'Station' );
    </db:modify>

    <db:modify id="insertEmptyAddress" connection="conn">
        INSERT INTO Address (user_id, type) VALUES
            ( '<%= validator.getUserId()%>',
              '1');
    </db:modify>


<%
        // The operation was a success, forward the request to the next step
        if (insertUser.intValue() == 1 && insertEmptyAddress.intValue() == 1) {
            conn.commit();
%>
        <jsp:forward page="Step2.jsp"/>
<%
        }
    }
```

```
      catch (Exception exc) {
        conn.rollback();
        // SQL Exception occurred, the User id is in use, retry required
        validator.setError("userId", "The ID is already in use.
➥ Choose a different ID");
      }
%>
<jsp:forward page="Step1.jsp"/>
```

Figure 6.12

Error message generated when the user ID is already in use

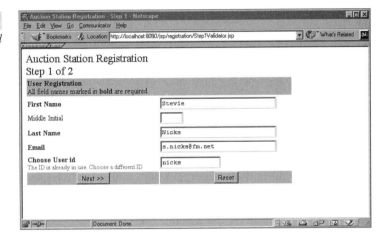

When operating on more than one table, as when inserting rows in the Users and Address tables, you need to provide *transactional integrity*. A transaction is a set of operations that act as though they were a single, atomic operation. Either all of them are completed successfully or none of them are operated on. In this case, either the user and address information was inserted in the tables or none of the information was entered. In a nontransactional situation, the database would be in an inconsistent state if one SQL statement executed without a problem and another didn't. You can use the connection reference to specify the transaction scope; all SQL updates executed using this connection can be committed or rolled back together using the `commit()` or `rollback()` methods defined on the `java.sql.Connection` interface.

A *transaction* is identified by four properties referred to as its ACID test. The mnemonic ACID stands for Atomic, Consistency, Integrity, and Durability.

On a successful insertion, a JSP representing the next step of the registration process is displayed.

Obtaining Password and Address Information: Step 2

The next step of the registration process is to obtain the password and address information from the user. This is done starting with Step2.jsp, which was the JSP invoked when AddUser.jsp successfully inserted the user information in the database. The page flows are as shown in Figure 6.13.

Figure 6.13

Page flows for step 2 of the registration process

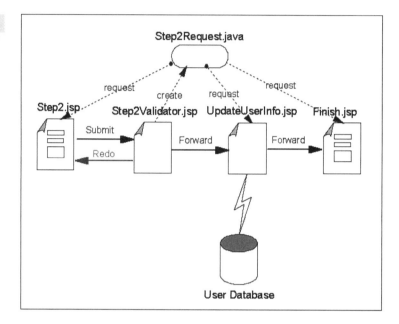

The password information includes the password itself and a challenge question-answer combination that the user can use in case he or she forgets the password.

To obtain a password from a user, you need to follow these rules of thumb while designing the HTML form:

- Security is key. Accept the password in password input fields.

- Use the POST parameter-passing mechanism for submitting the form. This will prevent the password from showing up in the URL.

- Provide a duplicate field for accepting the password. This will ensure that the chances of the user having entered a misspelled password are minimized unless the user misspelled it in both the fields.

- The user may forget the password, so you should provide mechanisms for the user to obtain the original password. One way is to mail the password to the specified email address, and the other is to provide a challenge question-answer combination. If the user forgets a password, you (the JSP) can prompt the user with the challenge question provided and check the user's answer with the one in the table .

You should also provide fields for accepting the address information. Lastly, store the user information provided in the first step as hidden fields. You cannot use the Step1Request bean instance to pass the information because you marked the bean type as request. This implies that the instance is invalidated after the page is generated and sent to the browser.

 Hidden fields are not displayed by the browser. They are useful for passing information by embedding them within name-value parameters. Alternatively, you could pass the information as session data by setting the Step1Request bean instance type as session.

Table 6.4 describes the fields used in forms for the second step of the registration process.

Table 6.4   Form Fields in Step2.jsp

Field	Description
password	Password field that accepts the user's password
password2	Duplicate password field that is used to detect a possibly misspelled password
challenge	Text field that accepts the challenge question
answer	Text field that accepts the answer to the challenge question
street1	Text field that accepts the user's street address
street2	Additional text field that accepts an optional second line for the street address
city	Text field that accepts the city
state	Text field that accepts a two-letter representation of the state
country	Text field that accepts the country information: You could replace this with a drop-down list containing the names of all the countries you want to constrain the input to.
phone	Text field that accepts the phone number
firstName	Hidden field that stores the user's first name
lastName	Hidden field that stores the user's last name
midInitial	Hidden field that stores the user's middle initial
email	Hidden field that stores the user's email address
userId	Hidden field that stores the user's choice of user ID

Create the request bean for the form, Step2Request. Be sure to provide fields and getter and setter methods for the hidden fields as well. Provide the process method for validating the field values. The process method will depend on your business logic and database constraints to validate the values. However, you can assume that the values passed in the hidden fields are correct because they are obtained from the validated Step1Request instance. The hidden fields are initialized as shown in Listing 6.21 .

Listing 6.21   Step2.jsp: Setting the Values of the Hidden Fields from the Step1Request Instance

```
<%@ taglib uri="../as-taglib.tld" prefix="as" %>
<jsp:useBean id="validator2"
    class="station.auction.registration.Step2Request" scope="request"/>
<jsp:useBean id="validator"
    class="station.auction.registration.Step1Request" scope="session"/>
...
<form name="registration" method="post" action="Step2Validator.jsp">
...
<input type="hidden" name="userId" value="<%= validator.getUserId()%>">
<input type="hidden" name="firstName" value="<%= validator.getFirstName()%>">
<input type="hidden" name="midInitial" value="<%= validator.getMidInitial()%>">
<input type="hidden" name="lastName" value="<%= validator.getLastName()%>">
<input type="hidden" name="email" value="<%= validator.getEmail()%>">
</form>
```

After AddUser.jsp successfully inserts the user information in the database, it forwards the request to Step2.jsp. The output of Step2.jsp is as shown in Figure 6.14.

Figure 6.14

Output of Step2.jsp

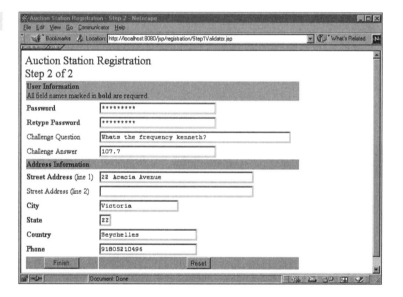

Create Step2Validator.jsp, which creates the Step2Request bean instance, sets the form parameters in the instance and forwards the request based on the result of the process method. On successful validation, the request is passed to UpdateUserInfo.jsp to update the rows in the tables with the passed information. The UpdateUserInfo.jsp executes two SQL UPDATE statements that set the rows in the Users and Address tables for the user with the password and address information. The two SQL operations are operated as a single transaction and committed/rolled back together as shown in Listing 6.22.

Listing 6.22   UpdateUserInfo.jsp: Updating the Rows in the User and Address Tables with the User Information

```
<%@ taglib uri="../db-taglib.tld" prefix="db" %>
<jsp:useBean id="validator2"
    class="station.auction.registration.Step2Request" scope="request"/>

<db:connection id="conn" url="jdbc:odbc:auction"/>

<db:modify id="updateUser" connection="conn">
        UPDATE Users SET
            password  = '<%= validator2.getPassword()%>',
            challenge = '<%= validator2.getChallenge()%>'
        WHERE user_id='<%= validator2.getUserId()%>'
</db:modify>

<db:modify id="insertAddress" connection="conn">
        UPDATE Address SET
            street_1 = '<%= validator2.getStreet1()%>',
            street_2 = '<%= validator2.getStreet2()%>',
            city     = '<%= validator2.getCity()%>',
            state    = '<%= validator2.getState()%>',
            country  = '<%= validator2.getCountry()%>',
            phone    = '<%= validator2.getPhone()%>'
        WHERE user_id='<%= validator2.getUserId()%>
</db:modify>

<%
    // Check if the operation was a success
    if (updateUser.intValue() == 1 && insertAddress.intValue() == 1) {
        conn.commit();
%>
    <jsp:forward page="Finish.jsp"/>
<%
    } else {
    // Rollback the transaction
conn.rollback();
validator2.setError("user_id", "No matching user id");
%>
    <jsp:forward page="Step2.jsp"/>
<%
    }
%>
```

On a successful execution of the update operation, the JSP forwards the request to the finish page, Finish.jsp. In this page, you need to indicate the successful registration by the user. You can do this by printing a thank you in the finish page and sending an email containing the user information to the user-specified email address as shown in Listing 6.23.

Listing 6.23   Finish.jsp: Generating the "Thank You" Page and Sending the Email Containing the User Information

```
<jsp:useBean id="validator2"
    class="station.auction.registration.Step2Request" scope="request"/>
<%@ taglib uri="../as-taglib.tld" prefix="as" %>
<% String name = validator2.getFirstName() + " " + validator2.getLastName(); %>
<html>
<title>Successful Registration</title>
<body>
<h1>Successful Registration</h1>

Thank you for registering with Auction Station,
<i><%= name%></i>
<p>

Please login to access the page for a personal browsing experience.
<a href="login.jsp">Login</a>

<%@ include file="Footer.html" %>

</body>
</html>

<as:email smtpHost="mail.auction.station.net">
   <as:from address="service@auction.station.net">Auction Station</as:from>
   <as:to address="<%= validator2.getEmail()%>"><%= name%></as:to>
   <as:subject>Welcome to Auction Station</as:subject>
   <as:body>
   Dear <%= validator2.getFirstName()%>,

   Thank you for registering with Auction Station.

   This automated reply is for your reference only.

   User ID: <%= validator2.getUserId()%>
   Password: <%= validator2.getPassword()%>
   Challenge Word: <%= validator2.getChallenge()%>

   Please visit us again soon at http://www.auction.station.net

   Best regards,

   The Auction Station Team

   </as:body>
</as:email>
```

Figure 6.15 displays the finish page for a successful registration.

Figure 6.15

Successful completion of the registration process

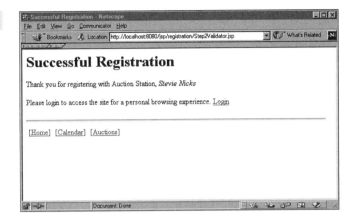

Providing User Login

Now that you have completed the registration part, you can allow the registered users to log on to the system to access privileged parts of the site. Unregistered users can browse the category listings, but in order to bid or to sell an item, they need to provide their identity in the form of login information made up of the name-password combination.

In Auction applications as well as in other Web-based applications, security is of prime importance. You can provide a degree of security using the login mechanisms. The following is a summary of some benefits of authentication.

- **Authentication**—You can authenticate a user and thereby prevent a malicious user from using the user ID frivolously. One of the reasons for authentication is to provide non-repudiation.

- **Non-repudiation**—You can identify actions performed by a user, including illegal ones such as selling live organs on the site and proxy bidding, using the login information. When the user sets an item for listing, the action is reflected in the database as a row with information including the user ID and a time-stamp. This associates the action with the user. If any of the actions infringe on the policies of the site, you can penalize the user as per your legal policies using the information in the database as proof.

- **Authorization**—Some parts of the site, such as the administrative sections, may require extra privileges. You can assign these privileges to certain users based on their user ID.

There are other alternatives for authenticating users, such as digital certificates. For reasons of simplicity, we will use the simple name-password logon mechanism. After a successful authentication, the user is allowed to browse the protected portions of the site, as shown in Figure 6.16.

Figure 6.16

Protecting portions of the Web site using a log in

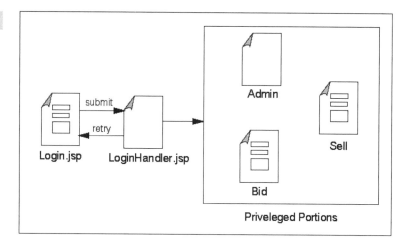

Authenticating Users Using the Name-Password Mechanism

The user submits the user ID and password for validation using the form in Login.jsp. The page is designed as a bare-bones HTML fragment without the enclosing html, head, and body tags to allow it to be reused (included) within another page. It contains text fields for accepting the user's name and password and a submit button as shown in Listing 6.24. The output of the page is shown in Figure 6.17.

Listing 6.24 Login.jsp: Accepting the User's Information for Logging On

```
<form method="POST" action="LoginHandler.jsp">
<table>
<tr><td>Sign-in Name</td></tr>
<tr><td><input name="userId" type="text" size="10">
    </td></tr>
<tr><td>Password</td></tr>
<tr><td><input name="password" type="password" size="10">
    </td></tr>
</table>
  <input type="submit" value="   Login   ">
</form>
<a href="Forgot.jsp">Forgot your password?</a>
<br>New User <a href="../registration/Step1.jsp"><b>Sign Up</b></a>
```

The JSP posts the data to LoginHandler, which queries the Users database and checks whether the name and password combination matches. This can be done using a simple SELECT query against the Users table.

```
SELECT * FROM Users WHERE user_id='<%= userId%>' AND password='<%= password%>'
```

Figure 6.17

Log in page containing data entered by a user

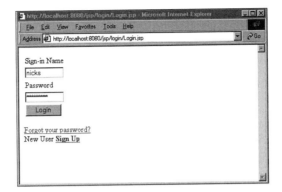

This selects all rows in the Users table that have the user ID and password as the one passed by the JSP expression. If the user had provided incorrect values, no matching rows would be returned on the execution of the query. You can execute the query using the database taglib we created earlier, as shown in Listing 6.25 .

Listing 6.25   LoginHandler.jsp: Authenticating the User by Querying the Users Table Using the ID-Password Combination

```
<%@ taglib uri="../db-taglib.tld" prefix="db" %>

<jsp:useBean id="userId" class="java.lang.String" scope="session"/>

<%
    userId = request.getParameter("userId");
    String password = request.getParameter("password");

    if (userId != null && password != null) {
%>

<db:connection id="conn" url="jdbc:odbc:auction">
</db:connection>

<db:query id="getUser" connection="conn">
SELECT * FROM Users WHERE user_id = '<%= userId%>' AND
password = '<%= password%>'
</db:query>
```

If the combination is correct, the ResultSet, getUser, returns a single row. You can forward the request to the necessary start or welcome page in this case and back to Login.jsp if the values are incorrect as shown in Listing 6.26.

Listing 6.26   LoginHandler.jsp: Forwarding the Request to Welcome or Retry Page Based on the Success of the Authentication

```
<%
        if (getUser.next()) {
        // Forward to the Welcome/start page
%>

<jsp:forward page="index.jsp"/>

<%
        }
    }
    // Return for a retry
%>

<jsp:forward page="Login.jsp"/>
```

 Note

When forwarding requests to another page using relative URLs, ensure that the page you are forwarding to is in the same directory as the page you are forwarding from. If it is in another directory, the relative links and images specified using the relative URL naming scheme will refer to the directory from which the request has been transferred. As a result, your images will not be shown and the links will be broken. Absolute and root relative URLs are not affected, however.

Handling Lost Passwords

Thanks to the plethora of Web sites, the user ends up having several user IDs and passwords. Remembering all the combinations is not an easy task. A lost password might result in a defunct user ID if you don't provide mechanisms to recover the passwords. Different sites have different approaches to handling lost passwords. Two of the most common approaches are sending the passwords to the registered email ID or providing a challenge question and asking the user to provide the answer to it, the question and answer for which are provided by the user during registration.

For Auction Station, you will provide both these techniques to recover the lost password (see Figure 6.18). The page flows for the password recovery begin when the user visits the "Forgot Password" page, Forgot.jsp. The user then chooses one of the two recovery mechanisms and follows the respective processes. The page flows for the scenario are shown in Figure 6.19 .

Figure 6.18

Forgot password page with two scenarios for recovery

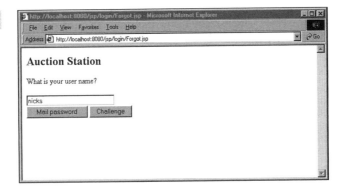

Figure 6.19

Page flows for the recover password scenario

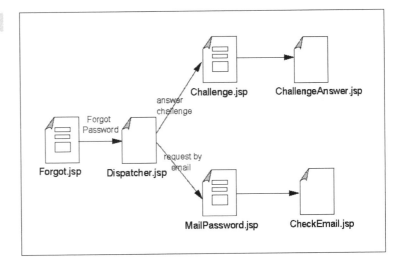

Developing Forgot.jsp

Users initiate the password recovery by visiting this page and entering the username, for which they had forgotten the password, and selecting one of the two mechanisms, "Mail Password" or "Challenge," by clicking on the buttons with the labels. This would translate into a simple form as shown in Listing 6.27.

Listing 6.27   Forgot.jsp: Page Displaying the Password Recovery Mechanisms

```
<html>
<title>Forgot your password?</title>
<body>
<h2>Auction Station</h2>
<p>
What is your user name? <br>
```

```
<form method="GET" action="Dispatcher.jsp">
<input type="text" name="userId" size="25" maxlength="50"><br>
<input type="submit" name="type" value="Mail password">
<input type="submit" name="type" value="Challenge">
</form>

</body>
</html>
```

There are two submit buttons for the same form. The two buttons have the same name, type. The value of the type field will be used to determine the action required for the form.

Dispatcher.jsp identifies the specific handler for the request, as shown in Listing 6.28. If the user selected the "Mail Password" button, the request would be forwarded to MailPassword.jsp, and to Challenge.jsp for the "Challenge" button. If the user did not enter any text in the userId field, Dispatcher.jsp returns the request to Forgot.jsp for a retry .

Listing 6.28   Dispatcher.jsp: Forwarding the Request to the Specific Handler

```
<%
    String userId = request.getParameter("userId");
    String type = request.getParameter("type");
    if (userId == null || userId.trim().length() == 0) {
      // No user id specified...retry
%>
        <jsp:forward page="Forgot.jsp"/>
<%
    }
    // Check if the password needs to be mailed
    if ("Mail Password".equalsIgnoreCase(type)) {
%>
    <jsp:forward page="MailPassword.jsp"/>
<%
    }
    if ("Challenge".equalsIgnoreCase(type)) {
%>
    <jsp:forward page="Challenge.jsp"/>
<%
    }
%>
```

Password Challenge Mechanism

In the password challenge mechanism, you need to find the challenge question for the user. Querying the Users table using the user ID returns the challenge question for the particular user, as shown in Listing 6.29.

Listing 6.29   Challenge.jsp: Retrieving the Challenge Question for a User from the Database

```
<html>
<title>Forgot your password?</title>
<body>
<h2>Auction Station</h2>
<p>

<db:connection id="conn" url="jdbc:odbc:auction">
</db:connection>

<db:query id="challenge" connection="conn">
SELECT Challenge  FROM Users WHERE user_id = '<%= userId%>'
</db:query>
```

If no matching rows were found, it implies that the user had not provided a valid user ID. You should forward the request back to Forgot.jsp for a retry.

```
<%
    if (!challenge.next()) {
%>
<jsp:forward page="Forgot.jsp"/>
```

If the user had not provided a challenge question during registration, this mechanism is not useful, and you should display an error message indicating this. You can find out if the challenge was provided by checking whether the column for that row is null .

```
<%
    }
    String question = challenge.getString(1);
    if (question == null) {
        out.println("<font color=\"red\">You did not set a challenge
➡question</font>");
        return;
    }
%>
```

You need to provide a field that accepts the user's answer and a form to submit the values as well. You also need to set the userId as a hidden field to make the value traverse the two request sessions.

```
Your challenge question is:
<p>
<as:error color="blue"><%= question%></as:error>
<p>

What is your lost password answer?<br>

<form method="POST" action="ChallengeAnswer.jsp">
<input type="hidden" name="userId" value="<%= request.getParameter("userId")%>">
<input type="text" name="answer" size="35" maxsize="50"/><br>
```

6

```
<as:error><%= errMsg%></as:error><br>
<input type="submit" value="Continue">
</form>
</body>
</html>
```

The Challenge page for user *nicks* is shown in Figure 6.20.

Figure 6.20

Challenge page for user nicks

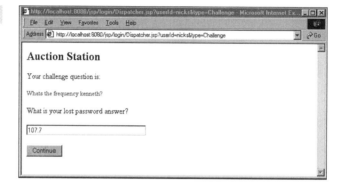

The user submits the answer for the challenge question to ChallengeAnswer.jsp. The JSP checks whether the answer matched the one in the table. This is done using a SELECT statement that returns a row from the Users table for a particular user ID. If the string in the database matches the one entered by the user, it prints the password, as shown in Listing 6.30 .

Listing 6.30   ChallengeAnswer.jsp: Retrieving the Password from the Table by Querying the Table Using the User ID and Challenge Answer

```
<%@ taglib uri="../as-taglib.tld" prefix="as" %>
<%@ taglib uri="../db-taglib.tld" prefix="db" %>
<%
        String userId = request.getParameter("userId");
        String answer = request.getParameter("answer");
%>

<html>
<title>Forgot your password?</title>
<body>
<h2>Auction Station</h2>
<p>

<db:connection id="conn" url="jdbc:odbc:auction">
</db:connection>

<db:query id="challenge" connection="conn">
SELECT answer, password  FROM Users WHERE user_id = '<%= userId%>'
</db:query>
```

```
<%
    if (!challenge.next()) {
%>
<jsp:forward page="Forgot.jsp"/>

<%
    }

    String dbAnswer = challenge.getString(1);
    if (answer == null || !answer.equalsIgnoreCase(dbAnswer)) {
%>
    <jsp:forward page="Challenge.jsp">
        <jsp:param name="answerMsg" value="Your answer doesn't match the
➡one in our records"/>
    </jsp:forward>
    }
<%
    }
    String password = challenge.getString(2);
%>

Your password is:
<p>
<as:error color="blue"><%= password%></as:error>
<p>

Please login again with your user id and password.
<br>
Happy Auctioning
</body>
</html>
```

If the user entered the same answer as the one provided during registration, ChallengeAnswer.jsp generates the password for user *nicks*, as shown in Figure 6.21 .

Figure 6.21

Password retrieved for user nicks using the Challenge mechanism

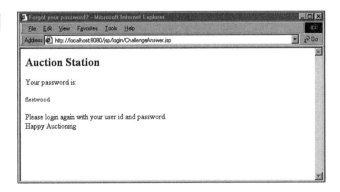

Password Emailing Mechanism

The password emailing mechanism is one of the safest methods to retrieve and transmit the password to a user. In this mechanism, the user enters his or her user ID and email address. These values are used to query the table to retrieve the password. The password information is then emailed to the user using the email ID. The JSP requires the email information to weed out requests from bogus users.

The technical details are similar to the Challenge mechanism except that the MailPassword.jsp accepts an email address instead of the answer to the challenge question. When the user sends out the email address, the JSP executes a SQL query using the email and user ID values in the WHERE clause.

```
SELECT f_name, l_name, password FROM Users WHERE user_id = '<%= userId%>' AND
➡email = '<%= email%>'
```

If a row is retrieved using this SELECT query, it implies that the email and user ID match the ones in the table and the information is valid. The JSP creates an email using the email custom tags and sends the password, as shown in Listing 6.31.

Listing 6.31   CheckEmail.jsp: Sending an Email to the User Providing the Password Information

```
<db:connection id="conn" url="jdbc:odbc:auction">
</db:connection>

<db:query id="verifyEmail" connection="conn">
SELECT f_name, l_name, password FROM Users WHERE user_id = '<%= userId%>' AND
➡email = '<%= email%>'
</db:query>

<%
    if (!verifyEmail.next()) {
%>

<jsp:forward page="MailPassword.jsp">
    <jsp:param name="emailMsg" value="The email you provided doesn't match with
➡our records" />
</jsp:forward>
<%
    }
%>

<as:email>
    <as:from address="service@auction.station.net">Auction Station Agent
➡</as:from>
    <as:to address="<%= email%>"></as:to>
    <as:subject>Your Auction Station Password</as:subject>
    <as:body>
        Hi <%= verifyEmail.getString(1)%>
```

```
            Your password for accessing Auction Station with the user name,
➥<%= userId%>
            is <%= verifyEmail.getString(3)%>

Happy Auctioning.
    </as:body>
</as:email>
```

You can also give a visual cue to the user to head to his or her inbox to find the email containing the password that was sent out, as shown in Figure 6.22 .

Figure 6.22

Providing a visual cue informing the user of the email containing the password that was sent out

Performing Database Connection Pooling

In the JDBC applications we created so far, we performed the following steps:

1. Load the JDBC Driver.
2. Obtain a connection from the Database Manager.
3. Perform database operations using the connection.
4. Close the connection.

This simple method is rather inefficient: Loading the driver and obtaining a connection is an expensive operation. No, you don't need to pay royalty fees for each connection! It's expensive because of the overhead involved in the process. Also, DBMSes have a limit on the number of active connections that can be made with each database, so if a connection is to be created for each request, the limit will be breached easily.

We will create a mechanism to pool or reuse database connections. In your JDBC application, you will pick up an instance from the pool and release it back when you are done with your database work, to make it available for another program.

Database pooling can be implemented by using three custom classes that we will build:

- DBConnectionManager
- DBConnectionPool
- DBConnection

DBConnectionManager

The DBConnectionManager keeps a collection of pools. Each pool provides connections to a particular database. We require only a single instance of the DBConnectionManager because we need a single point of contact in our JDBC applications. This can be easily implemented using the *singleton* pattern.

 The singleton pattern ensures that only one instance of the class can be created and accessed.

You can enforce the singleton behavior by storing a static instance of the same class it is defined in as a field (singleton) and providing a public static accessor method for the instance (getSingleton).

```
package station.auction.db;
import java.util.Hashtable;

public class DBConnectionManager {
    protected static DBConnectionManager singleton = new DBConnectionManager();
public static DBConnectionManager getSingleton() {
    return singleton;
}
}
```

You can prevent an application from creating more instances of this class by reducing the visibility of the constructor by making it a private constructor. Thus the class can be instantiated only within itself, either as a field variable or within a method.

```
private DBConnectionManager() {
    super();
}
```

The DBConnectionManager will be holding a DBConnectionPool for every database it is providing database connection pooling for. To speed up access to these pools, we will be using a Hashtable that maps the DBConnectionPool with its name.

```
    protected Hashtable pools = new Hashtable();
```

There are two types of containers used to store collections.

- Containers such as arrays and Vectors that store objects sequentially. An object can be retrieved by specifying its index in the container. Searching for a particular object implies a sequential search unless the collection is sorted.

- Containers such as Hashtable and Map that store objects along with a key. The key can be used to randomly access a particular object and thereby speeds searches.

The DBConnectionManager class provides a getConnection method that returns a DBConnection instance by providing its URL, database driver name, user ID, and password for making the connection. It uses these parameters to construct the key and map and retrieve a DBConnectionPool. If a pool does not exist for a particular type of a connection, a DBConnectionPool instance is created for the type of connection and added to the Hashtable. It then delegates the request to the specific DBConnectionPool to return a database connection.

```java
public DBConnection getConnection(String url, String driver, String userid,
➥String password) {
    try {
        String key = url + " " + driver + " " + userid + " " + password;
        DBConnectionPool ref = (DBConnectionPool) pools.get(key);

        if (ref == null) {
            ref = new DBConnectionPool(url, driver, userid, password);
            pools.put(key, ref);
        }
        return ref.getConnection();

    } catch (Exception exc) {
        exc.printStackTrace();
    }

    return null;
}
```

DBConnectionPool

This class is responsible for pooling the DBConnection instances to allow them to be reused by different applications. We will be using a data structure called a *queue* to store the instances. The JDK contains an implementation of the queue available in the sun.misc package.

As the name suggests, a queue represents an orderly collection of objects that works on the First-In First-Out *(FIFO)* principle. An object added first to the structure, using the enqueue method, will be the first to be retrieved using the dequeue method.

A stack, on the other hand, works on the Last-In-First-Out (LIFO) principle. The last object added using the push method will be the first to be retrieved using the pop method.

Lastly, a computer program operates on the *GIGO* principle: Garbage-In-Garbage-Out. As you code, so shall you reap!

```
package station.auction.db;

import java.sql.Connection;
import java.sql.DriverManager;
import sun.misc.Queue;

public class DBConnectionPool {
    protected String driver = null;
    protected String url = null;
    protected String userid = null;
    protected String password = null;

    protected Queue connPool = new Queue();
    protected int poolSize = 25;
```

The DBConnection instances are retrieved from the queue within the getConnection method. If the queue has no elements within it, in other words it is empty, you need to create a new instance of a DBConnection using the DatabaseManager and pass the database attributes to it.

```
public DBConnection getConnection() throws java.sql.SQLException,
➡InterruptedException {
    if (connPool.isEmpty()) {
        Connection con = DriverManager.getConnection(url, userid, password);
        DBConnection dbcon = new DBConnection(con, this);
        return dbcon;
    }

    synchronized(connPool) {
        return (DBConnection) connPool.dequeue();
    }
}
```

After the JDBC application is done with using the connection, it returns it to the pool using the releaseConnection() method.

```
public void releaseConnection(DBConnection con) {
    synchronized(connPool) {
        // Add check for pool size
        // con.close() if pool size at maximum
        connPool.enqueue(con);
    }
}
```

Note

You need to perform the `enqueue` and `dequeue` operations on the queue within a `synchronized` block. This ensures that only a single thread operates on the queue at the instance of time. During this time, it locks the queue instance while performing the operation within the synchronized block. Any other thread that tries to access the queue will be blocked during this time.

You can limit the active instances of the database connections in the queue by specifying a `poolSize`. You can provide accessor methods for this field.

```
public int getPoolSize() {
    return poolSize;
}
public void setPoolSize(int newPoolSize) {
    poolSize = newPoolSize;
}
```

Within the `releaseConnection` method, you can check whether the number of active connections is more than the pool size.

DBConnection

6

This class is a wrapper for the `java.sql.Connection` instance returned by the `DatabaseManager`. We do this in order to provide a `release()` method to the class. If `java.sql.Connection` were a class, we would have directly extended from the class and added the extra method. Luck isn't on our side: `Connection` is an interface. You can provide the method using the *proxy pattern*. Using the proxy pattern, you delegate responsibility to the actual `Connection` instance. The actual instance is stored as a field in the class and set in the constructor along with the `DBConnectionPool` to which the instance belongs.

```
package station.auction.db;

import java.sql.Connection;

public class DBConnection implements java.sql.Connection {
    DBConnectionPool pool = null;
    protected Connection original = null;
public DBConnection(Connection conn, DBConnectionPool pool) {
    super();
    original = conn;
    this.pool = pool;
}
```

You need to implement all the methods defined in the Connection interface and delegate the requests to the original instance.

```
public void clearWarnings() throws java.sql.SQLException {
    original.clearWarnings();
}
public void close() throws java.sql.SQLException {
    original.close();
}
public void commit() throws java.sql.SQLException {
    original.commit();
}
public java.sql.Statement createStatement() throws java.sql.SQLException {
    return original.createStatement();
}
public boolean getAutoCommit() throws java.sql.SQLException {
    return original.getAutoCommit();
}
public String getCatalog() throws java.sql.SQLException {
    return original.getCatalog();
}
public java.sql.DatabaseMetaData getMetaData() throws java.sql.SQLException {
    return original.getMetaData();
}
public int getTransactionIsolation() throws java.sql.SQLException {
    return original.getTransactionIsolation();
}
public java.sql.SQLWarning getWarnings() throws java.sql.SQLException {
    return original.getWarnings();
}
public boolean isClosed() throws java.sql.SQLException {
    return original.isClosed();
}
public boolean isReadOnly() throws java.sql.SQLException {
    return original.isReadOnly();
}
public String nativeSQL(String sql) throws java.sql.SQLException {
    return original.nativeSQL(sql);
}
public java.sql.CallableStatement prepareCall(String sql) throws
java.sql.SQLException {
    return original.prepareCall(sql);
}
public java.sql.PreparedStatement prepareStatement(String sql) throws
java.sql.SQLException {
    return original.prepareStatement(sql);
}
public void rollback() throws java.sql.SQLException {
    original.rollback();
}
```

```
public void setAutoCommit(boolean autoCommit) throws java.sql.SQLException {
    original.setAutoCommit(autoCommit);
}
public void setCatalog(String catalog) throws java.sql.SQLException {
    original.setCatalog(catalog);
}
public void setReadOnly(boolean readOnly) throws java.sql.SQLException {
    original.setReadOnly(readOnly);
}
public void setTransactionIsolation(int level) throws java.sql.SQLException {
    setTransactionIsolation(level);
}
```

You can now add the release method that recycles the connection instance into the pool.

```
public void release() {
    pool.releaseConnection(this);
}
```

Performing Database Pooling Within Your JDBC Application

You can easily introduce database pooling in your JDBC applications—JSPs, Taglibs, and JavaBeans—by replacing the code

```
String driver = <driver name>
Class.forName(driver);
Connection conn = DatabaseManager.getConnection(<db_url>, <user_id>,
<password>);
...
conn.close();
```

with the code

```
DBConnection conn = DBConnectionManager.getSingleton().getConnection(<db_url>,
        <driver_name>, <user_id>, <password>);
...
conn.release();
```

Database pooling is one of the key areas for obtaining performance improvements, and you can observe the improvements when the number of requests for the JDBC application increases.

Next Steps

In this chapter, you learned how to access databases from within Java programs and JSPs. The techniques described in this chapter use JDBC and its `java.sql.*` API for connecting to the database and executing queries and modifications.

You also created a custom database tag library to perform database queries and modifications. You saw its application in the registration module and the modified calendar of events application.

You can perform database operations within JSPs if your requirements are smaller. For larger projects, you will need to separate the tasks to the Web designer, Web integrator, server-side developer, and database modeler. That's where application development architecture comes into the picture. You will learn more about it in the next chapter.

Chapter 7

Using the Model 2 Architecture to Develop an Auction Items Catalog

In this chapter, we will develop the Auction item catalog module, which allows a user to browse through the product categories and view the items listed in the site.

The Web Application Model

We will be using a Web application model described in the "IBM Application Framework for e-Business." This model is also called the Model 2 Architecture and is a must for developing robust Web applications or e-businesses.

A Web application is a dialogue between the user and the system. Sending requests made up of data as HTML form field values represents one part of this dialogue, and the server's response, the other. An application on the Web server processes these requests and performs a combination of these three operations:

- Understands the requests and executes some business logic using the request data
- Forwards the requests to another application based on the values of the processed data obtained by executing the business logic
- Generates display pages from the processed data, such as a table to display the calendar for the month

You could incorporate all these operations into a single JSP, but separation of responsibility is a big concern. We have also used JavaBeans and the form-handling technique to address some of these issues. In this chapter, we will modify and enhance the form-handling technique to implement robust Web-based dialogues. For this we will use the time-tested *Model-View-Controller* (MVC) paradigm in the form of the command bean pattern. The MVC paradigm provides a set of three components to handle the different functional aspects of a Web application:

- **Controller**—This handles the forwarding of the request to the correct handler. The handlers in this case are command beans that perform a particular operation. This consists of the fulfillment of the interaction objective. The objective of this operation is the creation of the model or view helper JavaBeans. This could be the development of a bean instance that represents a particular month's calendar or the insertion of a record in the Users table during the user registration process.
- **Model or view-helper JavaBeans**—These are view-helper bean instances created by the controller and fed to the presentation layer for developing the output.
- **View or presentation layer**—This consists of the logic required for developing the response in the form of the generated page. For the Calendar application, it implies the laying out of a table containing information about the month. The view develops the response using the model developed by the calendar.

Controller

The *controller* plays a key role in the Web application. All requests are submitted to the controller. The controller invokes the necessary business logic by delegating the request to command beans and passes the result to the view. It can perform additional roles apart from redirecting, such as the following:

- Check whether the request information is valid
- Perform security checks to determine whether the user is authorized to access the page
- Pass the request data to the business logic, as in setting the input properties of command beans
- Set the output of the business logic—the result of the command—as request information and pass the request to the view

The interaction between the different components is shown in Figure 7.1.

Figure 7.1

Interaction between the Model-View-Controller components for a Web-based application

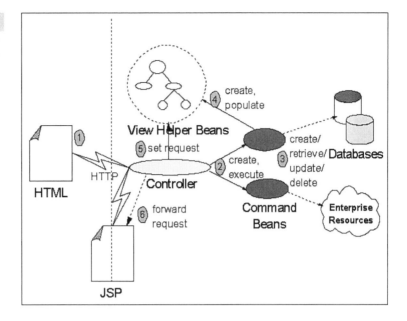

Command Beans

Command beans implement the business logic for the Web application and provide data that will be used for developing the response. Business logic could range from obtaining calendar information to querying and manipulating data stores or any other external services, such as ERP implementations and workflow engines.

These beans execute a particular business process or command and create JavaBeans that can be easily consumed for display in the view component. Because these beans are basically Java classes, they can make use of Java core packages as well as the multitude of enterprise-access Java libraries.

Model or View Helper JavaBeans

The model represents the internal state of the system represented by interacting business objects. At run-time this model comprises instances of view-helper JavaBeans created for a particular use case by a command bean.

View or Presentation Layer

The *view* is a set of JSPs that consume the view-helper beans created by the command beans to produce the response. The controller interacts with the command beans to set the data as request parameters. The views extract the view helper JavaBean instances from the request to generate the response using expressions and scriptlets.

Developing the Database Schema for the Catalog

For our application, we will be creating an Auction item catalog module that allows users to browse through the different categories in AuctionStation. A category can have either subcategories or items listed in it. We will develop a module that provides a uniform mechanism to browse both the subcategories and items.

In the Auction site, users can list their items for auctions. For small and highly targeted auction sites, you can list all the items together. However, as the listings and types of items in your site increase, the sheer number and lack of organization of the items can overwhelm a prospective bidder. You should allow the user to categorize the auction items and display only a subset of the items belonging to a particular category to help the user easily locate an item. This is similar to providing a book with a table of contents and an index that helps the reader easily locate a particular topic rather than providing all the content in a single chapter.

Now that you have gotten the hang of relational databases, you might have guessed the entities involved in the catalog. If you have a model that looks like the one in Figure 7.2, we think alike!

Figure 7.2

Entity relationships in the Auction site

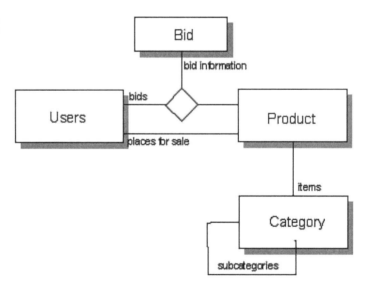

The Users table has already been created for the registration module in Chapter 6. Read on to get a more detailed explanation of the model. You can skip to the next section if you want to get to the Web enablement part of the auction items catalog.

Designing the Category Table

The Category table is an interesting element of this design. You can create a Category table specifying category information, such as name, category ID, description, image URL, and creation date.

```
CREATE TABLE Category  (
    cat_id VARCHAR(10) NOT NULL,
    name VARCHAR(50) NOT NULL,
    description VARCHAR(100),
    image_url VARCHAR(50),
    created TIMESTAMP,
    PRIMARY KEY (cat_id),
```

Each category has other subcategories nested within it. A simple two-level hierarchy can be obtained by creating another table, say SubCategory, having the same columns as Category as well as a foreign key relationship with it. The problem with this approach is the fixed level of subcategories and the requirement to create another identical table.

You can provide generic, multilevel nesting by providing a parent-child relationship in the Category table. You can achieve this by adding another column, `par_cat_id`, that refers to the parent category in the same table.

```
    par_cat_id VARCHAR(10)
)
```

 Note   You cannot enforce this parent-child relationship by a foreign key relationship because not all the categories have a matching `par_cat_id`-`cat_id` combination. For example, the root's `par_cat_id` field is `NULL` because it does not have a parent category.

The Product Table

You would need to create a Product table to store all the items. You can specify item information using the different columns of the table, such as name, description, creation date, minimum amount, bid increment amount, and end of bid date.

```
CREATE TABLE Product (
    prod_id VARCHAR(10) NOT NULL,
    prod_name VARCHAR(50) NOT NULL,
    description VARCHAR(100),
    url VARCHAR(50),
    image_url VARCHAR(50),
    min_amt DECIMAL(7, 2) NOT NULL,
    min_bid_inc DECIMAL(7,2) NOT NULL,
    bid_close TIMESTAMP NOT NULL,
    created TIMESTAMP,
    PRIMARY KEY (prod_id),
```

You also need to specify the user who inserted the item in the listing. You can do this by providing a column that stores the user ID in the Product table. You can further enforce *referential integrity* by providing a foreign key relationship on the column with the user_id column in the Users table. Using this relationship, you can constrain items that can be added to only those that have a matching user ID in the Users table.

```
user_id VARCHAR(15) NOT NULL,
    FOREIGN KEY (user_id) REFERENCES Users(user_id),
```

To catalog the items, you need to provide category information in the Product table. You can do this by adding another column, cat_id, that refers to an entry in a category table.

```
    cat_id VARCHAR(10) NOT NULL,
    FOREIGN KEY (cat_id) REFERENCES Category(cat_id)
)
```

The Bid Table

The Bid table stores information regarding the bids. The information includes the prod_id of the item being bid on, the user_id of the user bidding, the amount bid, and the creation date for the bid.

```
CREATE TABLE Bid (
        prod_id VARCHAR(10) NOT NULL,
        user_id VARCHAR(15) NOT NULL,
        amount DECIMAL(7, 2) NOT NULL,
        created TIMESTAMP,
```

You can set the primary key of the table as a compound key containing the prod_id and amount to prevent two users from bidding on the same item with the same amount. The database would generate an exception when this happens.

The prod_id and user_id columns are foreign key references for columns in the Product and Users tables. You can enforce this relationship with a foreign key relationship.

```
FOREIGN KEY (prod_id) REFERENCES Product(prod_id),
        FOREIGN KEY (user_id) REFERENCES Users(user_id)
)
```

Populating the Tables with Sample Data

Add the Product and Category tables to the AUCTION database. Populate the tables with sample data that you can use for the product catalog. The catalog contains different categories as listed in Figure 7.3.

Figure 7.3

Category hierarchy in Auction Station

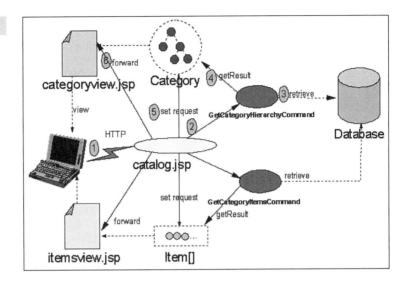

The SQL INSERT statements to create the equivalent categories are shown in Listing 7.1. You can set the created field to the timestamp representing the current date and time using CURRENT TIMESTAMP. Remember that the onus of specifying the correct parent category lies on you because no constraint checks exist in the table. You can end up with orphan categories if you specify a par_cat_id that does not match a cat_id of another category in the table, and you can end up with circular relationships if two categories have each other as parents.

Listing 7.1   PopulateItems.sql: Inserting the Different Categories for AuctionStation

```
INSERT INTO CATEGORY (CAT_ID, PAR_CAT_ID, NAME, DESCRIPTION, CREATED) VALUES
( '0', NULL, 'Root', 'Parent Category containing all the listings',
➥CURRENT TIMESTAMP),
( '1', '0', 'Antiques', 'Antiquities, books, furniture, metalware',
➥CURRENT TIMESTAMP),
( '2', '0', 'Computers', 'Computers, keyboards, modems', CURRENT TIMESTAMP),
( '3', '0', 'Electronics', 'Photographic equipment, Consumer electronics',
➥CURRENT TIMESTAMP),
( '4', '0', 'Miscellaneous', 'memorablia, clothing', CURRENT TIMESTAMP),
( '1.1', '1', 'Antiquities', 'Old Books, coins, treasures', CURRENT TIMESTAMP),
( '1.2', '1', 'furniture', 'sofa, love seats', CURRENT TIMESTAMP),
( '1.3', '1', 'Metal', 'Silver collections', CURRENT TIMESTAMP),
( '1.4', '1', 'Jewellery', 'Necklaces, earrings, brooches', CURRENT TIMESTAMP),
( '1.4.1', '1.4', 'Tiaras', 'royal headgear', CURRENT TIMESTAMP),
( '1.4.2', '1.4', 'Diadems', 'royal headgear', CURRENT TIMESTAMP),
( '2.1', '2', 'Hardware', 'Desktops, Servers, Notebooks, PDAs',
➥CURRENT TIMESTAMP),
( '2.2', '2', 'Software', 'Games, tools', CURRENT TIMESTAMP),
( '3.1', '3', 'Photography Equipment', 'Point and shoot cameras,
➥digital cameras', CURRENT TIMESTAMP),
```

7

Listing 7.1   continued

```
( '3.2', '3', 'Consumer Electronics', 'Audio, Radio, Calculators',
➥CURRENT TIMESTAMP),
( '4.1', '4', 'Clothing', NULL , CURRENT TIMESTAMP)
```

Add sample auction items by specifying the product details and bidding information. Each item also has an associated user (user_id) and a category (cat_id) as shown in Listing 7.2. Specify the bid closing time for these items as four days from the current time. You can do this using the date arithmetic CURRENT TIMESTAMP + 4 DAYS and CURRENT TIMESTAMP + 17 HOURS.

The product listings in this chapter and the rest of the book may not depict actual product information. The prices may be inflated or depreciated based on figures conjured entirely by me. Since these are item listings in an auction site, in any case the prices may not match retail ones. Please consult the dealers for authentic product information.

Listing 7.2   PopulateItems.sql: Inserting the Sample Auction Items in the Product Table

```
INSERT INTO PRODUCT (PROD_ID, PROD_NAME, CAT_ID, USER_ID, DESCRIPTION,
➥MIN_AMT, MIN_BID_INC, CREATED, BID_END) VALUES
('112', 'IBM Thinkpad 600X', '2.1', 'msahu', 'Ultra light notebook, with USB
➥and CD-ROM', 2500.0, 12.5, CURRENT TIMESTAMP, CURRENT TIMESTAMP + 4 DAYS),
('113', 'Workpad', '2.1', 'ken', 'Handheld with PalmOS', 499.9, 5.0, CURRENT
➥TIMESTAMP, CURRENT TIMESTAMP + 4 DAYS),
('114', 'Playstation', '2.1', 'ken', 'Sonys game console', 350.0, 5.0,
➥CURRENT TIMESTAMP, CURRENT TIMESTAMP + 4 DAYS),
('98323', 'Yamaha Distortion Emulator', '2.1', 'nicks', 'Distortion unit with
➥ MP3 converter', 225.0, 4.5, CURRENT TIMESTAMP, CURRENT TIMESTAMP + 17 HOURS)
```

You can even add a sample bid for the Yamaha Distortion Emulator courtesy citizen 'ken'.

```
INSERT INTO BID (PROD_ID, USER_ID, AMOUNT, CREATED) VALUES
('98323', 'ken', 250, CURRENT TIMESTAMP),
```

Developing the Model or View-Helper JavaBeans

You will now develop view-helper JavaBeans for the presentation layer. The view-helper beans represent the different entities in our application. The class diagram for the entities is shown in Figure 7.4.

Figure 7.4

Class diagram of the AuctionStation model created in TogetherSoft's Together/J

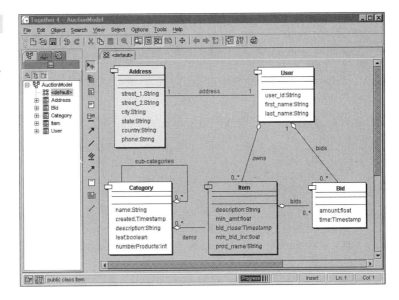

The model represents relationships between the interacting entities. In this model, the classes correspond directly to a table in the schema. The attributes of the classes map to columns in their respective tables. Additional methods will also be added as convenience methods for use by the JSP.

All our view-helper JavaBeans belong to the `station.auction.catalog` package. The classes in the model are described in the following sections.

Address

`Address` is the simplest class in our model. It contains the input and output properties for representing an address, as described in Table 7.1.

Table 7.1 Properties of the `station.auction.catalog.Address` JavaBean

Name	Type
street_1	String
street_2	String
city	String
state	String
country	String
phone	String
type	String
user (Association)	station.auction.catalog.User

The difference between the columns of the Address table and the properties of the class is in the definition of the user field. Here the type is `station.auction.catalog.User` instead of the string representing the user ID.

Define fields and accessor (getter and setter) methods using the properties. Add a constructor that sets the properties of the class, as in Listing 7.3.

Listing 7.3   Address.java: Defining Constructors for the Class That Set Some or All of Its Properties

```
public Address(String city, String state, String country) {
    setCity(city);
    setState(state);
    setCountry(country);
}
```

You can overload the constructors with extra parameters to suit your needs.

```
public Address(String street_1, String street_2, String city, String state,
➥String country, String phone) {
    this(city, state, country);
    setStreet_1(street_1);
    setStreet_2(street_2);
    setPhone(phone);
}
```

Constructors save you the trouble of setting the properties individually, as follows:

```
Address address = new Address();
address.setCity(city);
address.setState(state);
address.setCountry(country);
```

The problem with constructors having parameters is that you have to remember the order and sequence of the parameters while creating the instance.

Category

The `Category` class is built on the same lines as `Address`. It contains the input and output properties for a category, as described in Table 7.2.

Table 7.2   Properties of the `station.auction.catalog.Category` JavaBean

Name	Type
Name	String
description	String
image_url	String
created	java.sql.Timestamp
cat_id	String
par_cat_id	String

Category also has a parent-child relationship. A category has many subcategories, so Category has a one-to-many aggregation with itself. Define two properties: parent of type station.auction.catalog.Category and an indexed property, children, of type station.auction.catalog.Category[], to implement this relationship.

You can create an indexed property by following these steps:

1. Create a field of type java.util.Vector to hold the child instances.

   ```
   protected Vector fieldChildren = new Vector();
   ```

2. Provide methods that add instances to the collection. These constitute the setter methods for the indexed property as described in Table 7.3.

Table 7.3   Category.java   Setter Methods for the Indexed Property, children

Type of Addition	Method
| Append an instance in the collection | ```
public void addChild(Category child) {
    fieldChildren.addElement(child);
}
``` |
| Insert an instance at a particular location in the collection | ```
public void setChildren(int index,
              Category children) {
   fieldChildren.insertElementAt(
              children, index);
}
``` |
| Insert all the instances in the collection | ```
public void setChildren(Category[] children) {
   fieldChildren.removeAllElements();
     for (int i = 0; i < children.length; i++) {
       fieldChildren.addElement(children[i]);
     }
}
``` |

3. Add getter methods for the indexed property. Provide accessor methods that retrieve individual elements and the collection's elements as shown in Table 7.4.

Table 7.4   Category.java: Accessor Methods for the Indexed Property, children

Type of Addition	Method
| Get an instance at a particular location in the collection | ```
public Category getChildAt(int index) {
   return (Category)
          fieldChildren.elementAt(index);
}
``` |
| Obtain all the instances in the collection | ```
public Category[] getChildren() {
   Category[] children = new Category[fieldChildren.size()];
   fieldChildren.copyInto(children);
   return children;
}
``` |
```

4. Add additional convenience methods for the indexed property, such as one that returns the count of instances in the collection.

```
public int getChildCount() {
   return fieldChildren.size();
}
```

While setting the `parent` property in the `Category`, you can also add the `child` category to the parent `Category`.

```
public void setParent(Category parent) {
    fieldParent = parent;
    parent.addChild(this);
}
```

Create another indexed property, `items`, that represents the one-to-many aggregation with the `Item` class. This would require you to add the fields and methods for the indexed property as shown in Listing 7.4.

Listing 7.4 Category.java: Methods and Fields for the `items` Property

```
    protected Vector items = new Vector();

public void addItem(Item child) {
    items.addElement(child);
}

public Item getItemAt(int index) {
    return (Item) items.elementAt(index);
}

public int getItemCount() {
    return items.size();
}

public Item[] getItems() {
    Item[] children = new Item[items.size()];
    items.copyInto(children);
    return children;
}

public void setItems(Item[] children) {
    items.removeAllElements();
    for (int i = 0; i < children.length; i++) {
        items.addElement(children[i]);
    }
}

public void setItem(int index, Item children) {
    items.insertElementAt(children, index);
}
```

Add a boolean property, `leaf`, that determines whether the category is a leaf category—one that does not have any subcategories.

Lastly, define constructors for instantiating the bean.

```
public Category() {}

public Category(String cat_id, String par_cat_id, String name) {
    setCat_id(cat_id);
    setPar_cat_id(par_cat_id);
    setName(name);
}

public Category(String cat_id, String par_cat_id, String name, String
➥description, String imageURL,Timestamp created) {
    this(cat_id, par_cat_id, name);
    setDescription(description);
    setImage_url(imageURL);
    setCreated(created);
}
```

Item

Create the `Item` class with the properties representing its attributes and relationships for an item, as described in Table 7.5.

Table 7.5   Properties of the `station.auction.catalog.Item` JavaBean

Name	Type
name	String
description	String
image_url	String
created	java.sql.Timestamp
url	String
cat_id	String
prod_id	String
min_amt	float
min_bid_inc	float
user_id	String
bid_close	java.sql.Timestamp
user (association)	station.auction.catalog.User
bids (indexed property for the one-to-many relationship)	station.auction.catalog.Bid

7

User

Create the User class with the properties representing its attributes and relationships for a user, as described in Table 7.6.

Table 7.6   Properties of the `station.auction.catalog.User` JavaBean

Name	Type
user_id	String
firstName	String
lastName	String
initial	String
email	String
memberSince	java.sql.Timestamp
DOB	java.sql.Timestamp
address (association)	station.auction.catalog.Address
items (indexed property for the one-to-many aggregation)	station.auction.catalog.Item
bids (indexed property for the one-to-many relationship)	station.auction.catalog.Bid

Bid

Create the Bid class with the properties representing its attributes and relationships for a bid as described in Table 7.7.

Table 7.7   Properties of the `station.auction.catalog.Bid` JavaBean

Name	Type
amount	float
created	java.sql.Timestamp
user (association)	station.auction.catalog.User
item (association)	station.auction.catalog.Item
email	String
memberSince	java.sql.Timestamp
DOB	java.sql.Timestamp
address (Association)	station.auction.catalog.Address

Developing Command Beans for the Model

Command beans execute a particular command and return view-helper JavaBean instances. For the item catalog module, the command beans create and return view helper beans for the different entities.

You don't have to create or initialize the entire hierarchy of view-helper JavaBeans in the command bean. You can create a single instance, an array of instances, or a subset of the hierarchy.

We will define our command beans to conform to the following conventions. You can also use these as rules for creating your command beans.

- Name the Java classes or JavaBeans with the command they are executing, for example: `<Command_Name>Command`.

- Provide getter and setter methods for the input properties.

- Provide a `check()` method that verifies whether the bean is ready to execute the command.

- Provide an `execute()` method that performs the command and produces output in the form of view-helper JavaBean instances.

- Provide a `getResult()` method that returns the data produced in the `execute` method.

You can enforce the command design pattern by creating an interface that all your command beans should implement. The code for the interface is shown in Listing 7.5.

Listing 7.5   The Command Interface

```
package station.auction;
public interface Command {
    public boolean check() throws Exception;
    public void execute() throws Exception;
    public Object getResult();
}
```

For the item catalog module, we will create a set of command beans used for browsing the catalog and displaying the items. All the command beans created belong to the `station.auction.catalog.command` package.

GetMainCategoriesCommand

For our first command bean, we will develop a bean named `GetMainCategoriesCommand` that returns the main categories in the AuctionStation site as an array of `Category` instances.

SQL Statement for Obtaining the Main Categories

The main categories in the Category table are the rows whose parent category is
Root—all categories with the par_cat_id of 0. You can obtain them using a simple
SELECT statement:

```
SELECT cat_id, name, par_cat_id FROM Category WHERE par_cat_id = '0'
```

This would return the categories as shown in Listing 7.6.

Listing 7.6   Result of Executing the SELECT Main Categories Query

```
CAT_ID        NAME           PAR_CAT_ID
-----------   ------------   ------------------------------------------------------
1             Antiques       0
2             Computers      0
3             Electronics    0
4             Miscellaneous  0
```

Developing the GetMainCategoriesCommand JavaBean

Create a class, GetMainCategoriesCommand, that implements station.auction.
Command. Provide a property, cat_id, that represents the root category ID. Because
the root category's ID is already known, you can initialize the cat_id field to 0.

Create another field, result, to store the main categories. Because more than one
category can be returned, you need to store the result as an array.

```
protected Category[] result = null;
```

Implement the check() method to return only the Boolean value true because no
precondition checks are required.

```
public boolean check() throws Exception {
    return true;
}
```

Implement the execute() method that executes the SQL statement and initializes
the result field. Within the method, it creates a Statement, executes the query for
returning the first level categories, and creates Category instances from each row of
the ResultSet.

You can create arrays of an unknown size using a Vector.

1. Add all the Category instances to the vector.
2. After all instances have been added, initialize the size of the result (Category[])
   array to the size of the vector.
3. Copy the vector elements into the result field.

The code for the execute method is shown in Listing 7.7.

Listing 7.7   GetMainCategoriesCommand.java: Implementing the `execute()` Method

```
public void execute() throws Exception {
    String driver = "COM.ibm.db2.jdbc.app.DB2Driver";

    // Obtain a connection to the database
    DBConnectionManager dbcm = DBConnectionManager.getSingleton();
    DBConnection conn = dbcm.getConnection("jdbc:db2:auction", driver, null,
null);

    Statement categories = conn.createStatement();
    ResultSet rs = categories.executeQuery(
        "SELECT cat_id, par_cat_id, name, description, image_url, created " +
        "FROM Category WHERE par_cat_id = '" + cat_id + "'");

    // Create a Vector to store the categories
    Vector vect = new Vector();
    while (rs.next()) {
        // create a category for each row of the result set
        Category cat = new Category(rs.getString(1),
                                    rs.getString(2),
                                    rs.getString(3),
                                    rs.getString(4),
                                    rs.getString(5),
                                    rs.getTimestamp(6));
        vect.addElement(cat);
    }
    // Release the connection
    conn.release();
    result = new Category[vect.size()];
    vect.copyInto(result);
}
```

Implement the getResult() method to return the array of Category instance created in the execute method.

```
public Object getResult() {
    return result;
}
```

Testing `GetMainCategoriesCommand`

You can test the output of the command bean by adding a main method to the class. Within the method, create the command bean instance, set the cat_id property, execute the command, and print the results as shown in Listing 7.8.

Listing 7.8   GetMainCategoriesCommand.java: The Main Method That Prints the Result Categories Returned by the Command

```java
public static void main(java.lang.String[] args) throws Exception
{
    GetMainCategoriesCommand cmd = new GetMainCategoriesCommand();
    cmd.setCat_id("0");
    cmd.execute();
    Category[] cats = (Category[]) cmd.getResult();

    for (int i = 0; i < cats.length; i++) {
        Category aCat = cats[i];
        System.out.println(aCat.getName());
    }
}
```

GetCategoryHierarchyCommand

You might also be interested in displaying the hierarchy of categories. This will be useful in navigating through the categories to reach a particular item.

SQL Statement for Obtaining a Hierarchy of Categories

For displaying the hierarchy that would typically answer the question, "What are the subcategories of the category identified by the name 'Antiques'?" you could use the SELECT query used for obtaining the main categories by changing the par_cat_id in the WHERE clause accordingly.

```sql
SELECT cat_id, name, par_cat_id FROM Category WHERE par_cat_id = '1'
```

This query returns the categories within Antiques, such as Antiquities, Furniture, Metal, and Jewelry. However, it doesn't return the subcategories identified by the names Tiaras and Diadems because they are not the immediate "children" of the Antiques category.

To obtain even the subcategories, you need to perform a *single-level explosion* that will include the immediate child categories, subcategories of the children, and so on. To perform a single-level explosion, you need to use two advanced features of SQL:

- **Fullselect and UNIONs**—You have seen how to constrain rows returned by a query by using WHERE predicates containing relational operators such as equal (=), not equal (<>), greater than (>), and so on.

  Fullselects allow you to derive a result table from two other result tables using the set operators—UNION (union), EXCEPT (difference), and INTERSECT (intersection).

The `UNION` operand makes the fullselect derive a result table by combining two other result tables. If `UNION ALL` is specified, the result consists of all rows in the two result tables.

`UNION`s can be used to accumulate data from different tables. For example, to find the `cat_id` of categories whose parent is Antiques (`par_cat_id = '1'`) and the items of the products that were inserted by user ken (`user_id = 'ken'`), you can conveniently use the `UNION` fullselect.

```
SELECT cat_id FROM Category
    WHERE par_cat_id = '1'
UNION
SELECT cat_id FROM Product
    WHERE user_id = 'ken'
```

- **Common table expression**—A common table expression permits defining a result table with a table name that can be specified as a table name in any `FROM` clause of the fullselect that follows. The most popular usage of common table expressions is when the result needs to be derived by recursion, as shown in Listing 7.9.

Listing 7.9   Union.sql: Performing a Single-Level Explosion to Return All the Child Categories of Antiques

```
WITH RecCatList (cat_id, name) AS (
    SELECT ROOT.cat_id, ROOT.name
    FROM Category ROOT
    WHERE ROOT.cat_id = '1'
UNION ALL
    SELECT CHILD.cat_id, CHILD.name
    FROM RecCatList PARENT, Category CHILD
    WHERE PARENT.cat_id = CHILD.par_cat_id
    )
SELECT cat_id, name FROM RecCatList
```

The query might look a bit overwhelming at first sight, but it is a valuable mechanism for performing hierarchy-based searches at the data store end.

The query recursively obtains a set of the matching rows in the Category table. The first operand, referred to as the *initialization fullselect*, provides the starting point of the query. It obtains the root category from which the subcategories will be recursively obtained. In this case, it's the category with the `cat_id` 1 in the Category table. The result of this first fullselect goes into the common table expression `RecCatList`.

The second operand of the `UNION` uses `RecCatList` to obtain the subcategories by having the `FROM` clause refer to the common table expression instead of the Category table. The result goes back to `RecCatList` again. The second operand is used repeatedly until no more children exist.

The result of the query is

```
CAT_ID     NAME
---------  --------------------------------------------------
SQL0347W  The recursive common table expression "DB2ADMIN.RECCATLIST" may
contain an infinite loop.  SQLSTATE=01605

2          Computers
2.1        Hardware
2.2        Software
```

It is important to remember that with recursive common table expressions, it is possible to introduce an infinite loop. In this example, an infinite loop would be created if the search condition of the second operand that joins the parent and child were coded as

```
WHERE PARENT.cat_id = CHILD.cat_id
```

Note

The result produced by the query could be produced in a JDBC program without using a recursive common table expression. This approach, however, would require sending a new query for each level of recursion. Additional logic would also be required to accumulate the results and order them.

You can also control the depth of the hierarchy returned by the query. For example, you might be interested in returning only the first two levels of subcategories. You can do this by modifying the fullselect query by introducing a LEVEL column that keeps track of the depth. In the initialization fullselect, the value for the LEVEL column is initialized to 1. In the subsequent fullselect, the level from the parent is incremented by 1. To control the number of levels in the result, the second fullselect includes the condition that the parent level must be less than 3. This ensures that the second fullselect only processes subcategories to the third level. The SQL statement for controlling the depth is shown in Listing 7.10.

Listing 7.10   ControlledUnion.sql: Controlling the Depth of the Hierarchy Returned

```
WITH RecCatList (LEVEL, cat_id, name, description) AS (
     SELECT 1, ROOT.cat_id, ROOT.name, ROOT.description
        FROM Category ROOT
        WHERE ROOT.cat_id = '2'
     UNION ALL
     SELECT PARENT.LEVEL+1, CHILD.cat_id, CHILD.name, CHILD.description
        FROM RecCatList PARENT, Category CHILD
        WHERE PARENT.cat_id = CHILD.par_cat_id AND PARENT.LEVEL < 3
  )
SELECT cat_id, LEVEL, name, description FROM RecCatList
```

Developing the `GetCategoryHierarchyCommand` JavaBean

The `GetCategoryHierarchyCommand` requires two input properties, as necessitated by the SQL query:

- The `cat_id` of the category whose hierarchy has to be returned
- The depth or `level` of the hierarchy to be returned

You need to add fields and getter and setter methods for these input properties in the bean. The result of this command is the root of the hierarchy. You will need to add a field of type `Category` to store the root category as well.

```
public class GetCategoryHierarchyCommand implements Command {
    protected String cat_id = "0";
    protected int level = 3;
    protected Category root = null;
```

Implement the `check()` method to check whether the category specified using the input `cat_id` is a valid category. You can do this by querying the Category table using the specified `cat_id` as shown in Listing 7.11. If the category exists, the `ResultSet` has a row; otherwise, it is empty.

Listing 7.11   GetCategoryHierarchyCommand.java—`check()`: Determining Whether the Category Specified Using `cat_id` is a Valid Category

```
public boolean check() throws java.lang.Exception {
        String driver = "COM.ibm.db2.jdbc.app.DB2Driver";
        // Obtain a connection to the database
        DBConnectionManager dbcm = DBConnectionManager.getSingleton();
        DBConnection conn = dbcm.getConnection("jdbc:db2:auction", driver,
➥null, null);
        Statement category = conn.createStatement();
        ResultSet rs = category.executeQuery(
                "SELECT * FROM Category WHERE cat_id = '"+ getCat_id()+ "'");
        boolean found = false;
        if (rs.next()) {
                found = true;
        }
        // Release the connection into the pool
        conn.release();
        return found;
}
```

Implement the `execute()` method to execute the SQL statement containing the recursive common table expression. You will also need to create `Category` JavaBean instances and add them to their parent in the hierarchy. To do this you will need to create a `Hashtable` and add entries mapped by the `cat_id` to the `Category` instance. To add a category to the hierarchy, you will need to obtain an instance in the `Hashtable` whose `cat_id` is equal to its `par_cat_id`.

You can also obtain the product count for a category by querying the Product table using the cat_id column and using the COUNT function to obtain the count of the matching rows.

```
SELECT COUNT(*) FROM Product WHERE cat_id = 'cat_id'
```

This query, however, returns only the count of the products for the particular category without the ones in the subcategories. To obtain the counts of all the products, you can use another recursive common expression. To keep it simple, I have adopted a naming pattern for the categories that has the parent category's prefix. This way, by using the LIKE relational operator in the WHERE clause and the "%" wildcard character in the search string, even the subcategories are involved.

```
SELECT COUNT(*) FROM Product WHERE cat_id LIKE 'cat_id%'
```

The source for the execute() of the command bean is shown in Listing 7.12.

Listing 7.12   GetCategoryHierarchyCommand.java:—execute(): Building the Hierarchy of Categories

```
public void execute() throws Exception {
    String driver = "COM.ibm.db2.jdbc.app.DB2Driver";
    // Obtain a connection to the database
    DBConnectionManager dbcm = DBConnectionManager.getSingleton();
    DBConnection conn = dbcm.getConnection("jdbc:db2:auction", driver,
➥null, null);

    // SQL Statement to Obtain the Category hierarchies
    PreparedStatement catHierarchy = conn.prepareStatement(
      "WITH RecCatList (LEVEL, cat_id, par_cat_id, name, description) AS ( " +
      "        SELECT 1, ROOT.cat_id, ROOT.par_cat_id, ROOT.name,
➥ROOT.description" +
      "            FROM Category ROOT" +
      "            WHERE ROOT.cat_id = ? " +
      "        UNION ALL" +
      " SELECT PARENT.LEVEL+1, CHILD.cat_id, CHILD.par_cat_id, CHILD.name,
➥ CHILD.description" +
      "                FROM RecCatList PARENT, Category CHILD " +
      "                WHERE PARENT.cat_id = CHILD.par_cat_id AND
➥PARENT.LEVEL < ?)" +
      " SELECT LEVEL, cat_id, par_cat_id, name, description FROM RecCatList");

    // SQL Statement to Obtain the product count
    PreparedStatement prodCount = conn.prepareStatement(
      "SELECT COUNT(prod_id) FROM Product WHERE cat_id like ?");

    catHierarchy.setString(1, getCat_id());
    catHierarchy.setInt(2, getLevel());
    ResultSet rs = catHierarchy.executeQuery();
```

```
Hashtable map = new Hashtable();
// Iterate through the result set
while (rs.next()) {
    Category aCat = new Category(rs.getString("cat_id"),
                                 rs.getString("par_cat_id"),
                                 rs.getString("name"));
    aCat.setDescription(rs.getString("description"));

    // Obtain the product count
    prodCount.setString(1, aCat.getCat_id() + "%");
    ResultSet rs2 = prodCount.executeQuery();
    if (rs2.next()) {
        // Set the count in the category
        aCat.setNumberProducts(rs2.getInt(1));
    }
    // Add to the category hierarchy
    if (root == null) {
        root = aCat;
    } else {
        // find the parent to add to in the hierarchy
        Category parent = (Category) map.get(aCat.getPar_cat_id());
        if (parent != null) {
            aCat.setParent(parent);
        }
    } // end if-else
    // Add to the Hashtable
    map.put(aCat.getCat_id(), aCat);
}
conn.release();
}
```

Implement the getResult() method to return the root Category created in the exe-cute() method.

Testing the GetCategoryHierarchyCommand

To test the command, add a main method to GetCategoryHierarchyCommand. Create an instance of the command and set the cat_id and level properties. Execute the command and traverse through the hierarchy starting with the root returned by the getResult method as shown in Listing 7.13.

Listing 7.13   GetCategoryHierarchyCommand.java—main(): Obtaining the Hierarchy with the Category with cat_id '2.1' as the Root

```
public static void main(String[] args) throws Exception{
    GetCategoryHierarchyCommand cmd = new GetCategoryHierarchyCommand();
    cmd.setCat_id("0");
    cmd.setLevel(3);
    cmd.execute();
    Category result = (Category) cmd.getResult();
    if (result != null) {
```

Listing 7.13   continued

```
      System.out.println(result.getName());
   }
   for (int i = 0; i < result.getChildCount(); i++) {
      Category cat = result.getChildAt(i);
      System.out.println("\t" + cat.getName());
      // You could go deeper by traversing through the child
   }
}
```

GetCategoryItemsCommand

There are still the items of the category to be displayed. These items can be obtained by creating a `GetCategoryItemsCommand`. This command returns products in a particular category. It wouldn't be wise to return all the matching products, especially if the number of products is large. For one, it would take a long time to prepare the items for display in the page. You can address this problem by returning/displaying only a subset of the products in the items view.

You may also want to order the items based on one of the fields, such as the amount, name, or creation date, in either ascending or descending order.

SQL Statement for Obtaining the Products in a Category

You can achieve most of the functionality by means of a query on the `Product` table for the particular category.

```
SELECT prod_id, prod_name, min_amt, created, bid_end
FROM Product WHERE cat_id = ?
ORDER BY ? [ASC/DESC]
```

This query would return all the products in the table belonging to the category including ones on which bidding has been closed.

You can filter the items that are still open for bidding by augmenting the `WHERE` clause to test whether the `bid_end` timestamp is greater than the current time.

```
SELECT prod_id, prod_name, min_amt, created, bid_end
FROM Product WHERE cat_id = ? AND (bid_end > CURRENT TIMESTAMP)
ORDER BY ? [ASC/DESC]
```

Developing the `GetCategoryItemsCommand` JavaBean

You need to add the variables of the query string defined in Table 7.8 as input properties of the `GetCategoryItemsCommand` bean.

Table 7.8   Properties of the GetCategoryItemsCommand JavaBean

Name	Type	Description
cat_id	String	Category whose items need to be returned
pageSize	int	Maximum size of the result set to
pageNumber	int	The page number of the result set to be returned
orderByField	String	The order by field on the SELECT statement
ascending	boolean	Whether the results should be sorted in ascending or descending order

Implement the check() method to determine whether the category to be searched exists in the Category table, just as you did in GetCategoryHierarchyCommand.

Implement the execute() method to obtain the items that belong to a particular page, specified by the pageNumber and pageSize properties and sorted according to the orderByField property.

No standard SQL statement exists for returning a subset of the result rows using an index and the subset size. You need to implement this by providing your own logic.

Using the pageNumber and pageSize information, you can determine the start row number of the result: pageNumber * pageSize. You need to return all rows that lie between the start row number and start row number + pageSize as shown in Listing 7.14.

Listing 7.14   GetCategoryItemsCommand.java—execute(): Paging the Matching Items of a Specified Category

```
public void execute() throws Exception{
    // Obtain a connection to the database
    String driver = "COM.ibm.db2.jdbc.app.DB2Driver";
    DBConnectionManager dbcm = DBConnectionManager.getSingleton();
    DBConnection conn = dbcm.getConnection("jdbc:db2:auction", driver,
➥null, null);

    Statement items = conn.createStatement();
    ResultSet rs = items.executeQuery(
      "SELECT prod_id, prod_name, min_amt, created " +
      "FROM Product WHERE cat_id = '" + cat_id + "' " +
      "AND (bid_end > CURRENT TIMESTAMP) " +
      "ORDER BY " + getOrderByField() + " " + getAscending());

    int startFrom = getPageSize()*getPageNumber();
    int endAt = startFrom + getPageSize();
    int count = 0;
```

7

Listing 7.14 continued

```
        Vector vect = new Vector();
        while (rs.next() && count < endAt) {
            count++;
            if (count <= startFrom)
                continue;
            // create a category for each row of the result set
            Item item = new Item(rs.getString(1),
                    rs.getString(2), rs.getFloat(3),
                    rs.getTimestamp(4));
            vect.addElement(item);
        }
        conn.release();
        retVal = new Item[vect.size()];
        vect.copyInto(retVal);
}
```

You can also provide information, such as the total count of items in the category.
You can provide another method, getItemCount, to do this, as shown in Listing 7.15.

**Listing 7.15 GetCategoryItemsCommand.java—getItemCount(): Returning the Total
Count of Items in the Category**

```
public int getItemCount() throws java.lang.Exception {
        // Obtain a connection to the database
        String driver = "COM.ibm.db2.jdbc.app.DB2Driver";

        // Obtain a connection to the database
        DBConnectionManager dbcm = DBConnectionManager.getSingleton();
        DBConnection conn = dbcm.getConnection("jdbc:db2:auction", driver,
➥null, null);

        Statement prodCount = conn.createStatement();
        ResultSet rs = prodCount.executeQuery(
                "SELECT COUNT(*) FROM Product " +
                "WHERE cat_id = '" + cat_id + "'" +
                "AND (bid_end > CURRENT TIMESTAMP) " +);
        if (rs.next()) {
                return rs.getInt(1);
        }

        return 0;
}
```

You may want to accumulate information such as the array of items, count, page size,
and page number so that it can be used by the view JSP. The execute method has a
return type, java.lang.Object, implying that primitive values such as int and float
cannot be returned by the command bean. To work around this problem, you can
wrap the primitive values into objects such as java.lang.Integer and

`java.lang.Float`. In this case, there is more than one primitive value to be returned, so you need to create a *holder* class to store all the information. Create another class, `ItemsArray`, in the package `station.auction.catalog`. Add fields and getter and setter methods for the properties shown in Table 7.9.

Table 7.9 Properties of the `ItemsArray` Class

Name	Type	Description
items	station.auction.catalog.Item[]	The item array to be returned
count	int	The total count of items in the category
pageSize	int	Maximum size of the result set
pageNumber	int	The page number of the result set being returned

Alter the `execute()` method and the field storing the result value to use `ItemsArray`.

```
Item[] retVal = new Item[vect.size()];
vect.copyInto(retVal);

array = new ItemsArray(retVal, getItemCount(), getPageSize(), getPageNumber());
```

Implement the `getResult()` method to return the array created in the `execute` method.

GetItemInformationCommand

The `GetItemInformationCommand` command is executed to return a specific item's information. The specific item is identified by its `prod_id`. You can create an input property to specify this field as well as a `station.auction.catalog.Item` variable, `theItem`, to store the result.

The information about an item spans many tables: `Product`, `Users`, `Address`, and `Bid`. You can break up this query into one or more SQL SELECT statements and aggregate the results by creating appropriate view helper beans such as `Item`, `User`, `Address`, and `Bid` as shown in Listing 7.16.

Listing 7.16 GetItemInformationCommand—`execute()`: Obtaining Information About the Item

```
public void execute() throws Exception {
    DBConnection conn = DBConnectionManager.getSingleton().getConnection(
        "jdbc:db2:auction", "COM.ibm.db2.jdbc.app.DB2Driver", null,
➡ null);
    Statement categories = conn.createStatement();
    PreparedStatement userInfo = conn.prepareStatement(
    "SELECT city, state, country FROM Address WHERE user_id = ?");
```

Listing 7.16   continued

```
        ResultSet rs = categories.executeQuery(
          "SELECT p.cat_id, prod_id, p.prod_name, p.description, p.image_url, " +
          "p.url, p.min_amt, p.min_bid_inc, p.created, p.bid_end, " +
          "u.user_id, u.f_name, u.l_name, u.initial, u.email, u.dob, u.created " +
          "FROM Product p, Users u WHERE p.prod_id = '" + getProd_id() + "' " +
                                    "AND p.user_id = u.user_id" );

    if (rs.next()) {
        theItem = new Item(rs.getString(1), rs.getString(2),
            rs.getString(3), rs.getString(4), rs.getString(5),
            rs.getString(6), rs.getFloat(7), rs.getFloat(8),
            rs.getTimestamp(9), rs.getTimestamp(10));

        String user_id = rs.getString(11);
        User u = new User(user_id, rs.getString(12),
            rs.getString(13), rs.getString(14), rs.getString(15),
    rs.getDate(16), rs.getTimestamp(17));

        userInfo.setString(1, user_id);
        ResultSet rs2 = userInfo.executeQuery();
        if (rs2.next()) {
            Address a = new Address(rs2.getString(1),
              rs2.getString(2), rs2.getString(3));

            u.setAddress(a);
        } else {
            // set an empty address to prevent nulls
            u.setAddress(new Address());
        }

        theItem.setUser(u);
    }
    conn.release();
}
```

EXCURSION

Enter Enterprise JavaBeans

The shaky part in our command beans has been in extracting data from the different data-base tables to create and populate the view helper beans hierarchy. The development of the command beans requires the joint efforts of a programmer as well as a database mod-eler. It also has its share of hard-coded information, such as the table and column names within the beans. If only the tables of the database existed as a class hierarchy instead!

This is where Enterprise JavaBeans (EJBs) come into the picture. Entity EJBs map to table(s) in the database. A row in a table typically maps to an instance of the entity. You can obtain a particular instance or a set of matching instances by invoking finder methods on the bean's home interface. When this is done, the EJB container extracts the informa-tion from the database and syncs the container-managed fields in the entity bean with those values. Obviously some mapping is required to specify the persistence of the fields of the entity beans in the database tables. This can be done using some mapping tools by an EJB deployer.

The client of the bean doesn't have to deal with databases and database tables directly. The EJB specification also addresses the entire lifecycle of the entity, from its creation to its deletion. In all these cases, you don't have to write any SQL QUERY, INSERT, UPDATE, or DELETE statements because they are prepared by the persistence layer.

The EJB specification covers transactions, security, and naming services that are beyond the scope of this book. You can read about this in an IBM redbook I co-wrote: "Enterprise JavaBeans Development Using VisualAge for Java."

Developing Controllers Using Servlets and JSPs

The controller performs the routing of requests to the view after extracting the requests, setting parameters on one or more command beans, and setting the result from the command beans as a request parameter accessible to the presentation layer.

There are two options for implementing the controllers to do the operations:

- Using servlets
- Using JSPs with scriptlets

Using Servlets for Implementing the Controller

Servlets, as the name implies, service requests. *Servlets* are Java classes that implement one of the interfaces defined in the `javax.servlet.*` or `javax.servlet.http.*` packages. These servlets are then deployed or loaded into a servlet container. The container invokes method callbacks on the servlet's methods during different stages of its lifecycle and when a client requests service.

The basic interface, `javax.servlet.Servlet`, defines a set of five methods that have to be implemented to provide a service and for the lifecycle methods, as shown in Listing 7.17.

Listing 7.17   The `javax.servlet.Servlet` Interface

```
public interface javax.servlet.Servlet extends java.lang.Object {
    public void destroy();
    public javax.servlet.ServletConfig getServletConfig();
    public String getServletInfo();
    public void init(javax.servlet.ServletConfig);
    public void service(javax.servlet.ServletRequest,
➥javax.servlet.ServletResponse);
}
```

The method of importance is `service()`, which accepts the request providing additional information using the `ServletRequest` parameter and producing an output in the `ServletResponse` instance passed as the second parameter.

You will need to extend from an abstract class, `javax.servlet.http.HttpServlet`, to provide Web servicing. It redefines the `service` method using `HttpServletRequest` and `HttpServletResponse` classes.

```
public void service(javax.servlet.http.HttpServletRequest,
➥javax.servlet.http.HttpServletResponse);
```

The `HttpServletRequest` instance contains all the parameters associated with the particular request:

- The name-value parameters appended to the URL string typically in the GET method
- The form values passed using the POST protocol
- Header information mandated by HTTP

You can use the `HttpServletResponse` instance for generating your content. To generate a Web page that displays the current date and time, you would implement the `service` method as shown in Listing 7.18.

Listing 7.18   The `GenerateDate` Servlet That Generates a Web Page Displaying the Current Date and Time

```
import java.io.PrintWriter;
import java.util.Date;
public class GenerateDateServlet extends javax.servlet.http.HttpServlet {
    public void service(HttpServletRequest request,
➥HttpServletResponse response) {
        Date today = new Date();
        response.setContentType("text/html");
        PrintWriter out = response.getWriter();
        out.println("<html><title>Current date and time</title><body>");
        out.println(today.toString());
        out.println("</body></html>");
    }
}
```

EXCURSION

The Truth About Servlets and JSPs

I am sure you are feeling a sense of *déjà vu* seeing the servlet code. It seems awfully similar to the way we generated code using JSPs, especially within scriptlets. Notice the similarity in some of the objects—`response`, `request`, and `out`.

Sale order paid by Switch: £25.94
Balance due: £0.00

This shipment completes your order.
You can always check the status of your orders from the "Your Account" link at the top of each page of our site.

Thank you for shopping at Amazon.co.uk!

USt-ID, GB 727 2558 21

1166/gwxb11098/-1-/1RL/1RMH/2319/std-uk-dom/1344386/0710-21:53/0711-17:54

L.P.S. 11/2000

Please note we only accept returns of items that have been opened if they are defective. Please see "To return an item" below for details of how to return defective items to us.

Delivery charges, gift wrapping and other services

If you are returning an item because of error on our part or because it is defective, we will be happy to refund the delivery charges incurred in sending the item to you and your costs in returning it to us. Otherwise you will be responsible for those charges and the costs of any other services provided to you in connection with your purchase, for example gift wrapping.

Problems, Questions, Suggestions?
If you have any questions regarding this order, please contact us via:

Non-UK Residents Phone: +44 20 8636 9451
UK Residents **ONLY** Phone: 0800 279 6620
Non-UK Residents Fax: +44 20 8636 9401
UK Residents **ONLY** Fax: 0800 279 6630
E-mail: orders@amazon.co.uk

Reason for Return:

_____

_____

_____

_____

Thanks for shopping at Amazon.co.uk!
http://www.amazon.co.uk

amazon.co.uk™

At Amazon.co.uk, we want you to be delighted every time you shop with us. Occasionally though, we know you may want to return items, so below is our returns policy.

For books:
Our "no quibbles" guarantee means that if for any reason you are unhappy with your purchase you can return it to us in its original condition, within 30 days, and we will issue a full refund for the price you paid for the item.

For all other items:
We accept the return of all other items only if they are unopened and in their original condition. If you return goods, as detailed, within 30 days, we will issue a full refund for the price you paid for the item.

To return an item:
To return an item, please fill out the back of this delivery slip giving the reason for the return, wrap the package securely and send the package to the address below. In the case of a defective product, please provide a full description of the fault in the space provided and return the defective item in its original box (if any), with all warranty cards, licenses, manuals and accessories. Then send the package to the address below.

Amazon.co.uk
Returns Department
Ridgmont
BEDFORD
MK43 0ZA
United Kingdom

For your protection we recommend that you use a recorded-delivery service.

This returns policy does not affect your statutory

Invoice for gwxb11098 10 July, 2001

amazon.co.uk

www.amazon.co.uk

c/o Marston Gate
Ridgmont
MK43 0XP BEDFORD
United Kingdom, UK

Paid by:
Derek Voyce
16 Guillemot Close
Blyth, Northumberland NE24 3SN
United Kingdom, GB

Delivered to:
Derek Voyce
16 Guillemot Close
Blyth, Northumberland NE24 3SN
United Kingdom, GB

Invoice/Receipt for

Your order of 10 July, 2001

Order ID 026–4521180–9167602

Invoice number gwxb11098
10 July, 2001

Qty	Item	Bin	Description	Our Price	VAT Rate	Total Price
1	Java Server Pages from Scratch (From Scratch) Sahu, Maneesh 0789724596	(P–2–D14C82)	Paperback	£23.19	0.00%	£23.19

Shipping Subtotal

Order Total

1

In case you haven't heard before, JSPs are basically precompiled servlets. They are translated into servlets by the JSP precompiler in your JSP engine. A JSP provides the same functionality as its servlet counterpart, but it does it more elegantly. The servlet shown in Listing 7.17, for example, can be more elegantly written using the simple JSP shown in Listing 7.19.

Listing 7.19   JSP That Would Compile into the GenerateDate Servlet

```
<%@ page import="java.util.Date"%>
<html><title>current date and time</title><body>
<%= (new Date()).toString()%></body></html>
```

The norm has been to use servlets to implement the controller logic, as it can be developed by simple Java programming. Within the service method, the servlet creates and executes command beans, obtains the results, and forwards the requests to the presentation-layer JSPs.

For our first example, we will develop a servlet, MainCategoriesController, that obtains the subcategories of a specified category and forwards the request to a view JSP, categoryview.jsp, for display.

Create a class, MainCategoriesController, that extends from HttpServlet in the <jakarta-tomcat>\webapps\AuctionStation\WEB-INF\station\auction\catalog\controller directory. Import the necessary packages for the command and view beans. Implement the service method to do the following:

1. Extract the cat_id request parameter encoded into the URL. If the parameter is not specified, use the root category, "0".

2. Create an instance of GetMainCategoriesCommand and set the category obtained from the request. Execute the command and obtain the result.

3. Set the result as an attribute in the HttpRequest instance.

4. Forward the request using the ServletContext instance associated with the servlet to the appropriate JSP, passing the request and response instances.

The source of the servlet is shown in Listing 7.20.

Listing 7.20   MainCategoriesController.java: Controlling the Display of the Main Categories

```
package station.auction.catalog.controller;

import javax.servlet.*;
import javax.servlet.http.*;
import station.auction.catalog.Category;
import station.auction.catalog.command.GetMainCategoriesCommand;
```

Listing 7.20 continued

```java
public class MainCategoriesController extends HttpServlet {
    public void service(HttpServletRequest request,
➥HttpServletResponse response) {
        try {
            // Extract 'cat_id' from the request
            String category = request.getParameter("cat_id");
            if (category == null) {
                // Display the root category
                category = "0";
            }

            // Execute the command to return the array of categories
            GetMainCategoriesCommand cmd = new GetMainCategoriesCommand();
            cmd.setCat_id(category);
            cmd.execute();
            Category[] result = (Category[]) cmd.getResult();

            // Set result as a REQUEST_SCOPE attribute
            request.setAttribute("categories", result);

            // Forward the request to the View JSP
            ServletContext context = getServletContext();
            String jspToCall = "/jsp/catalog/categoryview.jsp";
            context.getRequestDispatcher(jspToCall).forward(request,
➥response);
        } catch (Exception exc) {
            // Redirect to the error page
        }
    }
}
```

Compile the servlet. You need to set <jakarta-tomcat>\lib\servlet.jar in the CLASSPATH to successfully perform the compilation.

Now, you need to make the servlet engine aware of the servlet's existence. To do this, you need to make an entry in the web.xml file stored in the WEB-INF directory.

 Note You can copy another Web application's structure, for instance, to reuse or modify definitions, such as web.xml or the directory structure of WEB-INF.

Add an entry for the servlet. The entry maps a shorthand name—controller for the physical servlet—station.auction.catalog.controller.MainCategoriesController as shown in Listing 7.21.

Listing 7.21   Web.xml: Making an Entry for the `MainCategoriesController` Servlet

```
<?xml version="1.0" encoding="ISO-8859-1"?>

<!DOCTYPE web-app
    PUBLIC "-//Sun Microsystems, Inc.//DTD Web Application 2.2//EN"
    "http://java.sun.com/j2ee/dtds/web-app_2.2.dtd">

<web-app>
    <servlet>
        <servlet-name>
            category
        </servlet-name>
        <servlet-class>
            station.auction.catalog.controller.MainCategoriesController
        </servlet-class>
    </servlet>
    ...
</web-app>
```

Restart Tomcat to make the changes in the servlet configuration take effect.

Create the view JSP, categoryview.jsp, in the directory mapped to the virtual `/jsp/catalog` directory: `<jakarta-tomcat>\webapps\AuctionStation\jsp\catalog`.

In the JSP, extract the categories instance from the request. Iterate through the elements of the array to print the category names as shown in Listing 7.22.

Listing 7.22   Displaying the Category Names by Iterating Through the Category Array

```
<%@ page import="station.auction.catalog.Category" %>
<jsp:useBean id="categories" class="station.auction.catalog.Category[]"
➥scope="request"/>
<%
    for (int i = 0; i < categories.length; i++) {
        Category aCat = categories[i];
%>
        <font size="+1"><%= aCat.getName()%></font><br>
<%
    }
%>
```

Launch your browser and type the location of the `MainCategories` servlet. The location of a named servlet is

`<host-name>/<webapp-name>/servlet/<servlet-name>`

Therefore, the `MainCategoriesController` servlet's location is either

`http://localhost:8080/AuctionStation/servlet/category`

or

`http://localhost:8080/servlet/category`

The generated page displays the main categories of the site, as shown in Figure 7.5.

Figure 7.5

Main categories of the site displayed using the combination of the `MainCategories Controller` *servlet,* `GetMainCategories Command`, *and* categoryview.jsp

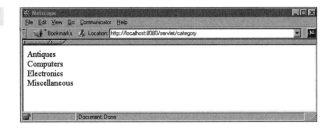

In this case, the servlet obtains the subcategories of the root category to `cat_id = "0"`. You can display the subcategories for a specific category by encoding the `cat_id` parameter in the URL as shown in Figure 7.6. In other words, you will need to append `cat_id=<cat_id>` after the URL just as in the `GET` parameter-passing mechanism.

Figure 7.6

Subcategories of the category with `cat_id "2"` *displayed by appending the* `cat_id` *name-value parameter as a query string*

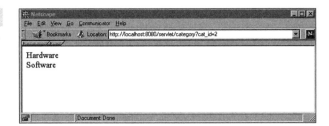

Using JSPs

Now that you know JSPs are essentially servlets, the use of JSPs might seem unnecessary. The problem with servlets is that making changes to your servlet code requires you to recompile your source file and restart the server to load the latest version of your servlet, unless your servlet engine provides servlet reloading.

JSPs allow you to make your change more easily and reflect these changes immediately without having to restart the server. JSP features, such as introspecting and setting properties on beans from the request parameters and the other tags, have also made life easier for the developer.

Migrating from servlets to JSPs is very simple. All you need to do is create a scriptlet that contains the `service` method's body. You would also need to add a page directive that specifies the packages and classes in addition to the servlet classes to be imported as shown in Listing 7.23.

Listing 7.23 Translating the `MainCategoriesController` Servlet into a JSP

```
<%@ page import="station.auction.catalog.*,
station.auction.catalog.command.*"%>
<%
// Extract 'cat_id' from the request
String category = request.getParameter("cat_id");
if (category == null) {
    // Display the root category
    category = "0";
}

// Execute the command to return the array of categories
GetMainCategoriesCommand cmd = new GetMainCategoriesCommand();
cmd.setCat_id(category);
cmd.execute();
Category[] result = (Category[]) cmd.getResult();

// Set result as a REQUEST_SCOPE attribute
request.setAttribute("categories", result);

// Forward the request to the View JSP
ServletContext context = getServletContext();
String jspToCall = "/jsp/catalog/categoryview.jsp";
context.getRequestDispatcher(jspToCall).forward(request, response);
%>
```

No special entries need to be made in the web.xml to identify the JSP.

Developing the Controller for the Catalog

The first controller that you will require for the item catalog module is the catalog controller, catalog.jsp. This JSP handles request for displaying categories and the item listing.

Figure 7.7 displays the flows between the different components.

Figure 7.8 shows the sequence diagram for displaying the categories.

Figure 7.7

Page flows between the different components of the item catalog module

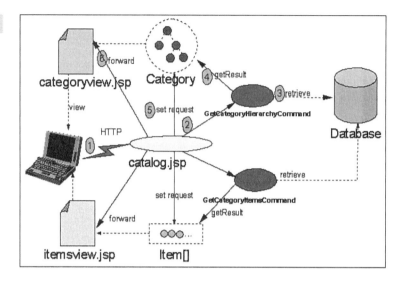

Figure 7.8

Sequence of events involving the catalog controller

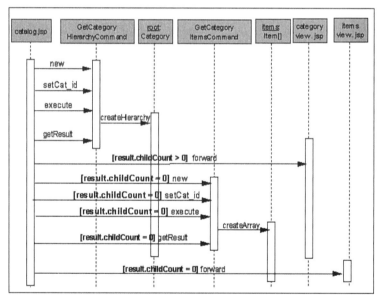

For the catalog.jsp, add the page directive to import the additional packages and classes.

```
<%@ page import="station.auction.catalog.*, station.auction.catalog.command.*"
errorPage="invalidCategory.jsp"%>
```

1. The sequence begins when the user sends a request to the server specifying the controller JSP. The request may or may not contain parameters that are appended to the URL as a query string.

2. The controller determines the category from the query string using the `cat_id` parameter. If this parameter is not specified, it uses the root category.

```
    String category = request.getParameter("cat_id");
    if (category == null) {
        category = "0";
    }
```

3. The controller executes the `GetCategoryHierarchyCommand` to obtain the sub-tree with the `Category` instance representing the specified `cat_id` as the root.

```
    GetCategoryHierarchyCommand cmd = new GetCategoryHierarchyCommand();
    cmd.setCat_id(category);
    cmd.setLevel(3);
    cmd.execute();
```

4. If the root category has no subcategories, you need to display the items instead. The controller then executes the `GetCategoryItemsCommand` to retrieve the items for the specified `cat_id`. The controller sets the result as a request parameter and forwards the request to itemsview.jsp to display the results.

```
    Category root = (Category) cmd.getResult();
    if (root.getChildCount() == 0) {
%>
        <jsp:useBean id="cmd2"
class="station.auction.catalog.command.GetCategoryItemsCommand">
            <jsp:setProperty name="cmd2" property="*"/>
        </jsp:useBean>
<%
        cmd2.execute();

        Item[] items = (Item[]) cmd2.getResult();
        pageContext.setAttribute("items", items,
PageContext.REQUEST_SCOPE);
%>
        <jsp:forward page="itemsview.jsp"/>
```

Notice that we have created an instance of the `GetCategoryItemsCommand` using the `jsp:useBean` tag, and set its properties by introspection using the `"*"` wildcard property. This will enable the request parameters to set as properties into the bean, as you will see while creating the Items View JSP.

5. The controller sets the category hierarchy as a request parameter and forwards the request to the categoryview.jsp for display.

```
<%
    }
    pageContext.setAttribute("root", root, PageContext.REQUEST_SCOPE);
%>
    <jsp:forward page="categoryview.jsp"/>
```

We haven't checked the validity of the `cat_id` passed in the request. If the `cat_id` is invalid, the command beans will throw an exception that will be handled by the `errorPage` specified in the page directive, invalidCategory.jsp. Alternatively, you can invoke the `check()` method on the command to check the preconditions before executing the command.

Developing a Controller for Viewing the Item Information

You can also develop a controller to view the details about a specific item. The controller extracts the `prod_id` of the product from the request and sets it as the `GetItemInformationCommand`'s input property. Finally, it sets the result—the `Item` instance for the product—as a request parameter and forwards it to the Product View JSP.

```
<%@ page import="station.auction.catalog.*, station.auction.catalog.command.*"
errorPage="invalidProduct.jsp"%>
<%
    String product = request.getParameter("prod_id");

    GetItemInformationCommand cmd = new GetItemInformationCommand();
    cmd.setProd_id(product);
    cmd.execute();

    Item anItem = (Item) cmd.getResult();
    pageContext.setAttribute("item", anItem, PageContext.REQUEST_SCOPE);
%>
<jsp:forward page="productview.jsp"/>
```

Developing JSPs for the Presentation Layer

You need to develop the JSPs named in the controller for displaying the information specified using the request parameters. You can obtain this information by using the `jsp:useBean` tag with the same ID or name as the one used to set the attribute in the controller.

Developing the Category View JSP

The first view, categoryview.jsp, displays the categories for the specified `cat_id`. The JSP implementing this view has the root `Category` instance at its disposal, thanks to the spoon-feeding by the controller. It can therefore generate the content using simple expressions and scriptlets on the view-helper instances.

Our strategy for the display will be to display the subcategories of the root along with the item count. Their subcategories will also be displayed. All the categories will be hyperlinked to display their information. This is done by appending the `cat_id` parameter to the URL for the controller, catalog.jsp. The source for categoryview.jsp is shown in Listing 7.24.

Listing 7.24   Categoryview.jsp: Displaying the Three-Level Category Hierarchy Using the Category **View-Helper Bean Instance Set by the Controller**

```
<%@ page import="station.auction.catalog.*" %>
<jsp:useBean id="root" class="station.auction.catalog.Category"
➥scope="request"/>
<table>
<%
    for (int i = 0; i < root.getChildCount(); i++) {
        Category aCat = root.getChildAt(i);
%>
<tr>
    <td>
    <font size="+1"><a href="/jsp/auction/catalog.jsp?cat_id=<%=
➥aCat.getCat_id()%>"><%= aCat.getName()%></a></font> <small>(<i><%=
➥aCat.getNumberProducts()%></i>)</small>
    <br><font size="-1">
<%
        for (int j = 0; j < aCat.getChildCount(); j++) {
            Category bCat = aCat.getChildAt(j);
%>
    <a href="/jsp/auction/catalog.jsp?cat_id=<%= bCat.getCat_id()%>">
➥<%= bCat.getName()%></a> 
<%
        }
%>
    </font><br></td>
</tr>
<%
    }
%>
</table>
```

The location identified by the controller, `http://localhost:8080/jsp/auction/catalog.jsp`, will generate an output as shown in Figure 7.9.

Figure 7.9

Main categories of the site displayed using the combination of catalog.jsp, GetCategoryHierarchy Command, *and categoryview.jsp*

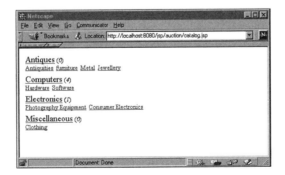

7

You can browse the subcategories by traversing the links. The controller forwards the requests to categoryview.jsp when the category has one or more subcategories. If it has none, it forwards the request to itemsview.jsp, described in the next section.

Developing the Items View JSP

The Items View JSP displays the following information:

- Items in the category that are still open for bidding.
- Basic item information, such as the name, price, and time left for the bid to close. This information is displayed in tabular columns.
- The items shown in the view can be sorted for any of the columns. This can be done by following a link on the table column names.

To accomplish this, you can make use of the Item view helper and the GetCategoryItemsCommand bean we developed earlier. Item provides most of the information needed to populate the tables. It provides the bid end timestamp, but you need to provide the user with more useful information, such as the time left. You can translate the bid_end property into a time-left string by adding another method to Item—getTimeLeftString—that calculates the difference between the current timestamp and the bid end and returns the required information, as shown in Listing 7.25.

Listing 7.25   Item.java: Returning the Time Left Information Calculated Using the Current Time and the Bid End Time

```java
public String getTimeLeftString() {
    long currentTime = new java.util.Date().getTime();
    long endTime = getBid_end().getTime();

    // find time left in minutes
    long diff = (endTime - currentTime)/(1000*60);
    if (diff < 0)
        return "Bid Closed";

    if (diff < 60) {
        return(diff + " minutes");
    } else {
        diff = diff/60;
        if (diff < 24) {
            return(diff + " hours");
        } else {
            diff = diff/24;
            return(diff + " days");
        }
    }
}
```

You can iterate through the element of the Item array and display the information in a table. To enable sorting of the table's contents by following the link in the table column header, you need to perform *URL rewriting*. You can encode the `orderByField` information by appending the value to the URL. For example, you can hyperlink the column for the minimum amount as follows:

```
<a href="catalog.jsp?orderByField=min_amt">Amount</a>
```

URL rewriting is the mechanism of encoding information into the URL. It encodes the information by setting name-value parameters, just as data is encoded in the GET method.

The side effect of this technique is that it disposes the other parameters that may be associated with the request, such as `ascending`, `pageSize`, and `pageNumber`. To retain the information you need to alter the query string associated with the particular request, you could append the name-value parameter to this query string :

```
<a href="catalog.jsp?<%= request.getQueryString()%>&&orderByField=min_amt">
➥Amount</a>
```

Note The parameter names that can be used in the request are the ones that have the same property names as the `GetCategoryItemsCommand`. Other names will be ignored because the `jsp:setParameter` tags used on the bean in the controller will not be able to match the parameter with the property.

The problem with this approach is the possibility of introducing duplicate requests into the query string. If the query string had the information that the `orderByField` was `prod_name`, appending the `orderByField` would make the new query string look like this:

```
orderByField=prod_name&&orderByField=min_amt
```

It would be difficult to determine the `orderByField` from such a request. The length of the URL has also increased unnecessarily. Our approach is to rewrite the URL by replacing existing parameters with the new values. You can do this by defining a `getNewQueryString()` method in your JSP that returns the modified query string using the original query string and the name-value to be inserted or modified.

```
<%! public final static String WHITE = "white";
    public final static String GRAY = "#EEEEEE";

    protected String getNewQueryString(String uri, String name, String value) {
        // check if the parameter already exists
        int i = uri.indexOf(name);
```

7

```
        if ( i == -1) {
            // No match was found append the name-value pair
            return uri + "&&" + name + "=" + value;
        }

        // Extract the string before the name and store it in a StringBuffer
        StringBuffer sb = new StringBuffer(uri.substring(0, i));
        sb.append(name).append("=").append(value);

        /* skip the parameter value and append the name-value parameters
           appearing after the parameter in the query string */
        String lastPart = uri.substring(i);
        int j = lastPart.indexOf("&&");
        if (j != -1) {
            sb.append(lastPart.substring(j));
        }

        return sb.toString();
    }
%>
```

You can now define String variables for storing the links representing requests for the sorted columns.

```
<%
    String  queryString = request.getQueryString();
    String _prod_name_order = getNewQueryString(queryString, "orderByField",
➥"prod_name");
    String _min_amt_order = getNewQueryString(queryString, "orderByField",
➥ "min_amt");
    String _bid_end_order = getNewQueryString(queryString, "orderByField",
➥ "bid_end");
%>
<table width="100%">
    <tr bgcolor="silver">
        <th><small><a href="catalog.jsp?<%= _prod_name_order%>">Product Name
➥</a></small></th>
        <th><small><a href="catalog.jsp?<%= _min_amt_order%>">Amount</a>
➥</small></th>
        <th><small><a href="catalog.jsp?<%= _bid_end_order%>">Bid Closes</a>
➥</small></th>
    </tr>
```

You can then add rows to the table for each item in the array returned by GetCategoryItemsCommand and set as a request parameter by the controller. You can display alternate rows with different colors to enhance readability. The columns of the row correspond to information obtained from a property of the Item instance.

```
<jsp:useBean id="array" class="station.auction.catalog.ItemsArray"
        scope="request"/>
<%
    boolean colored = false;
```

```
    Item[] items = array.getItems();
    for (int i = 0; i < items.length; i++) {
        Item anItem = items[i];
%>
    <tr bgcolor="<%= ((colored)?WHITE:GRAY)%>">
        <td> <a href="product.jsp?prod_id=<%= anItem.getProd_id()%>">
<%= anItem.getProdName()%></a></td>
        <td> <%= anItem.getMin_amt()%> </td>
        <td> <%= anItem.getTimeLeftString()%> </td>
    </tr>
<%
        // switch to other color
        colored = !(colored);
    }
%>
    <tr bgcolor="silver">
        <td><small> </small></td>
        <td><small> </small></td>
        <td><small> </small></td>
    </tr>
</table>
```

You can hyperlink the product name to display the details of the product when a user clicks it. The URL for the link refers to the product controller, product.jsp, and appending the prod_id parameter.

The view for the items of category '2.1' is shown in Figure 7.10.

Figure 7.10

Items view for the hard-ware subcategory

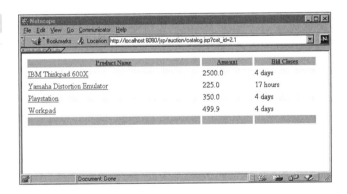

You can sort the items according to the bid end time by following the "Bid Closes" link as shown in Figure 7.11.

Figure 7.11

Items sorted according to the bid end field

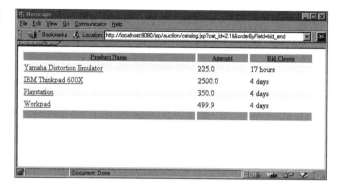

Providing Multipage Item Listing

The Items View JSP developed earlier displays only one page of items. You can set the page size by rewriting the URL with the request parameter. You can accommodate any number of items by setting an obscenely large `pageSize`. The problem with this approach is that the table will not be rendered until all the rows are obtained, which could frustrate a user.

To prevent this, you can provide a multipage listing for the items in the category whereby you display only a subset of all the results and items. You will also need to provide the user with controls to navigate through the entire set.

You can easily implement such a control using the information in the `ItemsArray` instance: the `count`, `pageSize`, and `pageNumber` properties.

You can provide links to each page of the result set. A page is the total count divided by the page size. You can do this by rewriting the URL with the `pageNumber` parameter, as shown in the scriptlet in Listing 7.26.

Listing 7.26   itemsview.jsp: Creating Links for the Item Information

```
<small>
<%
    int count = array.getCount();
    int pageNumber = array.getPageNumber();
    int pageSize = array.getPageSize();
    if (count > pageSize) {
        for (int i = 0, num = 0; i < count; i+= pageSize, num++) {
%>
        <a href="catalog.jsp?<%=
        getNewQueryString(queryString, "pageNumber", num + "")
                %>"><%= (num + 1) %></a> 
<%
        }
    }
%>
</small>
```

You can manually set the pageSize parameter in the URL to view the multipage listing, as shown in Figure 7.12.

Figure 7.12

Multipage listing for the items in the category when the pageSize is set to 2

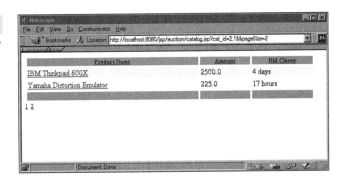

Displaying the Item Details

The item can also view the item details, such as the product description, the user, and the bid information. You can create another controller for the view, product.jsp.

In this JSP you need to extract the prod_id parameter from the request and set it on the GetItemInformationCommand object. Finally, you need to set the resultant Item instance as a request parameter and forward the request to the view JSP, as shown in Listing 7.27.

7

Listing 7.27   product.jsp: Developing the Controller for Displaying the Details of a Particular Item

```
<%@ page import="station.auction.catalog.*, station.auction.catalog.command.*"
errorPage="invalidProduct.jsp"%>
<%
    String product = request.getParameter("prod_id");

    GetItemInformationCommand cmd = new GetItemInformationCommand();
    cmd.setProd_id(product);
    cmd.execute();

    Item anItem = (Item) cmd.getResult();
    pageContext.setAttribute("item", anItem, PageContext.REQUEST_SCOPE);
%>
<jsp:forward page="productview.jsp"/>
```

The view is composed using the properties of the Item instance obtained from the request and its associated User, Address, and Bid instances.

```
<%@ page import="station.auction.catalog.*, java.sql.Timestamp" %>
<jsp:useBean id="item" class="station.auction.catalog.Item" scope="request"/>
<%
```

```
    User user = item.getUser();
    Address addr = user.getAddress();
    Bid hiBid = item.getHighestBid();
%>
```

You can embed the different properties of these beans in a table using JSP expressions, as shown in Listing 7.28.

```
...
<font size="+2"><%= item.getProdName()%></font><br>
<%= item.getDescription()%>
<%
    String imgUrl = item.getImage_url();
    if (!(imgUrl == null || imgUrl.trim().length() == 0)) {
        out.println("<center><img src=\"" + imgUrl + "\"></center>");
    }
%>
<table>
<tr>
<td width="80%">
<table width="100%">

<tr bgcolor="silver">
    <td colspan="2"><b>Item Information</b></td>
</tr>

<tr>
    <td>Minimum Amount</td>
    <td><%= item.getMin_amt()%></td>
</tr>

<tr>
    <td>Bid Increment</td>
    <td><%= item.getMin_bid_inc()%></td>
</tr>

<tr>
    <td>Bid Started</td>
    <td><%= item.getCreated().toGMTString()%></td>
</tr>

<tr>
    <td>Time Left</td>
    <td><%= item.getTimeLeftString()%></td>
</tr>

<tr bgcolor="silver">
    <td colspan="2"><b>User Information</b></td>
</tr>
```

```
<tr>
    <td>User</td>
    <td><%= user.getUser_id()%></td>
</tr>
<tr>
    <td>Location</td>
    <td><%= addr.getCity() + ", " + addr.getState() + " " +
        addr.getCountry()%></td>
</tr>


<tr bgcolor="silver">
    <td colspan="2"><b>Bid Information</b></td>
</tr>

<tr>
    <td># of Bids</td>
    <td><%= item.getBidCount()%></td>
</tr>

<tr>
    <td>Current Amount</td>
    <td><%= hiBid.getAmount()%></td>
</tr>

<tr>
    <td>Highest Bidder</td>
    <td><%= hiBid.getUser_id()%></td>
</tr>
</table>
```

7

You can also add a bid form that a user can use to place bids for the item after specifying the amount. The default amount shown in the amount field is computed using the current maximum bid amount and the bid increment, as shown in Listing 7.29.

Listing 7.29   productview.jsp: The Bid Form to Allow a User to Bid on the Item

```
<form action="/jsp/auction/bid.jsp" method="POST">
<table border="2" color="black">
<tr bgcolor="silver"><td><b>Enter Your Bid</b></td></tr>
<tr><td>
$ <input type="text" name="amount" value="<%= (hiBid.getAmount() +
item.getMin_bid_inc())%>">
<input type="hidden" name="prod_id" value="<%= item.getProd_id()%>">
</td></tr>
<tr><td align="center"><input type="submit" value="Place Bid"></td></tr>
</table>
</form>
```

The item information for the Yamaha Distortion Emulator is shown in Figure 7.13.

Figure 7.13

Item details displayed using the Product View JSP

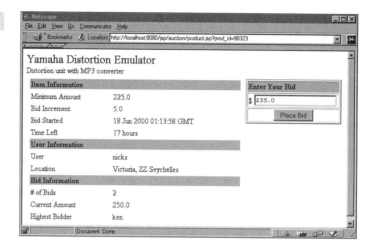

If the item specified an image URL, the page would include the image, as shown in Figure 7.14.

Figure 7.14

Item details, including the image displayed using the Product View JSP

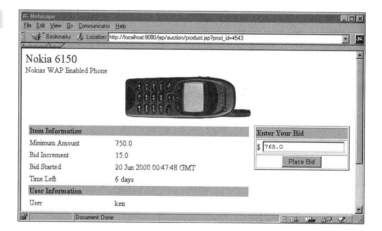

Summary

In this chapter, you have seen how to separate functionality using the command bean pattern. This design helps you reuse elements so that you can use a model in more than one view and a view as the output for more than one controller.

In this chapter, our command beans executed only JDBC commands. You can wrap any of your business logic within these beans—for instance, performing operations such as sending email and accessing non-database resources as well as Enterprise JavaBeans. To improve efficiency, you can also perform pooling on command beans like you did for database connections.

Most of the operations in this chapter were read-only operations required for browsing the catalog and hence could be executed by any user. Operations such as making bids and selling items, however, require inserts into the database. You would need to authenticate registered users and authorize them in different parts of the site to protect your resources. The next chapter looks at some authorization techniques to provide security.

7

Chapter 8

Developing Protected Portions of AuctionStation

So far, you have developed the auction items catalog module, which can be viewed by any user, even an unregistered one. The users can browse items and categories without having to log on to the system, but when they want to bid or sell items on AuctionStation, they have to authenticate themselves.

Authentication helps prevent misuse in situations when a user makes spurious bids, posts illegal item listings, or takes other actions that infringe your site usage policies. After authentication, all "protected" actions—such as bid or sell operations—will be attributed to the user performing them. You can penalize malevolent users by disabling their accounts or taking even stricter action.

What You Are Going To Do

In this chapter, you will look at some of the authentication techniques for protecting resources. You will develop the bid and sell portions of AuctionStation that can be accessed after a registered user authenticates him or herself.

You will also develop an administrative module where a user requires authorization to add categories to the catalog. Only a special type of user, the administrator, will be able to perform such tasks.

Using Tomcat's HTTP Authentication

The simplest way to protect Web resources is by making use of Tomcat's built-in authentication feature. A server administrator specifies the resources to be protected as well as the group or groups of users that can access them.

When a user tries to access a protected resource, the server challenges the user by opening a user-ID/password dialog. The user must then furnish this information and send it back to the server. The values supplied by the user are matched against those stored in a user data store. If they match, the user is allowed to access the resource; otherwise, the user is challenged with the dialog again.

Specifying User Information in Tomcat

Tomcat stores and uses user information against which the user's data is validated in the tomcat-users.xml file in the <jakarta-tomcat>\conf directory. Listing 8.1 shows an entry for user msahu, with a password ou812, having two roles: admin and tomcat.

Listing 8.1 Tomcat-users.xml: Specifying the User, Password, and Roles

```
<tomcat-users>
    <user name="tomcat" password="tomcat" roles="tomcat" />
    <user name="msahu" password="ou812" roles="admin, tomcat"/>
</tomcat-users>
```

A drawback is rather evident: storing the password on the file system without any encryption. This is not really recommended in light of the recent spurt in hacking activities. Other application servers have a more robust and sophisticated data store for authenticating the user's credentials. IBM's WebSphere Application Server, for example, uses and stores user information in a Lotus Notes Address Book (NAB) and a Lightweight Directory Access Protocol (LDAP) data store, which support encryption and access control.

Marking Protected Resources

Next, you need to specify the resources to be marked protected. You can do this in the web.xml file of the specific webapp. For AuctionStation, we will mark the files and directories within <jakarta-tomcat>/webapps/AuctionStation/jsp/confiden-tial/ as protected. You can do this by adding a security-constraint tag to the web.xml file stored in the <jakarta-tomcat>/webapps/AuctionStation/WEB-INF directory. Within the security-constraint tag, add a web-resource-collection tag specifying the Web resources to be protected: /jsp/confidential/* as well as the HTTP methods. Add an auth-constraint tag specifying the roles that can use the resource, as shown in Listing 8.2. In this case, specify the role name: "admin". All users specified in the tomcat-users.xml file with this role can access the mentioned resources. Add a login-config tag that specifies the type of authentication. Currently, Tomcat supports only Basic authentication. In *Basic authentication*, the user ID and password supplied by the user are base64-encoded and sent in the header.

This encoding is not foolproof because anyone tapping the wire can apply the base64 decoding algorithm to extract the user's values. However, it is certainly more secure than sending the data across without any encoding at all. Other more secure authentication methods exist but are not supported either by most of the browsers or by Tomcat.

Listing 8.2   web.xml: Protecting Resources by Adding Security Constraints and `login-config` Tags

```xml
<security-constraint>
    <web-resource-collection>
        <web-resource-name>Administrative Area</web-resource-name>
        <!-- Define the context-relative URL(s) to be protected -->
        <url-pattern>/jsp/confidential/*</url-pattern>

        <!-- If you list http methods, only those methods are protected -->
        <http-method>GET</http-method>
        <http-method>POST</http-method>
    </web-resource-collection>
    <auth-constraint>
        <!-- Anyone with the listed role- admin may access this area -->
        <role-name>admin</role-name>
    </auth-constraint>
</security-constraint>

<login-config>
    <auth-method>BASIC</auth-method>
    <realm-name>Administrators Area</realm-name>
</login-config>
```

Restart the server to make the security changes take effect.

HTTP Authentication in Action

For this application, you will create a protected area, `/jsp/confidential`, which is also specified as protected in web.xml. In this directory you will create a Web resource, important.html, an HTML document with possibly important information.

When the user tries to access the file using the browser, the server challenges the user, as shown in Figure 8.1.

If the credentials didn't match any of the admin users' credentials, the challenge dialog is redisplayed, as shown in Figure 8.2.

If the user provides information that matches one with the "admin" role in tomcat-users.xml, the specified resource is displayed, as shown in Figure 8.3.

8

Figure 8.1

The challenge user-ID/password dialog opened by the server to authenticate the user

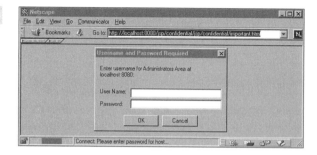

Figure 8.2

User prompted for a retry after an unsuccessful authorization

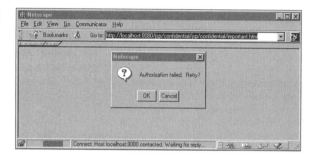

Figure 8.3

The important, confidential, and protected resource displayed in the browser after a successful authentication

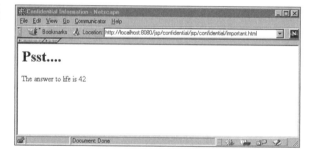

Problems with Server HTTP Authentication

You have seen one of the problems with Tomcat's HTTP Authentication dealing with the storage of user information directly on the file system. The second is the requirement of a manual insertion or deletion by a server administrator to manage the privileged users.

Another problem that is generic for most servers is in leveraging existing (maybe legacy) user registries. There is little chance that the Web server can access the information stored in such registries for authenticating the user. For AuctionStation, the user IDs and passwords are stored in the User table of the DB2 database, AUCTION. Tomcat is incapable of extracting information within databases for authentication. The solution for this problem is to develop a custom authentication module using either form-based or custom authorization.

Performing Custom Form-Based Authorization

One way to perform custom authorization is by displaying a form when the user attempts to access a "protected" resource. You cannot protect a resource by simple system administration, as you saw in the server HTTP authentication. You will need to embed code to perform the authorization. Thus, only JSPs and servlets can be marked as protected resources because they are the only resources within which custom code can be added. Static resources, such as HTML pages and images, are therefore outside the scope of custom authorization.

Adding Bids for Items

For the first form-based custom authorization, you will develop the module that allows a user to place bids for an item. The different JSPs in the module as well as the data flows between them are shown in Figure 8.4.

Figure 8.4

Data flows between the JSPs of the Add Bid module

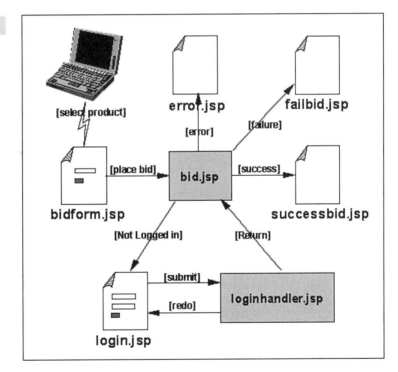

The bid use case begins when the user browses the item catalog and selects a particular item. The user then supplies a bid amount in the bid form displayed with the item, as shown in Figure 8.5 for the item named "Yamaha Distortion Emulator."

Figure 8.5

The Bid form displayed with a default bid amount displayed for the item

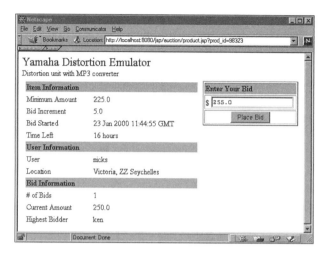

If the user has not logged on previously in the current session, the login page is displayed, prompting the user to provide the login information, as shown in Figure 8.6.

Figure 8.6

Displaying the login page to authorize the user

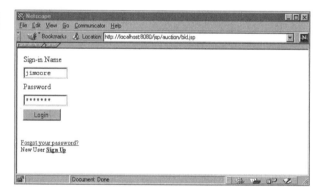

If the information provided by the user matches that of a user in the database, the add bid command is executed. If the user had logged on previously in the same session, the logon process is skipped and the command is executed directly. If the command executed successfully, the request is forwarded to the successbid page. On a failure, the request is forwarded to the failbid page, and on an error, to the error page specified in the page directive.

Performing Custom Authorization Using Information Stored in the Database

The custom authorization mechanism can be illustrated by a sequence diagram. Figure 8.7 shows the sequence of operations involved in authorizing a user. The user submits information, namely the prod_id and amount, to the controller, bid.jsp.

Figure 8.7

Sequence diagram for authorizing a user

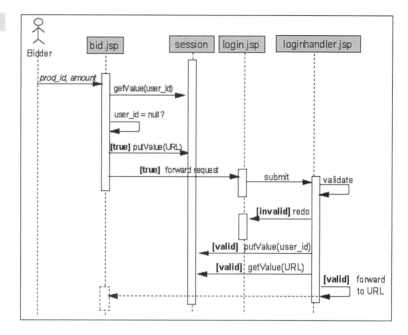

The sequence is initiated when the user submits information to a protected JSP. In this case, the user submits the bid information, specifying the product and the bid amount to bid.jsp. The bid form is stored in the product view JSP, which we created in the previous chapter, as shown in Listing 8.3.

Listing 8.3   productview.jsp: The Bid Form Displayed Along with the Product Information to Capture the User's Bid Data

```
...
<form action="/jsp/auction/bid.jsp" method="POST">
<table border="2" color="black">
    <tr bgcolor="silver"><td><b>Enter Your Bid</b></td></tr>
    <tr>
        <td> $ <input type="text" name="amount" value="<%= (hiBid.getAmount() +
item.getMin_bid_inc())%>"></td></tr>
    <tr>
        <td align="center"><input type="submit" value="Place Bid"></td></tr>
</table>
<input type="hidden" name="prod_id" value="<%= item.getProd_id()%>">
</form>
```

The controller checks whether a user_id attribute exists in the session implicit object.

8

EXCURSION

JSP Instance Variable Scopes

You have seen two scopes for JSP instance variables:

- **page**—The lifetime of the object is dependent on the JSP it is executing in.
- **request**—The object's lifetime is during the current request only. It can be accessed even in forwarded and included JSPs.

The session scope indicates that the lifetime of the object traverses more than one request until one of the following happens:

- The user closes the browser.
- The session times out. You can specify the timeout interval using the setMaxInactiveInterval method on the session.
- The session is invalidated programmatically using the invalidate() method.
- The specified attribute is removed from the session using the removeAttribute method.

Bid.jsp determines whether the user has logged in by checking for the existence of the user_id attribute in the session instance. If the attribute doesn't exist, identified by a null attribute value for user_id, bid.jsp forwards the request to the login page login.jsp. This custom authorization is a generic operation, not limited to bid.jsp alone. You can therefore create another JSP to store the scriptlet that does this check and forward operation, as shown in Listing 8.4.

Listing 8.4   checklogin.jsp: Checking Whether the User Logged In Already

```
<%
    String user_id = (String) session.getValue("user_id");
    if (user_id == null) {
        // Forward the request to the login page
%>
    <jsp:include page="/jsp/login/login.jsp" flush="true"/>
<%
    return;
    }
%>
```

The checklogin JSP can be included at the beginning of any controller JSP, such as bid.jsp, that requires custom authorization.

```
<%@ include file="/jsp/auction/checklogin.jsp"%>
```

Note
The page include directive instructs the JSP precompiler to include the source of the file into the main JSP before translating it into a Java servlet. You must exercise caution while naming your variables to ensure that they don't clash with any in the main JSP. You can also leave control blocks unterminated in the included JSP. Be sure to close them in the main JSP.

Next, you need to develop login.jsp, which contains a form that accepts the user's user ID and password for authentication. It is developed along the same lines of the login.html that you created in the User Registration module. The extra requirement is the need to store the original request as a URL with all the parameters encoded in the session. After the user successfully logs in, the user is displayed the same page specified by the URL.

We will create another JSP, StoreOriginalURL.jsp, that encodes all the request parameters along with the original request URI and stores this as an attribute, originalURL, in the session instance. This is done by declaring a method, storeOriginalURL, that accepts the original page's request and response implicit objects and constructs its equivalent URL by appending the request parameters to the request URI, as shown in Listing 8.5.

Listing 8.5   StoreOriginalURL.jsp: Storing the Original Request URL Along with the Request Parameters in the Session Instance

```
<%! public void storeOriginalURL(
        javax.servlet.http.HttpServletRequest request,
        javax.servlet.http.HttpSession session) {

    // Encode the request parameters in a query string
    StringBuffer sb = new StringBuffer(request.getRequestURI());
    java.util.Enumeration enum = request.getParameterNames();
    if (enum.hasMoreElements())
        sb.append("?");
    while (enum.hasMoreElements()) {
        String param = (String) enum.nextElement();
        sb.append(param + "=" + request.getParameter(param) + "&");
    }

    // Set the request string as a session variable
    session.putValue("originalURL", sb.toString());
    }
%>
```

8

StoreOriginalURL. jsp needs to be included within login.jsp using the page include directive. You also have to invoke the storeOriginalURL method declared in the JSP to construct and store the originalRequest attribute. You must also understand that the request might have been forwarded from the LoginHandler, which couldn't authenticate the user. In that case, the originalURL has already been set and you don't need to construct and store the attribute again. The source for login.jsp is shown in Listing 8.6.

Listing 8.6   login.jsp: Storing the Original Request URL and Displaying the Login Form

```
<%@ page import="java.util.Enumeration"%>
<%@ include file="/jsp/login/StoreOriginalURL.jsp"%>
<%
    String originalURL = (String) session.getAttribute("originalURL");
    if (originalURL == null || originalURL.trim().length() == 0) {
        storeOriginalURL(request, session);
    } else {
        // You were required to login in again
        out.println("<font color=\"red\" size=\"+1\">Relogin</font>");
    }
%>
<form method="POST" action="/jsp/login/LoginHandler.jsp">
<table>
<tr>
    <td>Sign-in Name
    </td>
</tr>
<tr>
    <td><input name="userId" type="text" size="10">
    </td>
</tr>

<tr>
    <td>Password
    </td>
</tr>
<tr>
    <td><input name="password" type="password" size="10">
    </td>
</tr>
</table>
  <input type="submit" value="   Login   ">
</form><br>
<small><a href="/jsp/login/Forgot.jsp">Forgot your password?</a><br>
New User <a href="/jsp/registration/Step1.jsp"><b>Sign Up</b></a>
</small>
```

Note
Notice that all the URLs specified in login.jsp, such as
/jsp/registration/Step1.jsp, are relative to the root instead of being relative
to the current page. When a page is included or forwarded from another JSP, the
base URL of the relative links is the URL of the page that received the request
initially.

The user furnishes the user ID and password in the form and submits the information. The form handler for the login page, LoginHandler.jsp, checks whether the
values match those stored in the Users table using custom db tags we created earlier.
If a row matching the SELECT statement using the user ID and password exists, the
user has been authenticated and authorized successfully and the request must be forwarded to the original page that required authorization. You need to forward the
request to the original URL obtained from the session instance. You can also store
the user ID as a session attribute, user_id, to enable the user to access other such
protected sections without having to log on again, as shown in Listing 8.7.

**Listing 8.7   LoginHandler.jsp: Authenticating the User Using the Specified User ID and
Password Parameters and Forwarding the Request to the Original URL Obtained from the
Session Attribute, originalURL**

```
<%@ taglib uri="../db-taglib.tld" prefix="db" %>
<db:connection id="conn" url="jdbc:db2:auction"
➥driver="COM.ibm.db2.jdbc.app.DB2Driver">
</db:connection>

<db:query id="getUser" connection="conn">
SELECT *  FROM Users WHERE user_id = '<%= request.getParameter("userId")%>'
          AND password = '<%= request.getParameter("password")%>'
</db:query>

<%
    if (getUser.next()) {
        // set the user id as a session parameter
        session.putValue("user_id", request.getParameter("userId"));

        // forward to the original page where authentication was required
        String originalURL = (String) session.getValue("originalURL");
        // Clean up the attribute
        session.removeAttribute("originalURL");
%>
        <jsp:forward page="<%= originalURL%>"/>
<%
    }
%>
<%-- Need to relogin --%>
<jsp:forward page="/jsp/login/login.jsp"/>
```

8

Executing the Add Bid Command

After the user has been authenticated and authorized, he or she can add a bid for the product. The sequence diagram for this operation (not including the authorization portions) is shown in Figure 8.8.

Figure 8.8

Sequence diagram for detailing the add bid use case

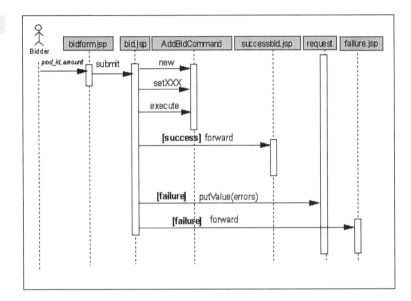

You need to create a command bean, AddBidCommand, that adds the bid by inserting a row in the Bid table. The bean has the properties defined in Table 8.1.

Table 8.1 **The Properties of** station.auction.catalog.command.AddBidCommand **bean**

Property	Type	Description
prod_id	String	The product ID of the item being bid
amount	float	The amount being bid on the item
user_id	String	The user ID of the user bidding on the item
result	Boolean	An output property of type Boolean (Boolean.TRUE or Boolean.FALSE) indicating whether the execute() method completed successfully.
errors	java.util.Hashtable	Output property storing the errors in the input parameters

You need to implement the check() method to determine whether the parameters provided are valid. This includes adding checks to determine whether the parameters are null or whether they are appropriate:

- Does an item with the `prod_id` exist in the Product table?
- Has bidding been closed on the product?
- Is the amount specified for bidding on the item greater than any available bid?
- Is the amount specified for bidding on the item compliant with the minimum bid increment?

You might obtain more than one error in the parameters supplied. You can accumulate these errors in the `errors` `Hashtable` instance and provide the same to the user while informing him or her of the problems encountered while adding the bid.

Implement the `execute()` method of the `Command` interface to add a bid by inserting a row in the Bid table. The SQL `INSERT` statement executed by the command bean checks whether the product has been closed to bidding by performing a `SELECT` query to return the item's `prod_id` whose `bid_end` column is greater than the current timestamp. It also sets the user's `amount` and `user_id`, as shown in Listing 8.8.

 Note   SQL data definition and modification statements can be executed in JDBC using the `executeUpdate` method defined on `java.sql.Statement` and `java.sql.PreparedStatement`. The return type of this method is `int`, specifying the number of rows affected by the operation. If the return value is 0, that indicates that the operation did not complete successfully or that the operation was a data definition command, such as creating or altering a table.

Listing 8.8   AddBidCommand.java: Implementing the `execute()` Method to Insert a Row in the Bid Table

```
public void execute() throws Exception {
    if (!check()) {
        ok = Boolean.FALSE;
        return;
    }

    String driver = "COM.ibm.db2.jdbc.app.DB2Driver";
    // Obtain a connection to the database
    DBConnectionManager dbcm = DBConnectionManager.getSingleton();
    DBConnection conn = dbcm.getConnection("jdbc:db2:auction",
➥driver, null, null);

    Statement insertBidStmt = conn.createStatement();
    int rows = insertBidStmt.executeUpdate(
        " INSERT INTO bid (prod_id, user_id, amount, created)" +
        " VALUES ( (SELECT prod_id from Product " +
        "               WHERE prod_id = '" + getProd_id() + "' " +
        "               AND BID_END > CURRENT TIMESTAMP)," +
        " '" + getUser_id() + "', " + getAmount() + ", CURRENT TIMESTAMP) ");
```

8

Listing 8.8 continued

```
    if (rows == 1) {
        ok = Boolean.TRUE;
    }

    // Release the connection
    conn.release();
}
```

Add bean tags in the controller, bid.jsp, that create an instance of the AddBidCommand and set the input properties on it. If the result of the execute operation is Boolean.TRUE, that indicates that the command executed successfully. The request must then be transferred to the successbid.jsp or failbid.jsp to display the status of the operation, as shown in Listing 8.9.

Listing 8.9 bid.jsp: Forwarding the Request to either successbid.jsp or failbid.jsp Based on the Result of the AddBidCommand

```
<%@ page import="station.auction.catalog.*, station.auction.catalog.command.*"
➥ errorPage="error.jsp"%>
<%@ include file="/jsp/auction/checklogin.jsp"%>

<jsp:useBean id="cmd" class="station.auction.catalog.command.AddBidCommand">
    <jsp:setProperty name="cmd" property="*"/>
    <jsp:setProperty name="cmd" property="user_id" value="<%= user_id%>"/>
</jsp:useBean>
<%
    cmd.execute();
    Boolean success = (Boolean) cmd.getResult();
    if (success == Boolean.TRUE) {
%>
    <jsp:forward page="successbid.jsp"/>
<%
    }
    pageContext.setAttribute("errors", cmd.getErrors(),
➥PageContext.REQUEST_SCOPE);
%>
<jsp:forward page="failbid.jsp"/>
```

Displaying the Status of the Bid

You need to create view JSPs to display the status of the bid operation:

- successbid.jsp on a successful operation
- failbid.jsp on a failure

In successbid.jsp, you can provide expression to display the values provided by the user. You can also provide a link to view the product by appending the prod_id parameter to the URL containing product.jsp, as shown in Listing 8.10.

Listing 8.10   successbid.jsp: Displaying the Bid Details Using the Request Parameters

```
Your bid has been recorded.
<p>
<table>

<tr>
<td><b>Item #: </b></td>
<td><a href="/jsp/auction/product.jsp?prod_id=<%=
➥request.getParameter("prod_id")%>">
<%= request.getParameter("prod_id")%></a></td>
</tr>

<tr>
<td><b>Your Bid: </b></td>
<td><%= request.getParameter("amount")%></td>
</tr>

</table>
```

Figure 8.9 displays the output of successbid.jsp when the bid for the product has been successfully recorded.

Figure 8.9

Page displayed on a successful bid

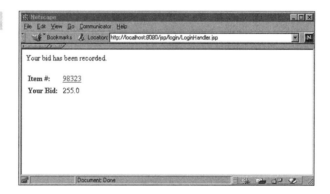

If the user bids on the item again at the same amount, the AddBidCommand instance returns a result, Boolean.FALSE indicating a failure. Bid.jsp sets the errors Hashtable instance returned by the command as a request parameter and forwards the request to failbid.jsp to display the problems. The source for failbid.jsp is shown in Listing 8.11. You can also provide a link to the previous page in the browser history using the javascript:history.go(-1) function. The parameter for the go function is the number of pages to go back or forward.

Listing 8.11   failbid.jsp: Displaying the Errors on a Failed Bid

```
<%@ page import="java.util.Enumeration"%>
<jsp:useBean id="errors" class="java.util.Hashtable" scope="request"/>
Your bid failed to record.

<ul><b>Reason: </b>
<%
    Enumeration enum = errors.elements();
    while (enum.hasMoreElements()) {
        String error = (String) enum.nextElement();
%>
<li><%= error%></li>
<%
    }
%>
</ul>

Please go <a href="javascript:history.go(-1)">back</a> to alter and place
➥your bid
```

Figure 8.10 displays the output of failbid.jsp when the user bids on the same item twice with the same amount.

Figure 8.10

Page displayed on a failed bid

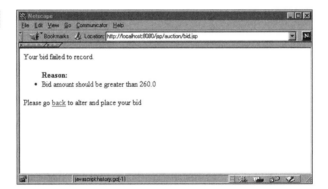

Placing an Item for Listing in AuctionStation

A user can also place an item for auction. A user does this by choosing a particular directory to list the item in and filling in the sell item form, sellform.jsp. The form data is submitted to sell.jsp for processing. It forwards the request to login.jsp to authorize the user just as in bid.jsp. On a successful authorization, sell.jsp attempts to add the item to the listing. On a successful add operation, it forwards the request to productview.jsp, which we created for the auction item catalog. On a failure, it forwards the request to failure.jsp, which displays the errors in the user data just as we did in failbid.jsp. The data flows between the pages are shown in Figure 8.11.

Figure 8.11

Data flows between the pages of the sell item use case

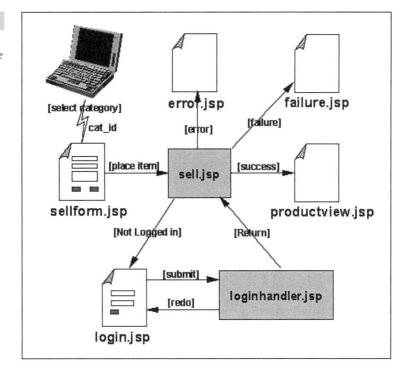

The user provides information in sellform.jsp. It provides different input fields to capture the user information regarding the item. The user needs to provide information regarding the product, such as the following:

- Item name
- Item description
- Minimum amount expected
- The bid increment amount
- The number of days the item is listed
- An optional item image URL
- An optional item URL

The category in which the item should be listed is provided as a hidden field. Its value is computed using the request parameter, cat_id, that is provided in the query string.

The source for sellform.jsp is shown in Listing 8.12. Notice the cat_id parameter appended to the query string.

Listing 8.12   sellform.jsp: The Form for Capturing Information About the Item to Be Placed for Listing

```
<form name="listItem" action="sell.jsp" method="POST">
<table>
<tr>
<td><b>Product Name: </b></td>
<td><input type="text" name="prod_name"></td>
</tr>

<tr>
<td valign="top"><b>Description: </b></td>
<td><textarea name="description" rows="5"></textarea></td>
</tr>

<tr>
<td><b>Minimum Amount ($): </b></td>
<td><input type="text" name="min_amt"></td>
</tr>

<tr>
<td><b>Bid Increment ($): </b></td>
<td><input type="text" name="min_bid_inc"></td>
</tr>

<tr>
<td><b>Bidding Closes in: </b></td>
<td>
<select name="bid_end">
<%
    for (int i = 1; i < 31; i++) {
        out.println("<option value=\"" + i + "\">" + i + "</option>");
    }
%>
</select> Days
</td>
</tr>

<tr>
<td><b>URL: </b></td>
<td><input type="text" name="url"></td>
</tr>

<tr>
<td><b>Image URL: </b></td>
<td><input type="text" name="image_url"></td>
</tr>
<tr>
<td><input type="submit" value="Auction Item"></td>
<td><input type="reset" value=" Reset "></td>
</tr>
</table>
```

```
<input type="hidden" name="cat_id" value="<%=
➥request.getParameter("cat_id")%>">
</form>
```

Figure 8.12 displays the output of the sellform.jsp with the fields filled with sample data.

Figure 8.12

Providing information about an item to be listed in the sell item form

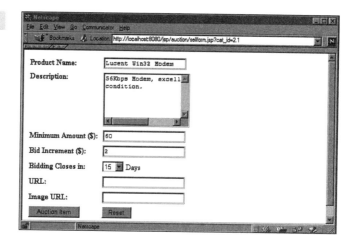

The information is submitted to the form handler and controller, sell.jsp for processing. The controller authorizes the user using the same technique used for bid.jsp by including checklogin.jsp. On a successful authorization, it inserts the item using a command bean, InsertItemCommand.

Executing the Insert Item Command

You need to create a command bean, InsertItemCommand, to add the item to the category listing. The bean contains fields and getter and setter methods for the properties listed in Table 8.2.

Table 8.2   The Properties of the `station.auction.catalog.command.InsertItemCommand` Bean

Property	Type	Description
prod_name	String	The name of the item being listed
description	String	Details about the item being listed
min_amt	float	The minimum bid amount for the item
min_bid_inc	float	The minimum bid increment for the item
bid_end	String	The number of days from the current date until which bids will be accepted for the item
image_url	String	The URL for an image for the item

Table 8.2 continued

Property	Type	Description
url	String	An option URL for the item
cat_id	String	The category in which the item should be placed for listing
user_id	String	The user ID of the user selling the item
result	String	An output property for the product ID of the item just inserted. If the item could not be inserted, the return value is null
errors	java.util.Hashtable	Output property storing the errors in the input parameters

Implement the check() method defined in the Command interface to determine whether the preconditions are met to execute the command. This would include checking whether the required fields are not null. The error information is stored within the errors Hashtable instance.

Implement the execute() method to do the following:

1. Obtain the product ID, prod_id, for the item. The prod_ids for the items are serial numbers. You can create a row in the Counter table that keeps track of the latest product count:

    ```
    INSERT INTO Counter (name, count) VALUES ('prod_id', 100)
    ```

    You can initialize the count to 100 that will be the prod_id for the first item added to the site.

2. Increment the count for the row with the name, prod_id, for each item added:

    ```
    UPDATE counter SET count = count + 1 WHERE name = 'prod_id'
    ```

3. Obtain count in the prod_id row of the Counter table; this value will be the prod_id for the item being added.

    ```
    SELECT count FROM counter WHERE name = 'prod_id'
    ```

4. Insert the item into the Product table providing the information provided by the user as well as the prod_id. The created field is the timestamp represented using the value CURRENT TIMESTAMP. The bid_end field is represented by the value CURRENT TIMESTAMP + x DAYS where x is the number of days in which the bid closes.

    ```
    INSERT INTO product (prod_id, prod_name, cat_id, user_id, description,
                min_amt, min_bid_inc, image_url, created, bid_end) VALUES
    (?, ?, ?, ?, ?, ?, ?, ?, CURRENT TIMESTAMP, CURRENT TIMESTAMP + ? DAYS )
    ```

5. Set the prod_id value for the item as the result if the SQL INSERT statement executed successfully.

The source for the execute() method is shown in Listing 8.13.

Listing 8.13   InsertItemCommand.java: Adding an Item for Listing in the Auction Site

```java
public void execute() throws Exception {
    String driver = "COM.ibm.db2.jdbc.app.DB2Driver";

    // Obtain a connection to the database
    DBConnectionManager dbcm = DBConnectionManager.getSingleton();
    DBConnection conn = dbcm.getConnection("jdbc:db2:auction", driver,
➥null, null);
    conn.setAutoCommit(false);

    // Increment the product ID count by 1
    Statement stmt1 = conn.createStatement();
    int done = stmt1.executeUpdate(
      " UPDATE counter SET count = count + 1 WHERE name = 'prod_id'");

    if (done == 0) {
        return;
    }

    // Get the prod id count for the product
    Statement stmt2 = conn.createStatement();
    ResultSet rs = stmt2.executeQuery(
      " SELECT count FROM counter WHERE name = 'prod_id'");

    long prod_id = 0;
    if (rs.next()) {
        prod_id = rs.getLong(1);
    }

    PreparedStatement stmt = conn.prepareStatement(
        "INSERT INTO product " +
        " (prod_id, prod_name, cat_id, user_id, description, min_amt, " +
        "            min_bid_inc, image_url, created, bid_end) VALUES " +
        " (?, ?, ?, ?, ?, ?, ?, ?, CURRENT TIMESTAMP, CURRENT TIMESTAMP + " +
➥getBid_end() + " DAYS )"
    );

    stmt.setString(1, prod_id + "");
    stmt.setString(2, getProd_name());
    stmt.setString(3, getCat_id());
    stmt.setString(4, getUser_id());
    stmt.setString(5, getDescription());
    stmt.setFloat(6, getMin_amt());
    stmt.setFloat(7, getMin_bid_inc());
    stmt.setString(8, getImage_url());
```

8

Listing 8.13   continued

```
        int rowsAffected = stmt.executeUpdate();
        if (rowsAffected == 1) {
            returnProd_id = prod_id + "";
            conn.commit();
        } else {
            conn.rollback();
        }
        conn.setAutoCommit(true);
        conn.release();
}
```

Developing the Controller

The controller, sell.jsp, is responsible for creating an instance of the
InsertItemCommand and setting the input properties used the request parameters. It
executes the command to return the prod_id of the item just added to the listing. It
then invokes the GetItemInformationCommand to return an Item instance representing
the particular item. It sets the result as a request parameter and forwards the request
to productview.jsp for display. If the insert operation was unsuccessful, it sets the
errors Hashtable obtained from the InsertItemsCommand instance in the
pageContext as a request scope variable and forwards the request to failure.jsp to display the errors. The sequence diagram for the use case is shown in Figure 8.13.

EXCURSION

Check This Out

Notice that by implementing the Model-View-Controller model, you can easily reuse the
different components—such as the **GetItemInformationCommand** and the view,
productview.jsp, used in the auction item catalog module—in other modules and applications as well.

The sequence diagram shown in Figure 8.13 can be translated into a scriptlet in the
controller, sell.jsp, as shown in Listing 8.14.

Figure 8.13

Sequence diagram detailing the sell item use case

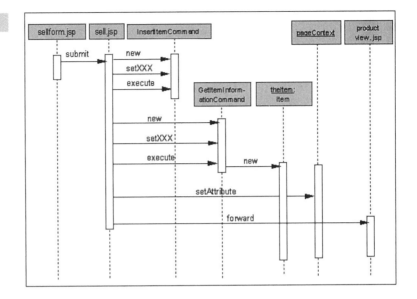

Listing 8.14   sell.jsp: Controlling the Data Flows Between the Different JSPs in the Add Item for Listing Use Case

```jsp
<%@ page import="java.util.Hashtable,
                 station.auction.catalog.Item,
                 station.auction.catalog.command.*"%>
<%@ include file="/jsp/auction/checklogin.jsp"%>
<jsp:useBean id="cmd"
      class="station.auction.catalog.command.InsertItemCommand">
    <jsp:setProperty name="cmd" property="*"/>
    <jsp:setProperty name="cmd" property="user_id" value="<%= user_id%>"/>
</jsp:useBean>
<%
    boolean precheck = cmd.check();

    String prod_id = null;
    if (precheck) {
        cmd.execute();
        prod_id = (String) cmd.getResult();
        System.out.println(prod_id);
    }

    if (prod_id != null) {
        GetItemInformationCommand cmd2 = new GetItemInformationCommand();
        cmd2.setProd_id(prod_id);
        cmd2.execute();
        Item theItem = (Item) cmd2.getResult();
        pageContext.setAttribute("item", theItem, PageContext.REQUEST_SCOPE);
%>
```

Listing 8.14   continued

```
        <jsp:forward page="/jsp/auction/productview.jsp"/>
<%   }
     pageContext.setAttribute("errors", cmd.getErrors(),
➥PageContext.REQUEST_SCOPE);
%>
<jsp:forward page="/jsp/auction/failure.jsp"/>
```

If no errors were encountered while adding the item for listing, the browser displays the item information, as shown in Figure 8.14.

Figure 8.14

The successful addition of the item for listing is marked by displaying the item information

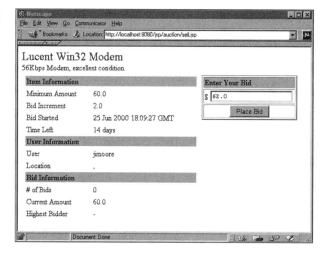

Performing Custom Authorization

You have seen how registered users can access the protected portions of the site for bidding and auctioning items. This authorization is performed by the form-based login that we reused from the user registration module. Now, we will develop an authorization routine that permits only a specific kind of users, the administrators, to use the protected resources.

This authorization routine is similar to the Client Authentication provided by Tomcat, except that you need to write extra code in your JSP to mark it as a protected resource.

Performing Custom Basic Authorization

In Basic authorization, the user ID and password are encoded according to the base64 encoding scheme and passed in the header. This provides additional security as compared to passing them without any encoding as request parameters in the form-based authorization.

To perform this authorization, we will create a JSP, authorize.jsp. This JSP checks whether the authorization header exists. If the header doesn't exist, we need to check whether the user has already logged on using the form-based login. You can find this out by checking whether the session attribute, user_id, has been set.

```
<jsp:useBean id="cmd"
    class="station.auction.catalog.command.AuthenticateAdminCommand"/>
<%
    String user_id = null;
    String password = null;
    String authHeader = request.getHeader("Authorization");
    if (authHeader == null) {
        System.out.println(user_id);
        // try obtaining the user id from the session
        user_id = (String) session.getValue("user_id");
```

If the authorization header exists, it implies that the request is a response to the challenge. You need to extract the user ID and password from the Authorization header. This information is encoded in the header. For example, the user ID msahu and password ou812 are encoded in the Authorization header as

```
Basic bXNhaHU6b3U4MTI=
```

It's hard to determine the name and password from this string. It has been encoded using the base64 encoding algorithm. Without the encoding, the header would be

```
Basic msahu:ou812
```

You can decode the user ID and password stored in the header using the Base64Decoder provided by Sun along with the standard packages of the Java Runtime Environment.

```
} else {
    // Extract the encoded user:password from the header
    // Basic .... After the sixth character in the header
    String encoded = authHeader.substring(6);

    // Decode the string
    sun.misc.BASE64Decoder decoder =
            new sun.misc.BASE64Decoder();
    String decoded = new String(decoder.decodeBuffer(encoded));

    // Locate the separator -> :
    int colonIndex = decoded.indexOf(":");
    user_id = decoded.substring(0, colonIndex);
    password = decoded.substring(colonIndex + 1);
}
```

Next, you can check whether the user is an administrator by executing the AuthenticateAdminCommand that checks whether the user ID and password match those of a user in the User table who is an administrator. An administrator is one whose type is 0 in the User table. The command's source is displayed in Listing 8.15.

Listing 8.15   AuthenticateAdminCommand.java: Authenticating Administrators

```java
package station.auction.catalog.command;

import java.sql.*;
import station.auction.db.*;

public class AuthenticateAdminCommand implements station.auction.Command {
    protected String user_id = null;
    protected String password = null;
    protected Boolean ok = Boolean.FALSE;

public boolean check() throws Exception {
   if (user_id == null)
      return false;
   return true;
}

public void execute() throws Exception {
    // Obtain a connection to the database
    String driver = "COM.ibm.db2.jdbc.app.DB2Driver";

    // Obtain a connection to the database
    DBConnectionManager dbcm = DBConnectionManager.getSingleton();
    DBConnection conn = dbcm.getConnection("jdbc:db2:auction", driver,
➥null, null);

    Statement stmt = conn.createStatement();
    String query = "SELECT * FROM users WHERE user_id = '" + getUser_id() +
➥   "' AND  type = 0 ";


    if (password != null) {
        query += " AND password = '" + getPassword() + "'";
    }

    ResultSet rs = stmt.executeQuery(query);
    if (rs.next()) {
        // ok fine
        ok = Boolean.TRUE;
    }
}

public Object getResult() {
    return ok;
}

public void setUser_id(String uid) {
    this.user_id = uid;
}
```

```
public String getUser_id() {
    return user_id;
}

public void setPassword(String pass) {
    this.password = pass;
}

protected String getPassword() {
    return password;
}
}
```

You can set the user ID and password extracted from the header or the session on the command instance and execute it. The result property of the command specifies whether the user is an administrator (Boolean.TRUE).

```
cmd.setUser_id(user_id);
cmd.setPassword(password);
cmd.execute();

Boolean ok = (Boolean) cmd.getResult();
```

If the user is not an administrator, you need to challenge the user for the user ID and password. This is done by sending the error code SC_UNAUTHORIZED in the response. You can also specify the realm Administrators by setting the header: WWW-Authenticate.

```
if (ok == Boolean.FALSE || user_id == null) {
    response.sendError(HttpServletResponse.SC_UNAUTHORIZED);
    response.setHeader("WWW-Authenticate", "BASIC realm=\"Administrators\"");
```

If the authentication was successful, the user_id attribute is set in the session.

```
} else {
    session.putValue("user_id", user_id);
%>
```

Notice that the if-else block has been left unterminated. This is because authorize.jsp cannot be used independently. It needs to be included using a page include directive into another JSP that requires authorization.

Adding Categories to the Site

We will now implement an administrative task to add categories to the auction site. Additional authorization has to be provided to prevent users from adding their own categories.

Creating the New Category Form

Create a form to accept information about the category to be added. The information includes

- Name
- Description

You also need to specify the parent category ID to which the category should be attached. This is provided as a hidden field, par_cat_id, whose value is computed using the cat_id request parameter, as shown in Listing 8.16.

Listing 8.16   categoryform.jsp: Form to Accept Information About the New Category

```
<form name="category" action="/jsp/admin/addcategory.jsp" method="POST">
<table>
<tr>
<td><b>Category Name: </b></td>
<td><input type="text" name="name"></td>
</tr>

<tr>
<td valign="top"><b>Description: </b></td>
<td><textarea name="description" rows="5"></textarea></td>
</tr>

<tr>
<td><input type="submit" value="Add Category"></td>
<td><input type="reset" value=" Reset "></td>
</tr>
</table>

<input type="hidden" name="par_cat_id" value="<%=
➥request.getParameter("cat_id")%>">
</form>
```

The page containing the form is displayed in Figure 8.15 filled with sample data.

Adding the Category to the Database

You can add the category by inserting a row in the Category table using the parameters provided by the user. You can either add a db custom tag or create a command bean to perform this operation. We will continue using the MVC design to implement this feature.

Create a command bean, AddCategoryCommand, that inserts a Category in the database. The cat_id for the new category is obtained by concatenating the parent's cat_id with the current child count of the parent category. The source for the command bean is shown in Listing 8.17.

Figure 8.15

Form filled with sample data to create a new category

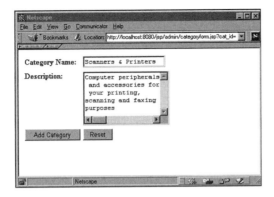

Listing 8.17 AddCategoryCommand.java: Command Bean to Add a Category

```java
package station.auction.catalog.command;

import java.sql.*;
import java.util.Hashtable;
import java.util.ResourceBundle;

import station.auction.Command;
import station.auction.db.*;

public class AddCategoryCommand implements station.auction.Command{
    protected String fieldPar_cat_id = null;
    protected String description = null;
    protected String name = null;

    protected String resultCat_id = null;

public boolean check() throws Exception {
    if (getPar_cat_id() == null || getName() == null)
        return false;
    return true;
}

public void execute() throws Exception {
    String driver = "COM.ibm.db2.jdbc.app.DB2Driver";

    // Obtain a connection to the database
    DBConnectionManager dbcm = DBConnectionManager.getSingleton();
    DBConnection conn = dbcm.getConnection("jdbc:db2:auction", driver,
➥null, null);
    conn.setAutoCommit(false);

    Statement stmt1 = conn.createStatement();
    ResultSet rs1 = stmt1.executeQuery(
        " SELECT COUNT(*) from Category " +
        " WHERE par_cat_id = '" + getPar_cat_id() + "'");
```

8

Listing 8.17   continued

```
        int count = 1;
        if (rs1.next()) {
            count = rs1.getInt(1);
        }

        String par_cat_id = getPar_cat_id();
        String cat_id = par_cat_id + "." + (count + 1);

        PreparedStatement stmt2 = conn.prepareStatement(
            " INSERT INTO Category (name, cat_id, par_cat_id, description,
➥created)" +
            " VALUES (?, ?, ?, ?, CURRENT TIMESTAMP)");
        stmt2.setString(1, getName());
        stmt2.setString(2, cat_id);
        stmt2.setString(3, par_cat_id);
        stmt2.setString(4, getDescription());

        int rowsAffected = stmt2.executeUpdate();
        if (rowsAffected == 1) {
            conn.commit();
            resultCat_id = cat_id;
        } else {
            conn.rollback();
        }
        conn.setAutoCommit(true);
        conn.release();
    }

    public Object getResult() {
        return resultCat_id;
    }

    public String getPar_cat_id() {
        return fieldPar_cat_id;
    }

    public void setPar_cat_id(String arg1) {
        fieldPar_cat_id = arg1;
    }

    public String getDescription() {
        return description;
    }

    public void setDescription(String arg1) {
        description = arg1;
    }

    public String getName() {
        return name;
    }
```

```
public void setName(String arg1) {
    name = arg1;
}
}
```

Creating the `AddCategory` Controller

Create the controller for the add category use case, AddCategory.jsp. The controller is responsible for authorizing the user, executing the `AddCategory` command, and forwarding the requests to one of the pages based on the result of the command. The data flows between the different JSPs are shown in Figure 8.16.

Figure 8.16

Data flows between the different pages for the add category use case

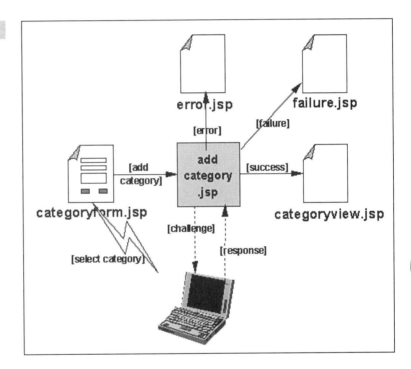

The controller receives the request to add the category from categoryform.jsp. It checks whether the user is in the administrator's role. You can include authorize.jsp to perform the authorization. On a successful authorization, the controller executes the command and forwards the request based on the result of the command. The source of addcategory.jsp is shown in Listing 8.18.

Listing 8.18   addcategory.jsp: Controlling the Sequence of Data Flows to Add Categories

```
<%@ page import="java.util.Hashtable,
                station.auction.catalog.Category,
                station.auction.catalog.command.*"%>
```

Listing 8.18   continued

```
        <%@ include file="/jsp/login/authorize.jsp"%>
        <jsp:useBean id="cmd2"
            class="station.auction.catalog.command.AddCategoryCommand">
            <jsp:param name="cmd2" property="*"/>
        </jsp:useBean>
<%
        boolean precheck = cmd2.check();

        String cat_id = null;
        if (precheck) {
            cmd2.execute();
            cat_id = (String) cmd2.getResult();

            Category category = new Category();
            category.setCat_id(cat_id);
            category.setPar_cat_id(request.getParameter("par_cat_id"));
            category.setName(request.getParameter("name"));
            category.setDescription(request.getParameter("description"));

            pageContext.setAttribute("category", category,
➥PageContext.REQUEST_SCOPE);
%>
            <jsp:forward page="/jsp/admin/categoryview.jsp"/>
<%
        } else {
            out.println("Could not create category");
        }
    }
%>
```

When the user attempts to add a category by submitting the category form, the controller launches the challenge dialog asking the user to specify her or his credentials, as shown in Figure 8.17.

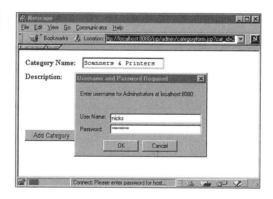

If the user specified an incorrect name-value combination or if the user is not an administrator, the retry dialog is displayed, as shown in Figure 8.18.

Figure 8.18

Retry dialog for accepting the credentials again

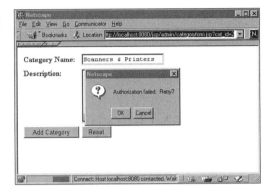

Creating the Category View

Create the view that displays the category information. The Category instance is obtained from the request and displays the attributes using expressions, as shown in Listing 8.19.

Listing 8.19   categoryview.jsp: Displaying the Category Information

```
<font size="+1">Category Information</font>

<jsp:useBean id="category" class="station.auction.catalog.Category"
➡scope="request"/>
<table>

<tr>
<td>Name: </td>
<td><%= category.getName()%></td>
</tr>

<tr>
<td valign="top">Description: </td>
<td><%= category.getDescription()%></td>
</tr>

<tr>
<td>Category ID: </td>
<td><%= category.getCat_id()%></td>
</tr>

<tr>
<td>Parent Category ID: </td>
<td><%= category.getPar_cat_id()%></td>
</tr>
</table>
```

8

If the authorization is performed successfully, the category view for the newly created `Category` instance is displayed, as shown in Figure 8.19.

Figure 8.19

Output of the add category operation

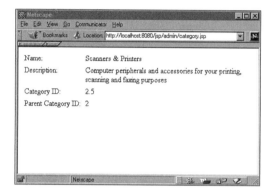

Summary

This chapter covered some of the authentication techniques that you can use for protecting your Web resources:

- Server authentication
- Custom authorization
- Custom form-based authorization

The next chapter will look at personalizing and customizing AuctionStation.

Chapter 9

Personalizing the Web Site

The difference between running a successful Web site and an unsuccessful one is gauged by the customer visits or "hits" to your site. A successful Web site obviously attracts more customers and provides some "sticky" characteristics that make users come back for more. Supplying a daily dose of cartoons and news or message boards and chat rooms can provide this sticky behavior. For business applications, however, stickiness is provided by *personalization*.

Personalization is a process of providing information and content customized to the user's needs and preferences. This is carried out by gathering and building up the user's profile and using this information while generating content. Personalization enables you to deliver content relevant to the user—for example, a section in Auction Station that tells the users the items they placed for listing and the items they bid on. You can also use the user's information for advertising and stealth marketing. For example, you can ask users to fill out a survey form about their hobbies and then you can target the user with advertisements of sports gear and fitness clubs if the user's preferences include sports and the outdoors. You can also perform data mining and data warehousing on data gathered about the site users' browsing habits, analyze the data, and provide information to the user. Sites that cross-sell products in their store can display a message to the user, for example: "People who bought this product also bought this other product...."

In this chapter, we will look at the personalization techniques that are easy to apply with JSPs—for example:

- Personalizing the look of a Web application
- Providing the user with a personal space for uploading and storing files
- Putting together a personal start page for the user using the information relevant to the user in the Auction site

We will start with personalizing the monthly calendar's look.

Customizing the Calendar's Look

In this section, we will break the monotony of the unistyle calendar generated by month.jsp by providing themes. These *themes* represent a particular style for the different HTML elements: the background of the page, the month name, and the day names of the generated calendar.

One approach for generating the stylized calendar would be to extract the HTML element's information for a specified theme and embed it directly into the HTML element for generating the month name's background, as shown following. The information about the themes can be stored in files, databases, or other data stores.

```
<tr bgcolor="<%= database.getColorForMonthName("theme")%>">
    <td colspan="7"> <font size="+2">
    <%= cal.getMonthName()%></font>
    </td>
</tr>
```

This rather naive approach complicates the presentation logic and makes it hard to maintain the JSP code. Reusing this technique for styling other pages is difficult as well.

To ease these customization pains, a more mature technology exists in the form of *Cascading Style Sheets*, CSS for short.

 **Note** CSS works with any CSS Level 1 compliant browsers like IE 3+ and Netscape 4+. Earlier browsers will ignore them.

Using Style Sheets

Cascading Style Sheets allow you to manage the look of the page separately from the content. Text styles and content can be modified independently of each other (see Figure 9.1), allowing Web pages to be updated more efficiently.

Styling the Page Using CSS Rules

To use plain HTML to display a heading with a font one size larger than the default and with a red foreground, you would nest a font tag within a header as follows:

```
<h1><font size="+1" color="red">header</font></h1>
```

If you have another header you want to display with the same style, you will have to repeat the nesting for the header text as well.

Figure 9.1

Figure 9.1

Separating style from content using CSS

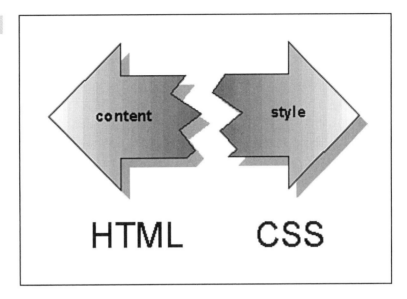

Using CSS, you can specify the style information for the header much more elegantly by providing *rules*. The structure of a rule is the name of the tag followed by one or more styles represented as name-value pairs stored within curly brackets, as shown following:

```
<tag name> { [<attribute-name>: <attribute-value>;]* }
```

You can specify the rule for styling the header tags using the following simple CSS rule:

```
h1 { color: red; font-size:large;}
```

This rule will cause all the level 1 header tags in the page to be displayed with a red foreground and a font one size larger than the default. An added benefit of using such CSS rules is the reduction in the Web page size that you achieve by stripping the nested font tags that were used to specify the color and font information. Your header tag would then be reduced to using the simple HTML element:

```
<h1>header</h1>
```

If you changed your mind about the look of the headers in the page and decided to display them with a blue background, you would only need to modify the CSS rule by adding the extra information as follows:

```
h1 { color: red; background: blue; font-size:large;}
```

9

Inheriting Rules

You can also display a subset of header tags underlined, retaining the other attributes (color red and large font), by specifying a `class` attribute in the header tag, as shown following:

```
<h1 class="underline">Underlined header</h1>
```

You will need to provide a corresponding CSS rule to underline the text. Your rule will not target a tag but the class specified with the `"underline"` value, as follows:

```
underline { text-decoration: underline; }
```

CSS employs a system of inheritance in which the child styles inherit properties from parent styles. The `h1` tag with the `underline` class is therefore displayed with the styles of the `h1` CSS rule as well as the underline rule. Any clashing styles will be overridden by the child styles defined in the underline rule. This cascade of rules is how CSS got its name!

Merging CSS and HTML

Now you need to merge the CSS rules with the tags in the Web document to obtain the desired effects. You can do this either by embedding the rules inline or by linking a stylesheet containing the rules to the document.

You can embed the rules within a script tag specified in the head of the HTML page, as shown in Listing 9.1. Figure 9.2 shows the output of the page in a browser.

Listing 9.1   embedcss.html: Embedding Style Sheet Rules Within the HTML Page

```
<html>
<head>
    <style type="text/css">
      h1 {color: red; font-size: large}
      .underline { text-decoration: underline; }
      </style>
</head>

    <body>
<h1>Red header, no font tag</h1>
<h1 class="underline">Underlined this time</h1>
    </body>
</html>
```

You can also store the CSS rules in a separate file, mystyles.css, and link them to the Web document using a `link` tag:

```
<link rel="stylesheet" type="text/css" href="mystyles.css"/>
```

You will obtain the same output as shown in Figure 9.2.

Figure 9.2

Embedding CSS rules to stylize a Web page

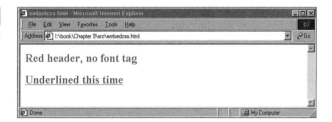

Styling month.jsp Using a Stylesheet

The easiest way to incorporate CSS rules in your Web page is by identifying styled tags in the Web document. Any tag that has color or size information is a candidate for a CSS transformation. Table 9.1 contains the tags in month.jsp identified for transformation.

Table 9.1   HTML Sections Being "CSS-ified"

HTML Section	CSS Rule	Modified Section
`<body>`	`body {background: white; }`	`<body>`

`<tr bgcolor="silver">`
`<td colspan="7"> `
` <font size="+2">`
`<%= cal.getMonth}Name()%></font>`
`</td>`
`</tr>`
	`.monthName {`
	`    background: silver;`
	`    font-size:large;`
	`}`
		`<tr>`
		`<td class="monthName"`
		`    colspan="7">`
		` <%= cal.getMonthName()%>`
		`</td>`
		`</tr>`

`<tr bgcolor="black" align="center">`
`<%`
`  for (int i = 1; i < 8; i++) {`
`    out.print("<td width=\"70\">");`
`    out.print(`
`      "<font size=\"-1\"" +`
`      "color=\"white\">");`
`|    out.print(`
`      cal.getDayName(i, true));`
`    out.println("</font></td>");`
`  }`
`%>`
`</tr>`
	`.weekName {`
	`    background: black;`
	`    color: white;`
	`    font-size: smaller;`
	`    text-align: center;`
	`}`
		`<tr>`
		`<%`
		`  for (int I = 1; i < 8; I++) {`
		`    out.print(`
		`      "<td width=\"70\"" +`
		`      " class=\"weekName\">");`
		`    out.print(`
		`      cal.getDayName(i, true));`
		`    out.println("</td>");`
		`}%>`
		`</tr>`

`out.print(`
`  "<td valign="top" height="57");`
 	
`if (cellNo < startCell ||`
`  cellNo > endCell) {`
`  out.print(`
`    " bgcolor=\"#999999\"> ");`
`}`
	`.noday {`
	`    background: #999999;`
	`}`
		`out.print(`
		`  "<td valign="top" height="57");`
		
		`if (cellNo < startCell ||`
		`  cellNo > endCell) {`
		`  out.print(`
		`    " class=\"noday\"> ");`
		`}`

`out.print(`
`  "><a href=\"" +`
`  "javascript:openWindow('" +`
`  day + "');\"><b>" + day +`
`  "</b></a>");`
`day++;`
`} // end if block`
 	
`out.println("</td>");`
	`.day {`
	`    background: white;`
	`    font-weight: bold;`
	`}`
		`out.print{`
		`  " class=\"day\"><a href=\"" +`
		`  "javascript:openwindow('"`
		`  day + "');\">" + day +`
		`  "</a>");`
		`day++;`
		`} // end if block`
		
		`out.println("</td>");`

9

You can store the CSS rules for the default style in a separate file, default.css, as shown in Listing 9.2, and link the style sheet to month.jsp by adding a `link` tag as shown in Listing 9.3.

Listing 9.2   default.css: The Default Style Sheet for month.jsp

```
body {background: white; }
.monthName { background: silver; font-size:large;}
.weekName { background: black; color: white; font-size: smaller;
            text-align: center;}
.day { background: white; font-weight: bold;}
.noday { background: #999999;}
```

Listing 9.3   month.jsp: Adding the Style Sheet to month.jsp

```
<jsp:useBean id="validator"
            class="station.auction.calendar.CalendarRequest"
            scope="request"/>

<jsp:useBean id="cal" class="station.auction.calendar.MonthBean"/>

<%      cal.setMonth(validator.getMonthAsInteger());
        cal.setYear(validator.getYearAsInteger());
        cal.update(); %>

<html>
<head>
<script LANGUAGE="Javascript">

  <!--
    function openWindow(day) {
      width = 600;
      height = 400;
      month = '<%= (validator.getMonthAsInteger() + 1) %>';
url='/jsp/calendar/2.1/daysevents.jsp\?month=' + month +
          '&&year=<%= validator.getYear()%>&&day=' + day;
      Win = open(url, 'as_events',
          'toolbar=0,location=0,directories=0,status=0,menubar=0,' +
          'resizable=1,width=' + width + ',height=' + height +
          ',scrollbars=yes');
      Win.focus();
    }
  //-->
</script>
<link rel="stylesheet" type="text/css" href="/jsp/calendar/2.1/default.css"/>
<title>Calendar</title>
</head>

<body>
    <table border="1">
    <tr>
        <td class="monthName" colspan="7"> <%= cal.getMonthName()%>
```

```
        </td>
    </tr>
    <tr>
    <%
        for (int i = 1; i < 8; i++) {
            out.print("<td width=\"70\" class=\"weekName\">");
            out.print(cal.getDayName(i, true));
            out.println("</td>");
        }
    %>
    </tr>
<%
    int startCell = cal.getStartCell();
    int endCell = cal.getEndCell();
    for (int cellNo = 0, day = 1; cellNo < 42; cellNo++) {
        if (cellNo%7 == 0) {
            out.println("<tr>");
        } // end check for start of row

        out.print("<td valign=\"top\" height=\"57\"");
        if (cellNo < startCell || cellNo > endCell) {
            out.print(" class=\"noday\"> ");
        } else {
            out.print(" class=\"day\"><a href=\"javascript:openWindow('" +
                day + "');\">" + day + "</a>");
            day++;
        } // end if block

        out.println("</td>");

        if (cellNo+1%7 == 0) {
            out.println("</tr>");
        } // end check for end of row
    } // end for-loop
%>
</table>

</body>
</html>
```

You will not notice any difference when you view the page in a browser and compare the output with the page generated by the earlier mechanism.

You can truly appreciate the use of CSS when you want to modify the look of the page. You can do this easily with CSS by modifying the style sheet or by attaching a new one to the document. You will create another style sheet, sunny.css, that can be attached to month.jsp. As the name suggests, the colors in the theme are rather bright (and will not be obvious in the grayscale colors of the book you are reading). The rules of the CSS are shown in Listing 9.4 .

Listing 9.4 sunny.css: Creating a New Style Sheet for the Sunny Theme

```
body {background: yellow; }
.monthName { background: orange; font-size:large;}
.weekName { background: red; color: white; font-size: smaller;
        text-align: center;}
.day { background: white; font-weight: bold;}
.noday { background: #ffcccc;}
```

You can easily switch the theme by setting the href of the link tag to point to sunny.css as shown following:

```
<link rel="stylesheet" type="text/css" href="/jsp/calendar/2.1/sunny.css"/>
```

Figure 9.3 shows the output of month.jsp shown with the "sunny" theme.

Figure 9.3

The Calendar displayed with the "sunny" theme (in black and white)

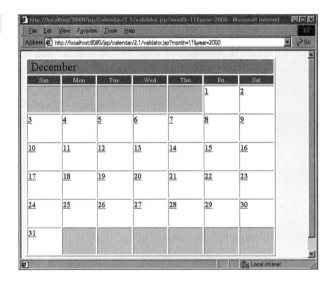

Allowing the User to Specify the Theme

We will now enhance our application to allow the user to customize the look by choosing a style for the calendar. We will permit the user to choose from one of the three available styles: default, contrast, and sunny. For each style in the list, there is an equivalent CSS. You can add more styles by creating CSS files for each entry in the list.

Create a JSP, customize.jsp, that generates the form containing the drop-down list of theme names as shown in Listing 9.5 and displayed in Figure 9.4. You can provide a hyperlink within month.jsp that can be followed to reach this page.

Listing 9.5   customize.jsp: Form for Specifying the Theme

```
<html>
<head><title>Customize your page</title></head>
<body>

<form action="/jsp/calendar/2.1/savechanges.jsp?<%= request.getQueryString()%>">
<table>
<tr><td><b>Select Theme: </b></td>
<td>
<select name="theme">
   <option value="contrast">Contrast</option>
   <option value="default">Default</option>
   <option value="sunny">Sunny</option>
</select>
</td></tr></table>
<input type="Submit" value="Submit">
</form>
</body>
</html>
```

Figure 9.4

Displaying the drop-down list of styles

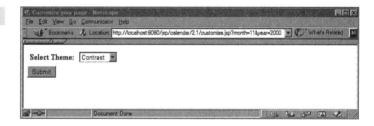

Using Cookies to Store Customization Information

You can use the style specified by the user to set the style sheet for month.jsp. You can also save this information to allow the user to view the calendar with the specified style on subsequent visits to the page. Because this data is rather trivial, you can store it as a *cookie*.

 Cookies are information sent by the Web server and stored by the browser on the client's file system. The browser sends the cookies obtained from the Web site back to the same server on subsequent requests. This way the server is able to remember the previous dialogues with the client based on the cookies it had set.

The part about the browser storing data from an unreliable source might seem like a potential security threat, especially with so many viruses floating around and causing havoc. Cookies, on the contrary, are innocuous bytes of text, incapable of harming even a sector of hard disk! For one, they are never executed on the client's machine, so there is never a risk of viruses. Secondly, the server has a limit to the amount of

9

data that it can send as cookies to the client. A Web site can set up to a maximum of 20 cookies, and the cookies themselves have a 4KB size limit. The browser will refuse to set any cookie that infringes these limits. Hence there is never a possibility of the server dumping megabytes of data as cookies on the client machine.

Cookies can also be used to identify users. A cookie containing the username can be sent to the client by the Web site after a user registers. When this happens, the user will not be required to log in to access the protected portions of the site because the same cookie can be used to authorize the user.

There is talk about cookies being a threat to a user's privacy. This may be true to the extent that a Web site may profile your actions and determine your interests by the searches you perform or the auction categories you generally browse. This way, it will be able to target banner ads and marketing content for the user. The point to note is that one site cannot access cookies of another that does not belong to the same domain.

If you are paranoid about the use of cookies, you can disable their use in your browser.

You can send a cookie in your JSPs using the Servlet Cookie API. The significant properties of the `Cookie` class are shown in Table 9.2.

Table 9.2 Significant Properties Of `javax.servlet.http.Cookie`

Property	*Description*
`name`	Specifies the name of the cookie. It should not contain any white characters or special symbols.
`value`	The value associated with the cookie.
`maxage`	Specifies the life of the cookie in seconds. After a cookie expires, it is purged from the client's machine.
`comment`	An optional comment.
`secure`	Whether the cookie should be encrypted.

Create a form handler for the "select styles" form, savechanges.jsp, which obtains the theme selected by the user and stores the information by sending a cookie to the user. Create a scriptlet in savechanges.jsp to create an instance of `Cookie`; set its `name`, `value`, `maxAge`, and `comment` properties; and add it to the `response` implicit object for sending it to the client. Finally, you can forward it to month.jsp to display the page updated with the new style, as shown in Listing 9.6.

Listing 9.6   savechanges.jsp: Saving the Theme Selected by a User in a Cookie

```
<%
    Cookie cookie = new Cookie("theme", request.getParameter("theme"));
    // Set the maximum age as an year
    cookie.setMaxAge(365 * 24 * 60 * 60);
    cookie.setComment("the theme style for the calendar");
    response.addCookie(cookie);
%>
<jsp:forward page="/jsp/calendar/2.1/month.jsp?<%=
➥request.getQueryString()%>"/>
```

You can set your browser properties to "Warn before accepting cookie." This allows you to analyze the cookie and take appropriate action when the server sends a cookie. Figure 9.5 shows the warning dialog displayed when savechanges.jsp attempts to set the "theme" cookie.

Figure 9.5

The warning dialog displayed by Netscape Navigator when the JSP sends a cookie

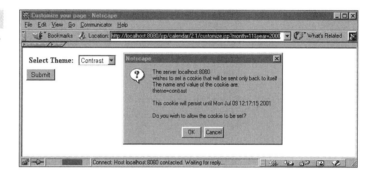

You can also determine the cookies associated with the page by typing `javascript:alert(document.cookie)` in the location field of your browser. Figure 9.6 displays the cookies in the document within an alert window. Notice the extra JSESSIONID cookie; the Web server sets this cookie for every session.

9

Figure 9.6

Displaying the cookies associated with the document using the JavaScript command

Within month.jsp, you need to obtain the cookies and set the style sheet to be linked. You can delegate this task to another JSP, stylesheet.jsp, that returns CSS content. To enforce this change, you need to modify the `href` property of month.jsp to point to this JSP.

```
<link rel="stylesheet" type="text/css"
➥href="/jsp/calendar/2.1/stylesheet.jsp"/>
```

Create the stylesheet.jsp that generates the CSS for month.jsp. Set the `contentType` of the page as `"text/css"`, indicating that CSS will be generated in the page instead of the default `"text/html"`. Extract the cookie named "theme" from the `request` implicit object. Construct the URL of the style sheet using the value in the cookie and include the style sheet using the URL to return the required CSS content, as shown in Listing 9.7.

Listing 9.7   stylesheet.jsp: Generating the Style Sheet from the "theme" Cookie

```
<%@ page contentType="text/css"%>
<%
    Cookie[] cookies = request.getCookies();
    String themeName = "default";
    for (int i = 0; i < cookies.length; i++) {
        if ("theme".equalsIgnoreCase(cookies[i].getName())) {
            themeName = cookies[i].getValue();
        }
    }
    String cssFile = "/jsp/calendar/2.1/" + themeName + ".css";
%>

<jsp:include page="<%= cssFile%>" flush="true"/>
```

Figure 9.7 displays the calendar with the "contrast" theme set by the user.

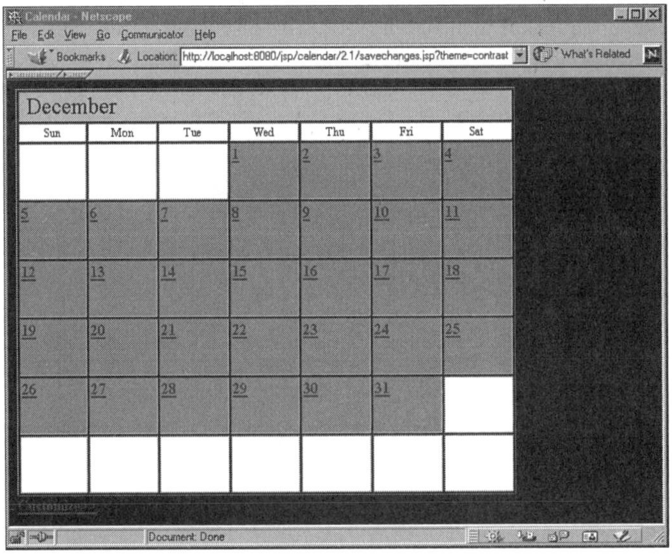

Figure 9.7

Displaying the calendar with the selected "contrast" theme

The next time the user views month.jsp using the same browser, the calendar is displayed with the selected theme. This personalization persists until the cookie expires, determined by its `maxAge` property.

Developing a Personal File Manager

In this section, we will build a Web-based file manager that enables users to upload and manage files. This will be useful when a user adds items for listing and wants to add images and links to the listing description.

In AuctionStation, every user will be provided a space on the Web server where they can upload and browse files for his or her personal use. You can create a top-level directory, users, in `<jakarta-tomcat>\webapps\AuctionStation` that holds all the user directories. Each user will have a directory named with his user ID within the users directory. You don't have to manually create the directories for each user—they will be created the first time the user attempts to upload a file or browse his personal space.

Developing a File-Upload Utility

You have seen some of the input tags for capturing user data. These inputs accept only text-based values. We will now use a form input to accept files from the client's file system and submit them to the server.

Create a form within a JSP, upload.jsp, for accepting input. You can perform user authentication using any of the techniques defined in the previous chapter. The form requires an `enctype` attribute whose value needs to be set to `"multipart/form-data"`, specifying the new MIME media type. Forms that submit only text-based information have an `enctype` `"application/x-www-form-urlencoded"`. Specify the form handler, uploadfile.jsp, in the `action` attribute and `"post"` as the request method. Add an input tag of type `"file"` and a submit button as shown in Listing 9.8. Figure 9.8 shows the file-upload utility in action, selecting the file dj.jpg from the local file system.

Listing 9.8   upload.jsp: Input Form for Uploading a File to the Server

```
<%@ include file="/jsp/auction/checklogin.jsp"%>
<html>
<title>AuctionStation: File Upload</title>
<body>
<h1>Hello <b><%= user_id%></b></h1>
Please specify the file to be uploaded or browse to select the file. <p>
<form action="/jsp/personal/savefile.jsp" method="post"
    enctype="multipart/form-data">
<input type="file" name="theFile">
```

Listing 9.8   continued

```
<br>
<input type="submit" value="Upload">
</form>
</body></html>
```

Figure 9.8

The file-upload utility in action

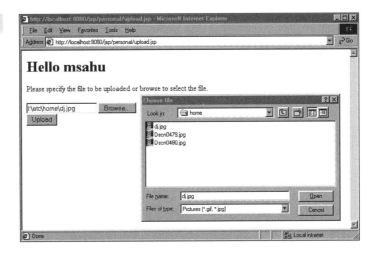

Developing the `UploadFilesCommand` Bean

When the user submits the form, the browser sends the form data and the content of the selected files. This data is encoded using the `multipart/form-data` mechanism. As of now, the Sun Servlet API do not support this encoding mechanism. We therefore need to develop a custom technique in the form of a JavaBean that extracts the files passed in the request.

The `multipart/form-data` encoding mechanism is described in detail in the Request for Comments (RFC) 1867.

An RFC is a document that specifies an Internet standards track protocol for the Internet community, and requests discussion and suggestions for improvements. Some of the important RFCs include RFC 2626, "Hypertext Transfer Protocol - HTTP/1.1." You can find a comprehensive list of RFCs at `www.ietf.org/rfc`.

In this encoding, a boundary is selected to separate the different fields and files. The boundary is a text string that is not present in any of the form data. Each field of the form is sent in the order of its occurrence separated by the boundary string. Each part also identifies the input name, content type, and filename.

Create a class, ServletStream, that extracts data from the request's input stream and returns either a line of text for obtaining the content-types, boundary and content-disposition strings, or the next 1,000 bytes containing parts of the attached file's body. It takes as input an instance of javax.servlet.http.ServletInputStream and extracts the relevant information using its readLine method in the getNextLine and getNext1000Bytes methods, as shown in Listing 9.9.

Listing 9.9   ServletStream.java: Reading Data from the ServletInputStream

```
package station.auction.personalization.command;

import java.io.*;
import javax.servlet.ServletInputStream;
import javax.servlet.ServletRequest;

public class ServletStream {
    protected int actual = 0;
    protected transient ServletInputStream sis = null;
    protected transient byte[] buffer = new byte[1000];

    public ServletStream() {
    }

    public ServletStream(ServletInputStream is) {
        setInputStream(is);
    }

    public ServletStream(ServletRequest request) throws Exception {
        this(request.getInputStream());
    }

    public void setInputStream(ServletInputStream is) {
        sis = is;
    }

    public String getNextLine() throws Exception {
        StringBuffer sb = new StringBuffer();
        actual = sis.readLine( buffer, 0, 1000);
        if (actual > 0) {
            for (int i = 0; i < actual; i++) {
                char b = (char) buffer[i];
                sb.append(b);
            }
            return sb.toString();
        }
        return null;
    }

    public byte[] getNext1000Bytes() throws Exception {
        actual = sis.readLine( buffer, 0, 1000);
        if (actual <= 0)
```

9

Listing 9.9   continued

```
            return null;
        byte[] data = new byte[actual];
        System.arraycopy(buffer, 0, data, 0, actual);
        return data;
    }

    public void finish() {
        try {
            sis.close();
        } catch (Exception exc) {
        }
    }
}
```

We will create another class, UploadFilesCommand, that parses the data using the ServletStream class we just created, extracts the encoded file, and stores the file in the user's personal directory. This class implements the Command interface that was used for developing the earlier command beans. It contains input properties as defined in Table 9.3.

Table 9.3   Properties of station.auction.personalization. command. UploadFilesCommand

Property	Type	Description
ServletRequest	javax.servlet ServletRequest	The request object containing the multipart form data and the attached file
directory	String	The directory in which the encoded files will be stored
errors	java.util.Hashtable	The errors obtained while executing the command

Implement a check() method that checks whether the request stream has a content type of "multipart/form-data" as shown in Listing 9.10. It also determines whether the uploaded file is larger than a permissible limit, to prevent malicious users from causing a possible "Denial of Service."

Denial of Service (DoS) is a form of attack on the Web server by hackers in which they try to overwhelm the server by sending spurious requests. Uploading many large files can easily tax the server.

Listing 9.10   UploadFilesCommand.java: Checking the Request for Validity

```java
public boolean check() throws Exception {
    if ( !(request.getContentType().startsWith("multipart/form-data")) ) {
      errors.put("contentType", "Form enctype should be multipart/form-data");
    }

    if ( request.getContentLength() > 50000) {
      errors.put("contentLength", "File is too large");
    }

    return errors.isEmpty();
}
```

For the input form present in the JSP described in Listing 9.8, the user had selected the file dj.jpg. The browser may send back the following data:

```
Content-type: multipart/form-data, boundary=ZGg4o23

-- ZGg4o23
Content-disposition: form-data; name="theFile"; filename="I:\etc\home\dj.jpg"
Content-Type: image/jpeg

...<contents of dj.jpg> ...
--ZGg4o23--
```

Implement the execute() method to do the following:

- Extract the boundary string from the line beginning with Content-type.
- For each form data part, beginning with the boundary string, check whether it contains the uploaded file. This is determined by the presence of the filename attribute in the Content-disposition line heading each part.
- If the part represents a file, extract the bytes from the stream until the boundary is encountered.
- Store the file in the specified directory.

The stream parsing is implemented in the execute(), getFileName(), and storeFile() methods, as shown in Listing 9.11.

Listing 9.11   UploadFilesCommand.java: Extracting the File from the Stream

```java
    protected String directory = null;
    protected ServletStream sst = null;
    protected ServletRequest request = null;
    protected String boundary = null;

public void setServletRequest(ServletRequest request) throws Exception {
    this.request = request;
    this.sst = new ServletStream(request);
}
```

Listing 9.11   continued

```java
public void execute() throws Exception {
    try {
        if (!check())
            return;
        boundary = sst.getNextLine();
        if (boundary.endsWith("\n")) {
            boundary = boundary.substring(0, boundary.length() - 2);
        }
        String contentDisposition = null;
        while ((contentDisposition = sst.getNextLine()) != null) {
            storeFile(contentDisposition);
        }
    } catch (Exception exc) {
    } finally {
        sst.finish();
    }
}

protected void storeFile(String contentDisposition) throws Exception {
    String fileName = null;
    String contentType = null;
    // check whether the form data is a file's content
    int index = contentDisposition.indexOf("filename");
    if (index == -1) {
        // It's a standard request parameter, does not contain a file
index = contentDisposition.indexOf("name");
        // You can extract the value and use it as required
        // As we aren't expecting a form we can skip
return;
    }
    // Get the file name from the content disposition string
    fileName = getFileName(contentDisposition.substring(index));

    // Get the content type. Not much we can do with it anyway
    String type = sst.getNextLine();
    contentType = type.substring((type.indexOf(' ') + 1));

    // Skip the next line
    sst.getNextLine();

    // Store the file in the given directory
    File aFile = new File(getDirectory(), fileName);
    FileOutputStream fos = new FileOutputStream(aFile);
    byte[] data = sst.getNext1000Bytes();
    while ( !getAsString(data).startsWith(boundary) ) {
        fos.write(data);
        data = sst.getNext1000Bytes();
    }

    fos.close();
}
```

```java
protected String getFileName(String latterHalf) {
    // Extract fileName stored within the quotes of the string
    // e.g. --> filename="I:\etc\home\dj.jpg"
    String fileName = latterHalf.substring(
                latterHalf.indexOf('"') + 1,
                latterHalf.lastIndexOf('"')
            );
    // Extract only the file name, minus the absolute path
    int slashIndex = fileName.lastIndexOf("\\");
    int backslashIndex = fileName.lastIndexOf("/");
    if (slashIndex != -1) {
        fileName = fileName.substring(slashIndex + 1);
    }
    if (backslashIndex != -1) {
        fileName = fileName.substring(backslashIndex + 1);
    }

    return fileName;
}

public String getAsString(byte[] data) {
    StringBuffer sb = new StringBuffer();
    for (int i = 0; i < data.length; i++) {
        char ch = (char) data[i];
        sb.append(ch);
    }
    return sb.toString();
}
```

As you might have noticed, this parsing technique is rather rustic and difficult to change. There are more sophisticated parsing techniques using tools such as IBM's Jikes Compiler, Sun's Java Compiler Compiler (JACC) and ANTLR that allow you to specify parsing rules and associated actions that are executed when text matching the rule is encountered in the input. These techniques are beyond the scope of this book. You can find a quick tutorial on such tools at www.antlr.org.

9

how too
prō nouns′ it

| JACC: *Jack* (as in Jack and the beanstalk) |
| ANTLR: Antler |

Developing the "Upload File" JSP

Create savefile.jsp, which executes the "Upload Files Command," using the JavaBean you just created. Before it does this, it checks whether the user has been authorized and whether the user's personal directory exists. After it executes the command, it forwards the request to list.jsp, which lists the files in the user's directory as shown in Listing 9.12. We will look at list.jsp in the next section.

Listing 9.12   savefile.jsp: Saving the File and Forwarding the Request to the List JSP

```
<%@ page import="java.io.*, station.auction.personalization.command.*"%>
<%! public final static String BASE_DIR =
        "i:/jakarta-tomcat/webapps/AuctionStation/users"; %>
<%@ include file="/jsp/auction/checklogin.jsp"%>
<%
    File userDir = new File(BASE_DIR, user_id);
    if (!userDir.exists())
        userDir.mkdir();

    UploadFilesCommand cmd = new UploadFilesCommand();
    cmd.setServletRequest(request);
    cmd.setDirectory(userDir.getAbsolutePath());
    cmd.execute();
%>
<jsp:forward page="list.jsp"/>
```

Managing Files in the Personal Space

After a user has uploaded files to her personal directory, you should allow her to browse her files and delete them as well.

Listing Files

In this section, we will list the user's files that were uploaded using the utility described earlier. We will continue to use the MVC design that we implemented in the previous chapter. The data flows between the different components are shown in Figure 9.9.

Developing the Model

First, you will need to develop the model, `FileInfo`, that contains information about a file in the directory listing. Table 9.4 lists the properties of the bean.

Table 9.4   Properties of `station.auction.personalization.FileInfo`

Property	Type	Description
name	String	The filename
length	String	The size in bytes of the file
lastModified	String	The date representing when the file was created or last modified
url	String	The URL of the file to be used in the listing

The properties of the bean are populated from a `java.io.File` instance within the constructor, as shown in Listing 9.13.

Figure 9.9

Data flows in the directory listing application

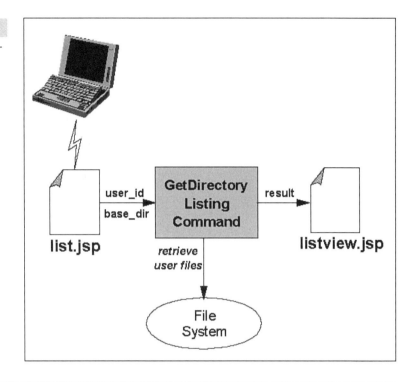

Listing 9.13   FileInfo.java: Populating the View Bean's Properties from a `java.io.File` Instance

```
public FileInfo(File afile) {
    setName(afile.getName());
    setLength(afile.length());
    setLastModified(afile.lastModified());
}

public void setLastModified(long modified) {
    this.modified = new Date(modified).toGMTString();
}
```

Developing the Controller

Create the command bean, GetDirectoryListingCommand, that retrieves all the files from the user's directory and returns an array of FileInfo objects. Table 9.5 lists the properties of the command bean.

9

Table 9.5 **Properties of** `station.auction.personalization.command.`
`GetDirectoryListingComm`

Property	Type	Description
user_id	String	The user ID of the user executing the command
base_dir	String	The absolute path for the root directory
result	Object	The result of the command that stores the array of FileInfo instances

Implement the `execute()` method to create the result array of `FileInfo` instances. It first checks whether the user directory exists, and if it doesn't, it creates the directory. It then iterates through all the files in the user directory and populates the result array of `FileInfo` instances from it as shown in Listing 9.14.

Listing 9.14 **GetDirectoryListingCommand.java: Creating the Array of** `FileInfo` **Instances**

```
File root = new File(getBase_dir());
    File adir = new File(root, getUser_id());
    // First time initialization
    if (!adir.exists()) {
        adir.mkdir();
    }

    String[] files = adir.list();
    result = new FileInfo[files.length];
    for (int i = 0; i < files.length; i++) {
        File afile = new File(adir, files[i]);
        result[i] = new FileInfo(afile);
        result[i].setUrl("/users/" + getUser_id() + "/" + afile.getName());
    }
}
```

Create the controller JSP, list.jsp, that executes the command to create the model and forward the request to the view as shown in Listing 9.15.

Listing 9.15 **list.jsp: Developing the Controller JSP for the Directory Listing Application**

```
<%@ page import="station.auction.personalization.FileInfo" %>
<%@ include file="/jsp/auction/checklogin.jsp"%>
<jsp:useBean id="cmd"
class="station.auction.personalization.command.GetDirectoryListingCommand"/>
<%
    cmd.setUser_id((String) session.getAttribute("user_id"));
    // Make sure you set the same directory as the one in the Upload command
    cmd.setBase_dir("i:/jakarta-tomcat/webapps/AuctionStation/users");
    cmd.execute();
    pageContext.setAttribute("content", (FileInfo[]) cmd.getResult(),
                             PageContext.REQUEST_SCOPE);
%>
<jsp:forward page="listview.jsp"/>
```

Developing the View

Finally, you need to develop the view that iterates through the result array to create the directory listing. You can include the `openWindow` JavaScript function that you created earlier to launch URLs in a new window. You will also add a function, `goUrl`, that sets the document in the current window as the upload page.

```
<script language="JavaScript">
<!--
    function openWindow(url) {
        width = 600;
        height = 400;
        Win = open(url, 'files',
            'toolbar=0,location=0,directories=0,status=0,menubar=0,' +
            'resizable=1,width=' + width + ',height=' + height +
            ',scrollbars=yes');
        Win.focus();
    }

    function goUrl() {
        this.window.location ="/jsp/personal/upload.jsp";
    }

-->
</script>
```

We will display alternating rows of files in the listing with different background colors to enhance readability. To do that, we will use CSS and set the class attribute of the rows with alternating class names (`row1`, `row2`). We will also need to specify the rules for the two classes in an embedded CSS style tag.

```
<style type="text/css">
   .header { background: gray; color: white; font-weight: bold;
➥text-align: left}
   .row1 {background: silver; font-size: smaller;}
   .row2 {background: white; font-size: smaller;}
</style>
```

You can provide the directory listing by iterating through the array of `FileInfo` instances and format the output using tables as shown in Listing 9.16. Figure 9.10 displays the directory listing for a user after the file dj.jpg has been uploaded.

Listing 9.16   listview.jsp: Developing the View for the Directory Listing Application

```
<%@ page import="java.io.*, java.util.Date" %>
<jsp:useBean id="content" class="station.auction.personalization.FileInfo[]"
             scope="request"/>
<html>
<head>
   <!-- The JavaScript functions and the style tag go in here -->
</head>
<body>
```

Listing 9.16   continued

```
<table width="100%">

<tr class="header">
<td> </td>
<td>Name</td>
<td>Size</td>
<td>Last Modified</td>
</tr>

<%
    int row = 2;
    int length = content.length;
    for (int i = 0; i < length; i++) {
        row = (row == 1)? 2: 1;
%>
        <tr class="row<%= row%>">
          <a href="javascript:openWindow('<%= content[i].getUrl()%>')">
            <%= content[i].getName()%></a></td>
           <td><%= content[i].getLength()%></td>
           <td><%= content[i].getLastModified()%></td>
        <tr>

<%
    }
%>

</table>
</html>
```

Figure 9.10

Directory listing for a user's personal directory

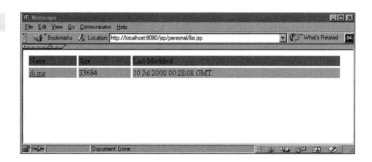

Figure 9.11 shows the directory listing after the image N6150.jpg has been uploaded. Clicking on the file's hyperlink causes a new window to be launched displaying the selected file.

Figure 9.11

Displaying a file from the directory listing

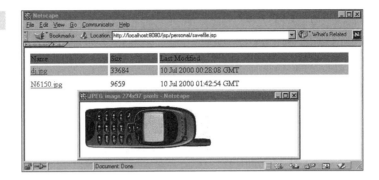

Deleting Files

In this section, we will develop a submodule that allows users to delete files from their personal directory. To do this, we will enhance list.jsp to allow users to select their files and invoke the delete action using a submit button.

One possible way to allow users to select more than a single file is by using input check box fields for each file in the listing. Modify the JSP code in Listing 9.16 to include a form embedding the table, an extra column for the check boxes, and submit buttons for deleting and uploading files, as shown in Listing 9.17. Figure 9.12 shows the directory listing with the check boxes for selecting files.

Listing 9.17   listview.jsp: Modifying the View to Allow the User to Select Files for Deletion

```
...
<form action="/jsp/personal/filemanager.jsp">

<table width="100%">

<tr class="header">
<td> </td>
<td>Name</td>
<td>Size</td>
<td>Last Modified</td>
</tr>

<%
    int row = 2;
    int length = content.length;
    for (int i = 0; i < length; i++) {
        row = (row == 1)? 2: 1;
%>
        <tr class="row<%= row%>">
            <td><input name="deletions" type="checkbox"
                    value="<%= content[i].getName()%>"></td>
            <td>
```

Listing 9.17   continued

```
                <a href="javascript:openWindow('<%= content[i].getUrl()%>')">
                    <%= content[i].getName()%>
                </a></td>
                <td><%= content[i].getLength()%></td>
                <td><%= content[i].getLastModified()%></td>
            <tr>

    <%
        }
    %>

    </table>
    <input type="submit" name="actionb" value="Delete Selected Files">
    <input type="button" name="actionb" value="Upload File"
        onClick="javascript:goUrl()">
    </form>
    </table>
    </body></html>
```

Figure 9.12

Providing check boxes to select multiple files for deletion

Create filemanager.jsp, which deletes the selected files from the user directory. Create a scriptlet that identifies the submit button used for sending the form data in listview.jsp. If the button is the delete button, determine the selected files from the "deletions" input field. Obtain a handle on the selected files in the user directories using the java.io.File class, and delete them using the delete() method as shown in Listing 9.18. At the end of the operation, you can forward the request to list.jsp to display the latest directory listing.

 Note You should be very cautious in handling filenames received from the user because the form data can easily be spoofed. If the user specified ".." in the filename, a file in the parent directory could be deleted. You can also provide checks to determine whether the specified file exists before you attempt to delete it.

Listing 9.18   filemanager.jsp: Deleting the Selected Files

```jsp
<%@page import="java.io.File"%>
<%@ include file="/jsp/auction/checklogin.jsp"%>
<%! public final static String BASE_DIR =
       "i:/jakarta-tomcat/webapps/AuctionStation/users"; %>
<%! protected String truncate(String original) {
       if (original.length() > 15) {
           original = original.substring(0, 13) + "..";
       }
       return original;
   }
%>
<%
  String button = request.getParameter("actionb");
  if (button.equalsIgnoreCase("Delete Selected Files")) {

       String[] files = request.getParameterValues("deletions");
       if (files != null) {
           File root = new File(BASE_DIR);
           File userroot = new File(root, user_id);
           for (int i = 0; i < files.length; i++) {
               // Check for illegal data
               if (files[i].indexOf("..") != -1) {
                   continue;
               }
               File afile = new File(userroot, files[i]);
               afile.delete();
           }
       }
   }
%>
<jsp:forward page="/jsp/personal/list.jsp"/>
```

Currently, filemanager.jsp handles only deletions. You can enhance this JSP to execute operations provided by a file management utility—for example:

- Rename files
- Create directories
- Move files
- Copy files

These tasks are left as an exercise for you!

Developing MyAuctions, MyBids, and MySpace

One of the primary objectives of personalization is to enable the users to access their information easily. For AuctionStation, the portions relevant to the users may include the items they bid on (MyBids), the items they placed for listing

(MyAuctions), and the files in their personal directory (MySpace). In this section, we will create a JSP, loggedinframe.jsp, that contains this information.

Identifying the User

Add an authorization routine to the JSP to determine the user ID of the person logged in. You can use custom tags for database queries to display the first and last name of the user. This information is retrieved from the Users table using the db:query tag and displayed using the db:foreach tag, as shown in Listing 9.19.

Listing 9.19   loggedinframe.jsp: Displaying User Information

```
<style type="text/css">
    .header { background: silver; font-weight: bold;}
    .name { font-size:smaller; font-weight:bold; text-align:center}
</style>
<base target="mainview">
<%@ taglib uri="jsp/db-taglib.tld" prefix="db" %>
<%@ include file="/jsp/auction/checklogin.jsp"%>

<db:connection id="conn" url="jdbc:db2:auction"
               driver="COM.ibm.db2.jdbc.app.DB2Driver">
</db:connection>
<%-- ----------------------- Who am I --------------------- --%>
<db:query id="whoamiStmt" connection="conn">
        SELECT f_name, l_name
        FROM Users WHERE user_id = '<%= user_id%>'
</db:query>
<p class="name">
<db:foreach query="whoamiStmt">
  <%= whoamiStmt.getString(1)%>
  <%= whoamiStmt.getString(2)%>
</db:foreach>
</p>
```

Displaying MyItems

To display MyItems, you can retrieve rows from the Items table that have a user_id of the user logged in. You can display the name of the item in the page and hyperlink the item to item.jsp to allow the user to access the complete details about the item, as shown in Listing 9.20. The item names are truncated to 15 characters using the truncate method in Listing 9.18.

Listing 9.20   loggedinframe.jsp: Displaying MyItems

```
<%-- ----------------------- Get My Items --------------------- --%>
<table border="1" width="100%">
<tr class="header">
<td>My Auctions</td>
</tr>
```

```
<db:query id="myItemsStmt" connection="conn">
        SELECT prod_id, prod_name
        FROM Product WHERE user_id = '<%= user_id%>'
        ORDER BY created DESC
</db:query>

<db:foreach query="myItemsStmt">
  <tr><td>
  <a href="/jsp/auction/product.jsp?prod_id=<%= myItemsStmt.getString(1)%>">
  <%= truncate(myItemsStmt.getString(2))%>
  </a></td></tr>
</db:foreach>
```

Displaying MyBids

Similarly, you can display MyBids in the page by retrieving rows from the Bid table and hyperlinking the bid to the associated item, as shown in Listing 9.21.

Listing 9.21   loggedinframe.jsp: Displaying MyBids

```
<%-- --------------------- Get My Bids---------------------- --%>
<tr class="header">
<td>My Bids</td>
</tr>

<db:query id="myBidsStmt" connection="conn">
        SELECT p.prod_id, p.prod_name
        FROM Product p, Bid b
        WHERE b.user_id = '<%= user_id%>'
        AND b.prod_id = p.prod_id
        ORDER BY b.created DESC
</db:query>

<db:foreach query="myBidsStmt">
  <tr><td>
  <a href="/jsp/auction/product.jsp?prod_id=<%= myBidsStmt.getString(1)%>">
  <%= truncate(myBidsStmt.getString(2))%></a></td></tr>
</db:foreach>
```

Displaying MySpace

Finally, you can provide a hyperlink to the personal directory listing of the user for accessing MySpace, as shown in Listing 9.22. Figure 9.13 shows the output of loggedinframe.jsp for user msahu.

Listing 9.22   loggedinframe.jsp: Displaying MySpace

```
<%-- ---------------------- Get My Space -------------------- --%>
<tr class="header">
<td>
<a href="/jsp/personal/list.jsp">My Space</a></td>
```

Listing 9.22   continued

```
</tr>
</table>
</body>
</html>
```

Figure 9.13

Personalized information for user msahu

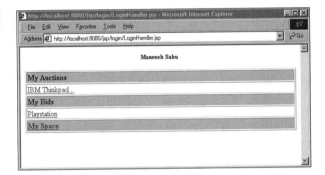

Connecting the Pieces

In this section, we will piece together the different components within the Auction module to build a sophisticated interface with navigational capabilities and personalized information. We will also create a site-wide look that contains a banner, sidebar, main view, and footer as shown in Figure 9.14.

Figure 9.14

Site-wide page style for AuctionStation

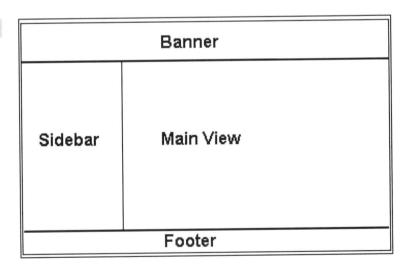

This section looks at two techniques for doing this:

- Using HTML frames
- Creating a JSP "template"

Using HTML Frames

HTML frames are an integral part of the HTML specification supported by most browsers. Using HTML frames, the browser window can be divided into a set of multiple, independently scrollable frames on a single screen, each with its own distinct URL. Each frame in the page is identified using a `frame` tag that refers to a page: HTML or JSP as specified in its `src` attribute. Multiple frames are integrated into a page using a `frameset` tag. A *frameset* specifies the layout of the frames embedded within it. It can lay them out either vertically or horizontally. A `rows` attribute in the `frameset` tag specifies the vertical layout of the embedded frames, and a `cols` attribute specifies the horizontal layout. Both attributes specify the position and height/width of each frame directly embedded in it. The height/width can be specified as follows:

- In absolute terms: the pixels size, such as 110 (pixels)
- As the percentage of the window it occupies, such as 50%
- As the remaining portion of the window: *

A simple frameset that lays out two frames, frame1.html and frame2.html, vertically is shown in Listing 9.23. You will need to create two HTML pages with the same names specified in the `src` of the frame tags. The output of the pages is displayed in Figure 9.15. You can lay them out horizontally by renaming `rows` to `cols` in the `frameset` tag. You can obtain a combination of the two layouts by nesting framesets.

Listing 9.23   frameset.html: Frameset for Displaying Frames Stacked Vertically

```
<frameset rows="*, *">
    <frame src="frame1.html">
    <frame src="frame2.html">
</frameset>
```

 Note   If you specify the height/width as * for more than one frame in the frameset, the height/width for each frame is computed as the remaining portion of the window's size divided by the number of frames marked with a height/width: *.

9

Figure 9.15

Frameset displaying two pages stacked vertically

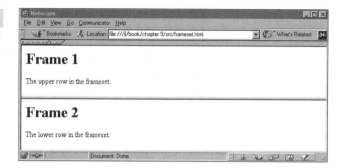

Creating Frames

You can easily accomplish the style in Figure 9.14 by creating a `frame` for each element—header, sidebar, main view, and footer—and integrating them into a page using `frameset` tags.

- The header is an HTML page that displays the banner image.

  ```
  <img src="/jsp/banner.gif">
  ```

- The sidebar is determined by the login status of the user. If the user has logged on, the personal page loggedinframe.jsp containing MyAuctions, MyBids, and MySpace is displayed. If not, notloggedinframe.jsp, containing a login form and the current month's calendar, is displayed, the source of which is as follows:

  ```
  <base target="_top">
  <table background="silver">
      <tr>
          <td><%@ include file="/jsp/login/login.jsp"%></td>
      </tr>
      <tr>
          <td><%@ include file="/jsp/calendar/smallmonth.jsp"%></td>
      </tr>
  </table>
  ```

- The main view displays the components we developed so far. The default page is the catalog listing, catalog.jsp, and is updated as the user navigates through the links.

- The footer provides hyperlinks to the main sections of the site.

  ```
  <base target="mainview">
  [<a href="/jsp/calendar/2.1/input.jsp">Calendar</a>] 
  [<a href="/jsp/auction/catalog.jsp">Auctions</a>] 
  [<a href="/jsp/registration/Step1.jsp">Register</a>] 
  [<a href="about.html">About Us</a>]
  <br><font size=-2>Auction Station is an imaginary Web Application,
              so don't go scouting the web for it</font>
  ```

The source of the page nesting these frames is shown in Listing 9.24. Figures 9.16 and 9.17 show the start pages when the user hasn't logged in and when the user msahu logs in.

Listing 9.24   frames.jsp: The Frame for Implementing the Site-Wide Style

```
<html>
<head><title>Auction Station</title>
</head>
<%
    String leftframeURL = "/jsp/personal/notloggedinframe.jsp";
    if (((String) session.getAttribute("user_id")) != null) {
        leftframeURL = "/jsp/personal/loggedinframe.jsp";
    }
%>
<frameset rows="110,*,10%" border="0" frameborder="0" framespacing="0">
<frame src="/jsp/header.jsp" name="banner">
        <frameset cols="20%,*" border="0" frameborder="0" framespacing="0">
                <frame src="<%= leftframeURL%>" name="sidebar">
                <frame src="/jsp/auction/catalog.jsp" name="mainview">
        </frameset>
    <frame src="/jsp/footer.jsp" name="footer">
    <noframes>
        <body>You require frames to view this page</body>
    </noframes>
</frameset>
</html>
```

Figure 9.16

The start page containing the different frames when the user hasn't performed a login

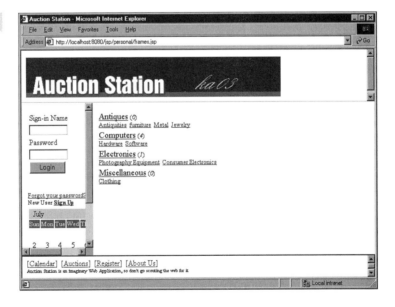

9

Figure 9.17

The start page when the user msahu logs in

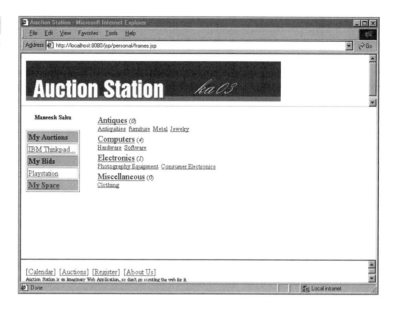

Targeting Frames

You can target hyperlinks to a named frame in the page. You can do this by either including a base tag in your HTML/JSP page or specifying the target frame. When the user clicks any link in the page, the contents are displayed in the targeted frame. In footer.jsp and loggedinframe.jsp, the target frame specified in the base tag is set to "mainview".

```
<base target="mainview">
```

There are also special targets such as "_top", which causes the window containing the frame to display the page specified in the hyperlink, and "_new", which causes a new window displaying the hyperlink page to be opened.

You can override the base targets for specific links by specifying a target attribute in them.

```
<a href="newcontent.html" target="_new">New</a>
```

Figure 9.18 shows the output when the user clicks the "Playstation" item in the sidebar frame.

Figure 9.18

Targeting links in the sidebar to the main view

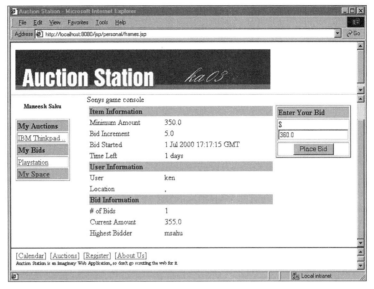

Using JSP "Templates"

Using frames, you can easily produce a site style for all your pages. They are efficient because only the modified frames are updated. For the page we developed earlier, only the "mainview" frame is refreshed to display the contents. In this section, we will develop a site-wide look without using frames.

The template mechanism displays pages by including content in different portions of the page and formatting them using tables. The style implemented using frames can be obtained by formatting the output of the different pages (frames) using tables. You can create an easily constructed JSP, noframes.jsp, that displays content without frames by including the different pages: header, footer, sidebar, and main view.

Because the header and footer elements are static, they are included at translation time using the page include directive. The sidebar displays either the login form or the personalized information based on the user login. The main view is computed from a request parameter, `href`, and in the absence of this parameter, displays the catalog listing. These two portions are displayed using the JSP include tags that include the output of the pages at runtime. Listing 9.25 displays the source for the noframes.jsp. Figures 9.19 and 9.20 display the output of the page based on the user login status.

9

Listing 9.25 noframes.jsp: The "Template" Including the Different Pages

```jsp
<html>
<head>
<%
    Object data = session.getAttribute("user_id");
    String sideURL = null;
    if (data != null)
        sideURL = "/jsp/personal/loggedinframe.jsp";
    else
        sideURL = "/jsp/personal/notloggedinframe.jsp";
    String mainURL = request.getParameter("href");
    if (mainURL == null || mainURL.trim().length() == 0)
        mainURL = "/jsp/auction/catalog.jsp";
    String title = request.getParameter("title");
    if (title == null)
        title = "";
%>
<title>AuctionStation: <%= title%></title>
</head>
<body>
<%@ include file="/jsp/header.jsp"%>
<table cellpadding="20">
<tr>
<td width="120" valign="top">
<jsp:include page="<%= sideURL%>" flush="true"/>
</td>
<td valign="top">
<jsp:include page="<%= mainURL%>" flush="true"/>
</td>
</tr>
</table>
<p>
<%@ include file="/jsp/footer.jsp"%>
</body>
</html>
```

To display a different page, you need to provide an href parameter containing its URL and append it to the location of noframes.jsp. The monthly calendar can be obtained by suffixing href=/jsp/calendar/2.1/month.jsp to /jsp/personal/noframes.jsp. The output is as shown in Figure 9.21.

Figure 9.19

The start page when the user hasn't performed a login

Figure 9.20

The start page when the user msahu logs in

Figure 9.21

Displaying the calendar using the template

 Note

When you are including content using the JSP include tags, special consideration must be given for chained JSPs: JSPs that develop content by forwarding requests to another, such as catalog.jsp. Such JSPs cannot be displayed because the original JSP's output stream has already been closed and there is no way that the template JSP including it can get a handle to its contents. To allow the output to be included, you will need to replace the JSP forward tags with include tags. You can easily substitute a forward tag, such as the following one in catalog.jsp

```
<jsp:forward page="/jsp/auction/itemsview.jsp"/>
```

with the following include tag:

```
<jsp:include page="/jsp/auction/itemsview.jsp" flush="true"/>
```

Summary

In this chapter, you performed the following tasks:

- Used CSS to style the content
- Used cookies to store information
- Uploaded files to the server
- Developed a Web-based file manager
- Used frames and JSP templates to piece the site's components together

In the next chapter, we will look at developing custom views using applets.

Developing Custom Views Using Java Applets

So far in this book, we have used HTML elements to develop our Web interfaces. The use of HTML elements allows any HTML browser to view our site. The problem with plain HTML is the limited set of controls and views that you can use for your Web pages. For example, there are no elements to display a hierarchy, like a tree view. The user has to traverse links and send additional requests to the server, as in the item catalog module when a user wants to browse all the categories listed in AuctionStation.

What You Are Going To Do

In this chapter, you will build a Java applet that displays AuctionStation's category hierarchy in a neat and intuitive tree view. Using this plug-in, you will also be able to select a particular category and view its properties.

Introducing Java Plug-Ins

When Java first came on the scene five years ago, it was primarily used for developing client-side applets. Applets allow you to develop animations and user interfaces using Java's standard, cross-platform package libraries. The first wave of Java brought along with it clever and glossy applets such as Nervous Text and image animation views that added sparkle to the Web landscape.

As the technology matured, several problems with using applets became apparent:

- Browsers were not up-to-date in their support of the current Java versions. Java has seen four major releases in its five years of existence starting with version 1.0, followed by 1.1, 1.2 (Java 2), and the latest, 1.3. Both the major browsers, Netscape and Internet Explorer (IE), were sluggish in providing support for the latest Java versions. Developers therefore had to tone down their enthusiasm in using the new features of the latest versions of Java in favor of the usage of their applets by the current browsers.

- Browsers like Microsoft's IE did not provide support for all the core packages of Java. IE in fact still doesn't support the JavaBeans and Remote Method Invocation packages.

- Because of the lack of browser support for the latest Java versions, browsers had to download the additional Java packages and classes not available in their runtime. This resulted in an increase in run and load times for the applet along with increased bandwidth usage.

As a result, the use of applets in Internet interfaces diminished over time. Applets, however, continued to flourish in intranet applications where bandwidth and browser compliance was not an issue. Information System managers could issue a decree forcing all employees to update their browsers or install fixpacks to view the Web interfaces built using applets.

Sun released the Java plug-in technology to address the noncompliance issues of the browsers. It provided a Java runtime environment for browsers to load and run applets. Users no longer had to download and install the latest version of the browser to keep in sync with the latest Java version. They only had to install the Java plug-in control that would load and execute the applets. The plug-in control provided all the core Java packages along with extension libraries such as the Java Foundation Classes. These libraries provide all you need to develop a sophisticated user interface.

Anatomy of an Applet

An applet is a Java application that can be embedded in an HTML page for viewing in a Web browser. It is a Java class that extends from `java.applet.Applet`. The `Applet` class defines a set of methods that you can override for use in the Web browser. These methods include

- `init()`—This method is invoked when the applet is loaded into the Web browser. It can be used like a constructor to initialize the applet. You can extract parameters passed to the applet within this method to perform your initializations.

- **destroy()**— This method is invoked when the applet is unloaded from memory. You can free any allocated resources with this method.

The applet is included in an HTML page using either the APPLET or OBJECT/EMBED tags. If you use the former tag, the applet is executed in the runtime environment provided by the browser. If you use the OBJECT/EMBED tag, the applet instance is loaded and run by the Java plug-in control. We will look in detail at the tags later on in the chapter.

Using the Java Plug-In Control

You must install the Java plug-in control to execute applets specified using OBJECT/EMBED tags. You can download a Java plug-in from the Sun site at http://java.sun.com/products/plugin/. The plug-in is also shipped along with the Java 2 Runtime Environment, so you don't have to install it separately if you have installed the runtime already.

After you install the plug-in on your system, a menu shortcut for the control panel is placed in the system menu. You can customize the plug-in settings by launching the Java Plug-in Control Panel. The Panel provides properties such as proxy settings that you can alter to suit your requirements. Most importantly, you must check the Enable Java Plug-in on the Basic tab to activate the plug-in in your Web browsers, as shown in Figure 10.1.

Figure 10.1

Enabling the Java plug-in control for Web browsers

10

Your First Applet

We will create an applet that displays the text "Auction Station" on a red background. You can achieve the same functionality using HTML elements. This example, however, is just to help you get jump-started with developing applets if you aren't already acquainted with them. If you have created applets before, you can skip to the section titled "Developing a Category Hierarchy View Applet."

Create a class, FirstApplet, that extends from the java.applet.Applet class. An applet is a visual element displayed in the browser. You can provide a red background by passing the java.awt.Color constant for red in the setBackground method. To display the text message, you can use a visual component, java.awt.Label. You can set the string "AuctionStation" as the constructor parameter while creating the Label instance. You also need to add the label within the applet to display it in the browser, as shown in Listing 10.1.

Listing 10.1 FirstApplet.java: Developing an Applet to Display the Text "AuctionStation" on a Red Background

```java
import java.applet.Applet;
import java.awt.Color;
import java.awt.FlowLayout;
import java.awt.Label;

public class FirstApplet extends Applet {

public void init() {
    setBackground(Color.red);
    setLayout(new FlowLayout());
    add(new Label("AuctionStation"));
}

}
```

Compile the applet to generate FirstApplet.class. Create a directory, applet, in the <jakarta-tomcat>/webapps/AuctionStation/jsp/admin directory and copy the class file into this directory.

Create a JSP file, firstapplet.jsp in the admin directory, that embeds the applet. Provide the jsp:plugin tag to embed the applet. Specify the applet class name using the code attribute and the directory containing the class file using the codebase attribute. Specify the height and width of the visible area for the applet as well as the Java Runtime Environment (JRE) version, 1.2, to be used for executing the applet, as shown in Listing 10.2.

Listing 10.2 firstapplet.jsp: Embedding FirstApplet in the JSP

```
<jsp:plugin type="applet"
            code="FirstApplet.class"
            codebase="/jsp/admin/applet"
            name="first"
            height="40"
            width="100"
            jreversion="1.2">
    <jsp:fallback>
        Plugin tag OBJECT or EMBED not supported by browser.
    </jsp:fallback>
</jsp:plugin>
```

Note

You should provide a jsp:fallback tag to indicate to users with browsers that do not support OBJECT/EMBED tags about the lack of support for plug-ins. This will encourage them to update their browsers to more contemporary ones.

Save the JSP and launch a browser to view the applet. If a plug-in was configured with the browser, you would obtain an output as shown in Figure 10.2.

Figure 10.2

Your first applet viewed in Netscape Navigator

If you were using a really primitive browser, such as Internet Explorer version 2.0, you would end up with an output as shown in Figure 10.3.

Figure 10.3

Viewing the plug-in in a primitive browser

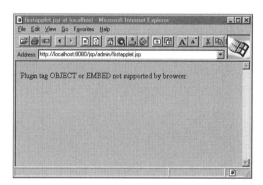

Passing Parameters to the Applet

In your first applet the label and color information has been hard-coded in the class. You might be interested in changing this information without having to recompile the applet. You can do this by specifying parameters in the embedding HTML/JSP document and extracting these parameters using the getParameter method within the Applet class.

You can pass parameters using the jsp:param tag in the JSP, secondapplet.jsp. Specify as many jsp:param tags as the parameters you want to pass, as shown in Listing 10.3.

10

Listing 10.3   secondapplet.jsp: Passing Parameters to the Applet

```
<jsp:plugin type="applet"
            code="ParameterApplet.class"
            codebase="/jsp/admin/applet"
            name="first"
            height="40"
            width="100"
            jreversion="1.2">

    <jsp:params>
        <jsp:param name="text" value="Auction"/>
        <jsp:param name="color" value="ffff00"/>
    </jsp:params>

    <jsp:fallback>
        Plugin tag OBJECT or EMBED not supported by browser.
    </jsp:fallback>
</jsp:plugin>
```

You can create another applet, ParameterApplet.java, that extracts the parameters in the init() method, as shown in Listing 10.4.

Listing 10.4   ParameterApplet.java: Using the Text and Color Parameters to Create the Text Label

```
import java.applet.Applet;
import java.awt.Color;
import java.awt.FlowLayout;
import java.awt.Label;

public class ParameterApplet extends Applet {

public void init() {
    String text = getParameter("text");
    if (text == null || text.trim().length() == 0)
        text = "AuctionStation";

    String colorParam = getParameter("color");
    Color color = null;
    if (colorParam == null || colorParam.trim().length() != 6) {
        color = Color.red;
    } else {
        int red = Integer.parseInt(colorParam.substring(0, 2), 16);
        int green = Integer.parseInt(colorParam.substring(2, 4), 16);
        int blue = Integer.parseInt(colorParam.substring(4), 16);

        color = new Color(red, green, blue);
    }

    setBackground(color);
    setLayout(new FlowLayout(FlowLayout.CENTER));
```

```
        add(new Label(text));
    }

}
```

Compile the applet and copy the class file to the applet directory as you did for
FirstApplet. The JSP's output will look like that in Figure 10.4 if you provided yellow as the background color (color="ffff00") and "Auction" as the text label.

Figure 10.4

*The Parameter applet
viewed in Netscape
Navigator*

Other Significant Applet Methods

An applet provides some methods that you can use in your class, as shown in
Table 10.1.

Table 10.1   Significant Methods of the `java.applet.Applet` Class

Method	Description
getImage()	Downloads an image and creates an in-memory object, Image, representing it.
getAudioClip()	Downloads an audio clip and creates an in-memory object, AudioClip.
getCodeBase()	Returns the URL from which the applet class is loaded.
getDocumentBase()	Returns the URL of the HTML page embedding the applet.
showStatus()	Displays a message in the status area of the Web browser.
getAppletContext()	Returns an object, AppletContext, that is useful for interacting with the browser. It contains methods such as showDocument() to display content in the browser windows.

10

Applet Restrictions

There are many restrictions with using applets that you must keep in mind while
developing Web interfaces.

Applets operate under a strict security model when they execute in a browser. This is
done to prevent users from getting affected by malicious applets on the net. By
default, every applet is an untrusted applet and cannot perform any of the following
operations:

- Access the local file system of the browser it is executing in
- Open network connections with a host apart from the one it originated from
- Access the system clipboard and system properties and send print jobs
- Manipulate the security properties on the system it is executing in
- Run native code

Applets have to be explicitly marked as trusted to operate without these restrictions. You need to digitally *sign* the applets to do this.

Developing a Category Hierarchy View Applet

We will now develop a tree view for viewing all the categories in the Web site. These categories are stored within the database, and you can reuse the GetCategoryHierarchyCommand to retrieve all the Category instances.

There are problems, however, with using the command bean or even a JDBC statement within an applet. An applet is executed on the client's machine, and the URL used for making the JDBC connection within the command bean, jdbc:odbc: AUCTION or jdbc:db2:AUCTION, may not be valid. The reason for this could be either that there is no jdbc:odbc:AUCTION connection configured in the ODBC user data source or the database server is not visible from the machine.

There are several approaches to providing the applet with the category information. Some techniques for passing such information are

- Computing the information within the JSP embedding the applet and passing the data in parameters. In this case the data is hierarchical, unlike the simple string information that we used for setting the label and color in ParameterApplet. You could create an XML structure for the category hierarchies and pass the XML string as a parameter to the applet. The problem with this approach is the additional steps involved in the creation of the XML structure within the JSP and parsing of the XML document to obtain the hierarchy.
- You can serialize or flatten the object hierarchy as a sequence of bytes and return this string as the output of a JSP. Within the JSP you can access this JSP, obtain the bytes, and deserialize the stream to construct the hierarchy in the applet again.

Serialization is a much more elegant mechanism to transmit such information. All it requires is that the objects being serialized/deserialized implement the java.io.Serializable interface. The data flows for displaying the categories are shown in Figure 10.5. The flow begins when the user loads the JSP containing the applet in the browser. After the applet is loaded, it requests information from the JSP by specifying its URL. The JSP then constructs the hierarchy of category instances, serializes the hierarchy, and sends this stream of bytes in the response. After the applet receives the response from the JSP, it deserializes the stream to construct the hierarchy within the applet as well. It then wraps the hierarchy with view-based objects to display them.

Figure 10.5

Data flows for the category view

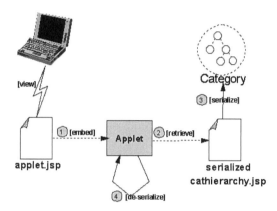

Returning the Serialized Category Hierarchy by a JSP

We will now create a JSP, serializedcathierarchy.jsp, that serializes the root `Category` of the hierarchy and sends it with the response. We will reuse the `GetCategoryHierarchyCommand` bean that returns a hierarchy of `Category` instances. You will need to specify an extremely large depth, say 10 for the level, to safely assume that the entire hierarchy will be returned. The value of the `cat_id` property for the bean is the `cat_id` of the root category, `"0"`. You can use a `jsp:useBean` tag to create the bean instance, as shown in Listing 10.5.

Listing 10.5   Serializedcathierarchy.jsp: Using the `GetCategoryHierarchyCommand` to Return the Entire Category Hierarchy

```
<%@ page import="station.auction.catalog.Category, java.io.*"
        contentType="java-serialized/Catalog"%>

<jsp:useBean id="cmd"
 class="station.auction.catalog.command.GetCategoryHierarchyCommand">
    <jsp:setProperty name="cmd" property="cat_id" value="0"/>
    <jsp:setProperty name="cmd" property="level" value="10"/>
</jsp:useBean>
```

To serialize the `Category` instance returned by the command, you have to use a set of classes that are defined in the `java.io` package: `OutputStream` and `ObjectOutputStream`. `OutputStream` is an abstract class that defines methods to write

10

bytes. ObjectOutputStream is a subclass used to write objects instead of dealing with bytes. It internally translates objects into bytes and is a critical component of the Java serialization mechanism.

To serialize the hierarchy, you have to encapsulate the response instance variable's OutputStream within an ObjectOutputStream instance. You can write the root to the stream by passing the root Category instance as a parameter to the writeObject method of the ObjectOutputStream instance, as shown in Listing 10.6. The writeObject method recursively serializes the entire hierarchy and writes it into the stream.

 Note

The root Category instance along with its hierarchy can be serialized because it implements the java.io.Serializable interface. If the object did not implement this interface, the writeObject method of ObjectOutputStream would throw a NotSerializableException.

Listing 10.6   Serializedcathierarchy.jsp: Sending the Serialized Root Object in the Response

```
<%
    cmd.execute();
    Category root = (Category) cmd.getResult();

    // send the serialized root across in the response's OutputStream
    ObjectOutputStream oos =
        new ObjectOutputStream(response.getOutputStream());

    oos.writeObject(root);
    oos.close();
%>
```

We have specified the contentType of the response as java-serialized/Catalog, a custom MIME type name that doesn't clash with any of the standard MIME types. This implies that if a user attempts to view the content generated by the JSP, the browser will display an Unknown File Type dialog instead of printing the serialized object in the browser, as shown in Figure 10.6.

Developing the CategoryViewApplet

Create an applet, CategoryViewApplet, that contains a tree view displaying the different categories as tree nodes. You can use the javax.swing.JTree component available in the Java Foundation Classes for the tree view. This component operates with the Model-View-Controller principle. It requires a TreeModel containing TreeNodes as display data.

Figure 10.6

The Unknown File Type dialog displayed when the user attempts to view the content generated by serialized-cathierarchy.jsp

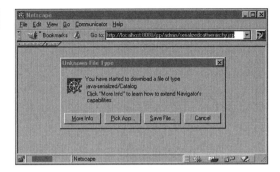

Developing a Model for the Tree View

Our `Category` hierarchy cannot be used directly by the `TreeModel`. We will need to wrap the `Category` instance in a `TreeNode` class, `CategoryTreeNode`. The `CategoryTreeNode` extends a `Swing` class, `javax.swing.tree.DefaultMutableTreeNode`, a default implementation for the `TreeNode` interface provided by JFC. The source for `CategoryTreeNode` is shown in Listing 10.7.

Listing 10.7 CategoryTreeNode.java: Wrapping the Category Instance with the `TreeNode` Interface

```java
package station.auction.applet;

import station.auction.catalog.Category;
import javax.swing.tree.DefaultMutableTreeNode;

public class CategoryTreeNode extends DefaultMutableTreeNode {
    protected Category theCategory = null;

    public CategoryTreeNode(Category aCategory) {
        theCategory = aCategory;
    }

    public Category getCategory() {
        return theCategory;
    }

    public String getCat_id() {
        return theCategory.getCat_id();
    }

    public String toString() {
        return theCategory.getName();
    }
}
```

10

The value returned in the public toString() method is used as the label for the node in the tree view. You can define additional public methods , getCategory() and getCat_id(), to return category information about the instance the node is encapsulating.

Deserializing the Category Hierarchy to Create the Tree Model

To create the tree view for the categories, you need to obtain the hierarchy of categories from the serialized object returned by serializedcathierarchy.jsp.

For the deserialization process, you need to obtain an InputStream for the URL of serializedcathierarchy.jsp and encapsulate the stream in a java.io.ObjectInputStream instance. This is almost the reverse of the process we applied in serializing the category hierarchy.

You need to create a java.net.URL instance using the URL string of the JSP and obtain the InputStream using the openStream method. The URL of the JSP is passed as a parameter to the applet by the embedding JSP.

After you obtain the root Category, you need to create the hierarchy of tree nodes that can be used to create the DefaultTreeModel instance that acts as the model for JTree. This is done in the createTree method shown in Listing 10.8 .

Listing 10.8 *CategoryViewApplet.*java—createTree(): Creating the JTree View from the Serialized Category Hierarchy Obtained from serializedcathierarchy.jsp

```
protected void createTree() {
    try {
        // Open an InputStream for the serialized file
        java.net.URL url = new java.net.URL(location);

        // Deserialize the Category hierarchy stored in the file specified
        // by the URL -> param
        java.io.ObjectInputStream ois =
            new java.io.ObjectInputStream(url.openStream());
        Category rootCat = (Category) ois.readObject();

        CategoryTreeNode root = createSubTree(rootCat);
        tree = new JTree(new DefaultTreeModel(root));
    } catch (Exception exc) {
        exc.printStackTrace();
        tree = new JTree();
    }
}
```

The TreeModel is generated by recursively creating a CategoryTreeNode for each Category node in the hierarchy, as shown in Listing 10.9.

Listing 10.9 *CategoryViewApplet*.java—`createSubTree()`: Recursively Creating the Tree Node Hierarchy

```
protected CategoryTreeNode createSubTree(Category cat) {
    CategoryTreeNode treeNode = new CategoryTreeNode(cat);
    for (int i = 0; i < cat.getChildCount(); i++) {
        CategoryTreeNode child = createSubTree(cat.getChildAt(i));
        treeNode.add(child);
    }
    return treeNode;
}
```

Initializing the Applet

Create an `init()` method for the `CategoryViewApplet` that extracts the parameters passed to the applet, namely the URL of serializedcathierarchy.jsp, and initializes the fields. You need to add the `JTree` instance created from the serialized object in the `getTree()` method to the applet for display. You can also embed the tree in a `JScrollPane` to provide scrolling. The source for the applet initialization is shown in Listing 10.10.

Listing 10.10 CategoryViewApplet.java: Initializing the Applet Using the Parameters Passed by the JSP

```
package station.auction.applet;

import java.applet.Applet;
import java.applet.AppletContext;
import java.awt.BorderLayout;
import java.awt.event.MouseEvent;
import java.awt.event.MouseListener;
import java.io.*;
import java.net.URL;

import javax.swing.JTree;
import javax.swing.JScrollPane;
import javax.swing.tree.DefaultTreeModel;

import station.auction.catalog.Category;

public class CategoryViewApplet extends Applet {
    protected JTree tree = null;
    String location = null;
    String url = null;
    String target = null;

    public void init() {
        setLayout(new BorderLayout());
        location = getParameter("serializedRoot");
        url = getParameter("url");
```

10

Listing 10.10   continued

```
        target = getParameter("target");
        add(new JScrollPane(getTree()));

    protected JTree getTree() {
        if (tree == null) {
            System.out.println("Creating Tree");
            createTree();
        }
        return tree;
    }
}
```

Compile the `CategoryTreeNode` and `CategoryViewApplet` Java source files and copy the class files to the applet folder retaining the directory structure specified by the package name, `station\auction\applet`. You also need to copy the additional files used by the applet, such as `Category` and the rest of the view helper classes. These classes are also stored in the applet directory retaining the directory structure representing their package name, `station\auction\catalog`.

Creating the JSP That Embeds the Applet

Create a JSP, applet.jsp, that embeds the `CategoryViewApplet`. Specify the applet in the code parameter, `station.auction.applet.CategoryViewApplet`, and the codebase, `/jsp/admin/applet`. Specify the URL returning the serialized root by creating the `serializedRoot` parameter, as shown in Listing 10.11.

Listing 10.11   applet.jsp: Embedding the `CategoryViewApplet`

```
<html>
<head><title> Category View </title>
<base target="View">
</head>
<body bgcolor="white">
<h3> Category Map   </h3>
<jsp:plugin type="applet"
            code="station.auction.applet.CategoryViewApplet.class"
            codebase="/jsp/admin/applet"
            name="view"
            jreversion="1.2"
            width="200"
            height="300">
    <jsp:params>
        <jsp:param name="serializedRoot"
value="http://localhost:8080/jsp/admin/serializedcathierarchy.jsp"/>
        <jsp:param name="url"
            value="http://localhost:8080/jsp/admin/category.jsp"/>
        <jsp:param name="target" value="View"/>
    </jsp:params>
```

```
    <jsp:fallback>
        Plugin tag OBJECT or EMBED not supported by browser.
    </jsp:fallback>
</jsp:plugin>
<p>
</body>
</html>
```

Open the page generated by applet.jsp in your browser. You will see the tree view containing the categories of your site, as shown in Figure 10.7.

Figure 10.7

The categories of AuctionStation displayed in the applet

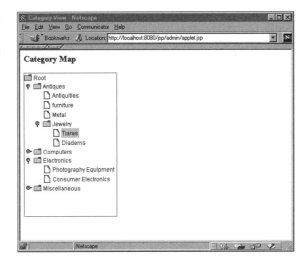

Viewing the Information of a Selected Category

Obviously, you want to do much more than just expand and collapse tree nodes representing the different categories. You may want to display the information about a category when the user double-clicks a particular node. You can enhance the application to detect user events such as double-clicking a node and display information about the specified category.

Detecting Mouse Double-Clicks

You can detect mouse double-clicks a particular component by listening to the java.awt.event.MouseEvent generated by it. You can do this by implementing the java.awt.event.MouseListener interface and the methods defined in it. When a particular mouse event occurs, a particular method of the interface is invoked. The MouseListener interface defines five methods for different mouse events:

```
public void mouseClicked(MouseEvent evt);
public void mousePressed(MouseEvent evt);
```

```
public void mouseReleased(MouseEvent evt);
public void mouseEntered(MouseEvent evt);
public void mouseExited(MouseEvent evt);
```

You can make `CategoryViewApplet` implement the `MouseListener` interface and add it as a listener to mouse events generated by the `JTree`.

```
public class CategoryViewApplet extends Applet implements MouseListener{
...
getTree().addMouseListener(this);
```

You can detect mouse double-clicks within the `mouseClicked` method.

```
public void mouseClicked(MouseEvent evt) {
    int clicks = evt.getClickCount();
    if (clicks > 1) {
        // User double clicked
```

Within the `if` block for the condition (`clicks > 1`), you can perform the display of category information.

Displaying the Category Information

You can display the category information in another Java component, such as a dialog or a frame, or within a browser window by providing a URL that can be constructed within the applet. The URL in this case is the URL of the Category View controller, passed as a parameter to the applet with the category ID obtained from the selected node appended as the query string.

You can obtain the category ID of the selected node in the tree view invoking the `getLastSelectedPathComponent` on the `JTree` instance. Because the node is an instance of `CategoryTreeNode`, you can invoke the `getCat_id()` method on it to return the information.

```
public String getCat_id() {
    CategoryTreeNode theNode = (CategoryTreeNode)
➥getTree().getLastSelectedPathComponent();
    if (theNode == null) {
      return "0";
    }
    return theNode.getCat_id();
}
```

You can display the information in a browser window using the `showDocument` defined in the `AppletContext` instance associated with the applet. You can show the category information by displaying the URL of the category JSP, as shown in Listing 10.12.

Listing 10.12   CategoryViewApplet.java: Displaying the Category Properties in the Target Browser Window by Constructing the URL of the JSP That Displays the Information

```java
public void mouseClicked(MouseEvent evt) {
    int clicks = evt.getClickCount();
    if (clicks > 1) {
        // User double clicked
        String cat_id = getCat_id();
        try {
            getAppletContext().showDocument(new URL(url + "?cat_id=" +
                cat_id), target);
        } catch (Exception exc) {
            showStatus("Malformed URL" + url);
        }
    }
}
```

Using Frames to Display the Pages

For our display, we will display both the output of applet.jsp and the category view in a single browser window. This is possible using an HTML element called frames. Frames allow you to display more than one page in the window by defining frame-sets containing multiple frames. Each frame acts as a minibrowser that displays a specified page.

For our view, create a HTML page, categories.html, and divide this page into two frames tiled vertically. You can do this by providing a `frameset` containing two `frames` displaying the necessary pages and specifying the `cols` property in the frame-set indicating the orientation of the frames, as shown in Listing 10.13.

Listing 10.13   categories.html: Creating Frames for the Applet and the Category Properties JSP

```html
<html>
<head><title>Category Map</title>
</head>
<frameset cols="50%,*" border="0" frameborder="0" framespacing="0">
    <frame src="applet.jsp">
    <frame src="/jsp/admin/category.jsp" NAME="View">
    <noframes>
        <body>You require frames to view this page</body>
    </noframes>
</frameset>
</html>
```

Figure 10.8 shows categories.html viewed in the browser. It displays the information about the root category as defined by the initial URL for the frame.

10

Figure 10.8

The categories of AuctionStation displayed in the applet

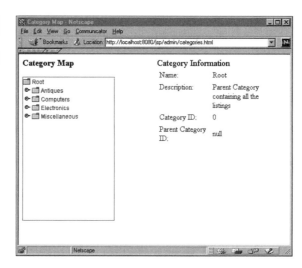

When the user double-clicks a particular category, the showDocument method passing the URL constructed using the view category JSP and the selected category's cat_id, and then the page is displayed in the targeted frame, as shown in Figure 10.9.

Figure 10.9

The information displayed for the selected "Tiaras" category

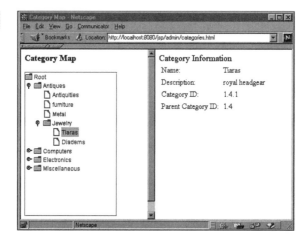

Summary

In this chapter, you performed the following tasks:

- Used the `jsp:plug-in` tag to embed an applet in the view
- Performed applet-JSP communication by passing serialized data
- Combined applets with JSP/HTML documents using frames to develop sophisticated interfaces

In this chapter, you learned to produce non-HTML content in the JSP in the form of serialized data that was used by the applet. In the next chapter, you will learn to enhance this technique to develop content for the wireless world.

Chapter 11

Developing Content for the Wireless World

So far we have been developing Web applications that can be viewed by machines with HTTP-compliant browsers. These machines include workstations, laptops, and servers. The past few years have seen the proliferation of wireless devices, such as mobile phones, pagers, and other hand-held devices. Mobile devices and wireless networks, however, have restrictions that prevent them from using HTML and HTTP efficiently. These devices cannot be ignored too long for any Web application because they constitute a big chunk of the devices connected to the Internet.

Why Develop for Wireless?

There are many reasons why mobile devices cannot be used to view standard Web documents. Most of these devices have low screen resolutions that are incapable of rendering graphics-intensive pages and can display only a few lines of text at the most. They operate with lower horsepower, smaller CPU, and low memory incapable of interpreting and rendering HTML pages. Input devices of these devices are limited in capability as well. Most devices have only numeric keypads that allow the user to enter data, and they lack mouse support, so the user cannot point and click.

The wireless networks, over which the devices operate, offer a peak transfer rate of only up to 10 Kb/s, with round-trip latencies of 5–10 seconds and unstable connections being common. HTTP operates on *Transfer Control Protocol* (TCP), which is not suited for such environments.

TCP is a connection-oriented protocol. It requires a dedicated connection between the server and the client while sending a message, the HTML page in this case. After the message is sent, it waits for an acknowledgement from the receiver. If the connection is unstable, as is the case for the wireless networks, the server will end up retrying and resending the entire lost message.

The *User Datagram Protocol* (UDP), on the other hand, is a connectionless protocol. It operates by sending the message without waiting for a reply or acknowledgement from the receiver. If the packets of the message are lost during transmission, the client times out and the user can request the page again.

Wireless Access Protocol (WAP) emerged to address the problems with HTTP. It provided solutions optimized to the needs of wireless communication. It operates on the connectionless UDP. It also utilizes binary transmission, unlike its text-based HTTP counterpart. This enables it to encode data, resulting in shorter transmission times and a lower likelihood of failure.

The Wireless Markup Language

WAP uses the Wireless Markup Language (WML) for sending content. WML pages are special types of XML documents that conform to the WML Document Type Definition (DTD). The tag set is very similar to that of HTML.

Table 11.1 shows the HTML and the WML equivalents for displaying "Auction Station" with the document title "Welcome" in their respective browsers.

Table 11.1 HTML and WML Content for Printing "Auction Station" with the Document Title "Welcome"

Welcome.html	Welcome.wml
`<html>`	`<?xml version="1.0"?>`
`  <head>`	`<!DOCTYPE wml PUBLIC "-//WAPFORUM//DTD WML`
	`1.1//EN" "http://www.wapforum.org/DTD/`
`    <title>`**`Auction Station`**`</title>`	`wml_1.1.xml">`
`  </head>`	
	`<wml>`
`  <body>`	`    <card id="card1" title="`**`AuctionStation`**`">`
`    <center>`**`Welcome`**`</center>`	`        <p align="center">`**`Welcome`**`</p>`
`  </body>`	`    </card>`
`</html>`	`</wml>`

The basic unit of content transmission of WML documents is a WML deck. A deck is similar to an HTML page in that it is identified by an URL. A deck contains cards that display the relevant information. You can navigate between cards of the deck without having to make a round trip to the server again. The card contains text and image laid out into one or more paragraphs. WML provides formatting and layout commands for these elements similar to those in HTML, the only exception being the lack of nested tables in WML pages.

The Wireless Access Protocol

WAP provides an application protocol for the wireless terminals, also known as user agents, to communicate to an application or Web server. Figure 11.1 shows the components involved in this network.

Figure 11.1

The WAP network structure

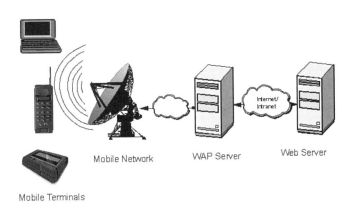

Mobile Network   WAP Server   Web Server

Mobile Terminals

WAP is similar to the Web model in the following ways:

1. The process is initiated when the user enters a URL in the mobile terminal's browser.
2. The terminal sends the request to a WAP gateway or server.
3. The WAP gateway routes the request to an application/Web server after creating a conventional HTTP request for the specified URL.
4. The Web server processes the request specified by the URL and returns WML content along with the HTTP header information.
5. The WAP gateway encodes the WML content to a binary form and sends the WAP response to the user agent.
6. The user agent decodes the WML contained in the response and displays the first card in the deck.

11

Testing Wireless Applications

For testing our wireless applications, we will use a WML emulator from Nokia, the Nokia WAP Toolkit 1.2. The toolkit simulates a generic WAP mobile phone as well as content encoders that would otherwise be performed by a WAP gateway. This toolkit is included in the companion CD, so you can get started with wireless application development without having to scour the Web for one.

Figure 11.2 shows the Nokia WAP emulator when it starts up. The left window displays the source of the WML document and a location field to enter the deck's URL, and the right window displays the output in the mock mobile terminal.

Figure 11.2

The Nokia WAP Toolkit

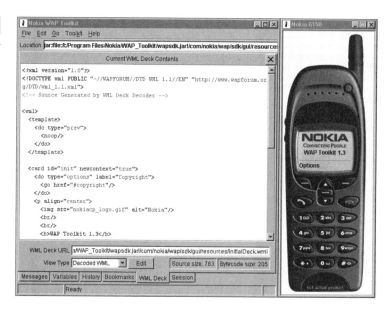

You can read the "Getting Started" guide available in the toolkit for more information about the controls.

Configuring Tomcat to Serve WML Documents

You will need to add MIME types to the Tomcat server configuration to allow it to serve files with the WML extensions. Add the following tags within the root web-app tag in web.xml, stored in the conf directory:

```
<mime-mapping>
    <extension>
        wml
    </extension>
    <mime-type>
```

```
        text/vnd.wap.wml
    </mime-type>
</mime-mapping>
```

Add similar tags to web.xml for the other MIME types shown in Table 11.2.

Table 11.2   MIME Types to Be Configured in Tomcat

Extension	MIME Type	Description
wbmp	image/vnd.wap.wbmp	Bitmap images for wireless devices
wmlc	application/vnd.wap.wmlc	WML pages in binary format
wmls	text/vnd.wap.wmlscript	WML Script
wmlsc	application/vnd.wap.wmlscriptc	WML Scripts in binary format

You can also specify index.wml as another welcome file for Tomcat. When you configure Tomcat to do so, the server will automatically serve the index.wml file located within the directory when only the directory is specified. This configuration is performed in web.xml by adding a `welcome-file` tag to the `welcome-file-list` tag, as shown in the following lines:

```
<welcome-file>
    index.wml
</welcome-file>
```

Developing the Start Page

In this section, we will create Auction Station's start page, a WML *deck*, index.wml. This deck will contain information about the site and provide links to the different sections as well.

Structuring a WML Deck

Each WML file requires the mandatory xml header and the DTD declaration shown following:

```
<?xml version="1.0"?>
<!DOCTYPE wml PUBLIC "-//WAPFORUM//DTD WML 1.1//EN"
        "http://www.wapforum.org/DTD/wml_1.1.xml">
```

As with well-formed XML documents, you will need to store the content within a `wml` root element. All the content in the WML page—text, images, and links along with the formatting information—is stored into one or more *cards*. To conform to the WML DTD, you need to specify a `card` tag for each card that you define in the deck.

11

Note

To improve readability in mobile terminals that usually have small monitors, you need to split large pages into more than one card. These cards are stored within a *deck*, and the user can navigate between the cards of these decks to obtain the required information—just as you would shuffle a pack of playing cards to find the queen of hearts!

We will create a deck and a card, index.wml, that displays the welcome message as shown in Listing 11.1. Create a directory, wap, within the AuctionStation webapp folder of Tomcat. Store the deck in this folder. Launch the Nokia Toolkit and enter the URL of the deck (`http://localhost:8080/wap/index.wml` or `http://localhost:8080/wap/` because index.wml is a welcome file) in the location field of the toolkit. The first card in the deck, card1, is rendered in the terminal as shown in Figure 11.3.

Listing 11.1 index.wml: Source of the Home Deck

```
<?xml version="1.0"?>
<!DOCTYPE wml PUBLIC "-//WAPFORUM//DTD WML 1.1//EN"
          "http://www.wapforum.org/DTD/wml_1.1.xml">

<wml>
  <card id="card1" title="Welcome">
    <p>
      <big>W</big>elcome to Auction Station, the latest Person-to-Person
      Auction Site.
    </p>
  </card>
</wml>
```

Figure 11.3

The bare-bones wireless start card for Auction Station

Adding a Banner Image

You can add images using the same tags that you used in HTML. There are restrictions, however, with using images. You must not go overboard with sprucing up the card with images. First, there is a restriction on the deck size, so you can't use large images. Second, large images in small monitors are square pegs in round holes and will frustrate the users completely by having them scroll vertically or horizontally to view the picture. Third, you can only use grayscale GIF or wireless bitmap (wbmp) formats for your images.

Add an `img` tag specifying the location in its `src` attribute and an alternate text in the `alt` attribute as shown following:

```
<img src="banner.gif" alt="Auction Station"/>
```

 Note Remember to add a slash (/) at the end of empty element tags such as `img`, `br`, and `hr`: `<br/>` and `<hr/>`.

You can center the image for display by embedding it in a paragraph tag. Ensure that you store it within the card element as shown in Listing 11.2. The output of the page is shown in Figure 11.4.

Listing 11.2   index.wml: Adding an Image to the Wireless Home Deck

```
<?xml version="1.0"?>
<!DOCTYPE wml PUBLIC "-//WAPFORUM//DTD WML 1.1//EN"
          "http://www.wapforum.org/DTD/wml_1.1.xml">

<wml>
  <card id="card1" title="Welcome">
  <p align="center">
    <img src="banner.gif" alt="AuctionStation"/>
  </p>
  <p>
    <big>W</big>elcome to Auction Station, the latest Person-to-Person
    Auction Site.
  </p>
  </card>
</wml>
```

Figure 11.4

Adding an image to the page

Adding a Site Map Card Containing Links

11

Now you need to add links to the other sections of the site such as the calendar, registration, and auction. You could simply append the links to the end of the welcome page, but notice that the screen in Figure 11.4 has already got the contents scrolled off. This is horribly inconvenient for the user to navigate. Alternatively, you could create another card that contains the site map as shown in Listing 11.3 and link this card to the welcome card.

Listing 11.3   index.wml: Adding Links to the Different Sections

```
<card id="sitemap" title="Site Map">
  <p>
    <a href="/wap/calendar.jsp">Calendar</a><br/>
    <a href="/wap/auction/catalog.jsp">Auctions</a><br/>
    <a href="/wap/register/step1.jsp">Register</a>
    <a href="/wap/index.wml">Home</a>
  </p>
</card>
```

You can add a link to the welcome card by specifying the `"links"` card in the `src` attribute. The URL of a card is its name prefixed by `"#"`—in this case, `"#sitemap"`. You can directly display a specific card from another deck by appending the card name to the deck's URL. The absolute URL of the site map card is `http://localhost:8080/wap/index.wml#sitemap`.

```
<a href="#sitemap">Site Map</a>
```

The output of the site map card when viewed is shown in Figure 11.5.

Figure 11.5

Providing a site map of links to the other sections of the site

What you have just done is the HTML way of hyperlinking documents or cards. WML includes navigation and event-handling models that are equivalent to JavaScript and HTML rolled into one. It's more suited to the needs of mobile terminals with their unwieldy input devices. Mobile phones have navigational buttons that can be assigned and pressed to follow a link instead of having to scroll to the particular hyperlink in the card and then follow it.

WML has elements such as the `do` tag that allow you to handle user events, such as selecting a particular option or pressing a particular navigational button. An event is bound to a particular task and executed when it occurs. You could replace the hyperlink with an accept option that is activated by pressing a navigation key. If more than one such accept option exists, a list of the options to choose from is displayed, which the user can choose from by using the navigation keys. The task handler for this event displays the specified card. The source for the event and task is shown following:

```
<do type="accept" name="sitemap" label="Site Map">
  <go href="#links"/>
</do>
```

Figure 11.6 displays the output of the two hyperlinking techniques in WML.

Figure 11.6

Hyperlinking to the site map card using links and accept options, respectively

Instead of defining the event bindings in individual decks, you can define them within a `template` element. When you do this, the event bindings are applicable for every card defined in the deck unless specifically overridden.

```
<wml>

<template>
   <do type="accept" name="sitemap" label="Site Map">
       <go href="#sitemap"/>
   </do>
</template>
..
<card ...>
```

 Tip

You can also store the site map card within a JSP, sitemap.jsp, so that it can be reused within another JSP generating WML content using a simple page include directive.

Displaying the Monthly Calendar

In this section you will display the monthly calendar formatted using WML tables. You can modify the monthly calendar JSP that we have been using throughout this book for wireless access by making a few changes.

The changes that you will need to make are as follows:

- Specify the `contentType` of the generated page as `text/vnd.wap.wml`:

  ```
  <%@ page contentType="text/vnd.wap.wml"%>
  ```

- Specify the XML header and DTD declaration for the WML deck. The XML header has to be the first line in the WML document and so does the JSP page directive need to be the first line in the JSP. The only way to do this is to append the XML header to the page directive:

  ```
  <%@ page contentType="text/vnd.wap.wml"%><?xml version="1.0"?>
  <!DOCTYPE wml PUBLIC "-//WAPFORUM//DTD WML 1.1//EN"
              "http://www.wapforum.org/DTD/wml_1.1.xml">
  ```

- Add a `wml` root element and the `template` containing the event bindings.

11

- Provide a card element and a paragraph (p) tag to store the monthly calendar's contents.

- Strip down the table by taking out any formatting information such as background colors and widths. Shorten the names of the days of the week to the first characters by hard-coding the values in the table header so that they fit in a small display. You need to specify the number of columns in the table in the table tag before you declare them. You can specify the alignment of text and images in the table in the align attribute in the table element. For each column, you need to specify L, C, or R for the left, center, or right alignments.

- Include the site map using the page include directive:

```
<%@ include file="/wap/sitemap.jsp"%>
```

The source of the modified calendar.jsp is shown in Listing 11.4. The output of the calendar is the current month, June 2000 in this case, as shown in Figure 11.7.

Listing 11.4   calendar.jsp: Generating a WML Deck to Display the Monthly Calendar

```
<%@ page contentType="text/vnd.wap.wml"%><?xml version="1.0"?>
<!DOCTYPE wml PUBLIC "-//WAPFORUM//DTD WML 1.1//EN"
                "http://www.wapforum.org/DTD/wml_1.1.xml">

<jsp:useBean id="cal" class="station.auction.calendar.MonthBean"/>

<wml>
<template>
   <do type="accept" name="sitemap" label="Site Map">
       <go href="#sitemap"/>
   </do>
</template>

<card id="card1" title="<%= cal.getMonthName()%> Calendar">
 <p>
   <table columns="7" align="CCCCCCC">
     <tr>
        <td>S</td> <td>M</td> <td>T</td> <td>W</td>
        <td>T</td> <td>F</td> <td>S</td>
     </tr>
<%
        int startCell = cal.getStartCell();
        int endCell = cal.getEndCell();
        for (int cellNo = 0, day = 1; cellNo < 42; cellNo++) {
            if (cellNo%7 == 0) {
                    out.println("<tr>");
            } // end check for start of row
            out.print("<td>");
            if (cellNo < startCell || cellNo > endCell) {
```

```
                        out.print(" ");
                } else {
                        out.print("<small>" + day + "</small>");
                        day++;
                } // end if block
                out.println("</td>");
                if (((cellNo+1)%7) == 0) {
                        out.println("</tr>");
                } // end check for end of row
        } // end for-loop
%>
    </table>
 </p>
</card>

<%@ include file="/wap/sitemap.jsp"%>

</wml>
```

Figure 11.7

Displaying the monthly calendar

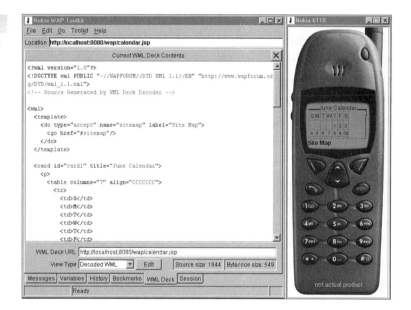

Note

Tables in WML involve plenty of restrictions. You cannot nest tables within another and you cannot align the contents of an individual cell. Tables, however, remain one of the popular formatting commands for text and images.

11

Developing the Auction Catalog Module

Next we need to generate the WML pages for displaying the auction catalog. We used the MVC technique using command beans to accomplish this for the HTML pages. An added advantage of the MVC technique is that you only need to modify the presentation layer to generate different content such as WML for wireless access. You could enhance the controller JSP to detect the source of the request, a WML browser or an HTML browser, and redirect the request to a page that is generating HTML or WML content.

One way to determine the source of the request is from the request headers. Some headers that you have been using are Cookies as you saw in Chapter 9, "Personalizing the Web Site," and Referer and Authorization information as you saw in Chapter 8, "Developing Protected Portions of AuctionStation." Other headers include the User-Agent, which specifies the browser that sent the request, and Accept, which specifies the MIME types the browser prefers. The header information can be obtained using the request implicit object. To retrieve the User-Agent, you can use request.getHeader("User-Agent") within your JSP.

Table 11.3 lists the request header values for a WML Browser, Nokia WAP toolkit, and an HTML browser, Netscape Communicator.

Table 11.3   Request Header Values for Nokia WAP Toolkit and Netscape Communicator

Header Name	Nokia WAP Toolkit	Netscape Communicator
User-Agent	Nokia-WAP Toolkit/1.3beta	Mozilla/4.72 (WinNT; I)
Accept	text/vnd.wap.wml,	image/gif, image/x-xbitmap,
	text/vnd.wap.wmlscript,	image/jpeg,image/pjpeg,
	application/vnd.wap.wmlc,	application/msword, */*
	application/vnd.wap.wmlscriptc,	
	image/vnd.wap.wbmp,	
	image/gif	

As you might have noticed, the User-Agent header value is specific to the browser being used. The Accept header, however, lists the MIME types that the browser is configured to use. You can make the assumption that the user agent is a WML browser only if the Accept header contains text/vnd.wap.wml in the list of MIME types.

You can implement this check within a scriptlet in the controller JSP as shown following:

```
<%
    boolean isWMLEnabled = false;
    String acceptHeader = request.getHeader("Accept");
```

```
        if (acceptHeader.indexOf("text/vnd.wap.wml") != -1) {
            isWMLEnabled = true;
        }
%>
```

While forwarding the requests to the presentation layer, you can check whether the user agent is WML-enabled and take action accordingly as shown following.

```
<%  if (isWMLEnabled) {   %>
        <jsp:include page="/wap/auction/categoryview.jsp" flush="true"/>
<%  } else {   %>
        <jsp:include page="/jsp/auction/categoryview.jsp" flush="true"/>
<%  } %>
```

In all the controllers, such as catalog.jsp, product.jsp, and bid.jsp, you need to add checks for the user agent and forward it to the right presentation JSP. You also need to create additional JSPs to generate WML decks for category listing, item listing, and bid status.

Displaying the Category Listing

You need to create a JSP, categoryview.jsp, that generates a WML deck for the category listing. The changes you need to make are to add the XML header, DTD declaration, and WML elements. We will display only one level of categories in each page. This JSP has the same JSP declarations, expressions, and scriptlets as the one in the HTML-generating JSP. The changes we made are to only make it WML-compliant, as shown in Listing 11.5. Figure 11.8 displays the catalog listing for the parent category.

Listing 11.5   categoryview.jsp: Generating the WML Deck for Displaying the Categories

```
<%@ page import="station.auction.catalog.*" contentType="text/vnd.wap.wml"%>
➥<?xml version="1.0"?><!DOCTYPE wml PUBLIC "-//WAPFORUM//DTD WML 1.1//EN"
➥"http://www.wapforum.org/DTD/wml_1.1.xml">
<jsp:useBean id="root" class="station.auction.catalog.Category"
➥scope="request"/>

<wml>

<card id="card1" title="Categories">
<p>
<table columns="1" align="L">
<%
    for (int i = 0; i < root.getChildCount(); i++) {
        Category aCat = root.getChildAt(i);
%>
<tr>
    <td>
<a href="/wap/auction/catalog.jsp?cat_id=<%= aCat.getCat_id()%>">
➥<%= aCat.getName()%></a> <small>(<i><%=
➥aCat.getNumberProducts()%></i>)</small>
```

11

Listing 11.5   continued

```
        </td>
    </tr>
    <%
        }
    %>
    </table>

    </p>
    </card>
    </wml>
```

Figure 11.8

Displaying the Auction Catalog

Displaying the Items Listing

You can similarly modify itemsview.jsp, the presentation JSP that displays the items in a category. The source for the JSP is shown in Listing 11.6. Figure 11.9 displays the item listing for the hardware category.

Listing 11.6   itemsview.jsp: Generating the WML Deck for Displaying the Items

```
<%@ page import="station.auction.catalog.*"
        contentType="text/vnd.wap.wml"%><?xml version="1.0"?>
<!DOCTYPE wml PUBLIC "-//WAPFORUM//DTD WML 1.1//EN"
➥"http://www.wapforum.org/DTD/wml_1.1.xml">

<jsp:useBean id="array" class="station.auction.catalog.ItemsArray"
                        scope="request"/>

<wml>

<card id="card1" title="Items">
<p>

<table columns="2" align="LL">
<%
    Item[] items = array.getItems();
    for (int i = 0; i < items.length; i++) {
        Item anItem = items[i];
%>
```

Listing 11.6   continued

```
<tr>
    <td> <a href="/wap/auction/product.jsp?prod_id=<%=
➡anItem.getProd_id()%>">
            <%= anItem.getProdName()%></a></td>
    <td> <%= anItem.getMin_amt()%> </td>
</tr>
<%
    }
%>
</table>

</p>
</card>
</wml>
```

Figure 11.9

Displaying the item list-
ing for the hardware
category

Displaying the Item Information Using Multiple Cards

The HTML page containing the item information, generated by productview.jsp,
contains lots of data that cannot be displayed in a single card. We will therefore split
the deck into several cards, each displaying a relevant set of information. To facilitate
easy navigation between the cards of the deck—item, info, user, bid, and place—you
will need to create a template that provides a link to every card in the deck. You can
also add a link to go back in the browser history, as shown in Listing 11.7.

Listing 11.7   productview.jsp: Generating the Template for the Item Information WML Deck

```
<%@ page import="station.auction.catalog.*, java.sql.Timestamp"
➡contentType="text/vnd.wap.wml"%><?xml version="1.0"?>
<!DOCTYPE wml PUBLIC "-//WAPFORUM//DTD WML 1.1//EN"
➡"http://www.wapforum.org/DTD/wml_1.1.xml">
<jsp:useBean id="item" class="station.auction.catalog.Item" scope="request"/>
<%
    User user = item.getUser();
    Address addr = user.getAddress();
    Bid hiBid = item.getHighestBid();
%>


<wml>
  <template>
```

11

Listing 11.7   continued

```
<do type="options" name="back" label="Back">
    <prev/>
</do>

<do type="accept" name="item" label="Item">
    <go href="#item"/>
</do>

<do type="accept" name="info" label="More Details">
    <go href="#info"/>
</do>

<do type="accept" name="user" label="User Details">
    <go href="#user"/>
</do>

<do type="accept" name="bid" label="Bid Details">
    <go href="#bid"/>
</do>

<do type="accept" name="place" label="Place Bid">
    <go href="#place"/>
</do>
</template>
```

The `Item` Card

Add a card, `item`, to the deck that displays the item name and description.

```
<card id="item" title="Item">
  <p>
    <big><%= item.getProdName()%></big><br/>
    <%= item.getDescription()%>
  </p>
</card>
```

Because this is the first card in the deck, it will be displayed in the WML browser if no card is explicitly specified as being the welcome card. If the user had selected "Playstation" from the category listing, the output would be as shown in Figure 11.10.

 Note You do have to provide the closing tags for the paragraph and WML elements if you expect to see it work!

The `"More Details"` Card

Add another card, `info`, that displays extra information about the item, such as the amount, bid increments, and start time, is shown following:

```
<card id="info" title="More Details">
  <p>
    Minimum Amount
    <b><%= item.getMin_amt()%></b>
    <br/>
    Bid Increment
    <b><%= item.getMin_bid_inc()%></b>
    <br/>
    Bid Started
    <b><small><%= item.getCreated().toGMTString()%></small></b>
    <br/>
    Time Left
    <b><%= item.getTimeLeftString()%></b>
  </p>
</card>
```

You can access the card by selecting the More Details option as shown in Figure 11.11.

Figure 11.10

Displaying the information about the Playstation.

Figure 11.11

Displaying the extra information about the item. Figure 11.11 (a) shows the navigation menu with the link to the details card and Figure 11.11 (b) shows the actual details when the user selects the option.

The "User Details" Card

You can display information about the user in a "User Details" card as shown following:

```
<card id="user" title="User Details">
  <p>
    User
    <b><%= user.getUser_id()%></b>
    <br/>
    Location
    <b><%= addr.getCity() + ", " + addr.getState()%></b>
  </p>
</card>
```

11

Figure 11.12

The user details for the item

The "Bid Details" Card

Lastly, you can add the card to display the bid details information, such as the number of bids, highest bidder, and current amount.

```
<card id="bid" title="Bid Details">
  <p>
    # of Bids
    <b><%= item.getBidCount()%></b>
    <br/>
    Current Amount
    <b><%= hiBid.getAmount()%></b>
    <br/>
    Highest Bidder
    <b><%= hiBid.getUser_id()%></b>
  </p>
</card>
```

Bidding on an Item

In this last section, we will use WML forms for submitting information to the server. WML forms are a little different from their HTML counterparts. You need to create input fields to accept user data and create a task and event handler to submit the data to the server. The input fields are similar to the HTML fields, accepting data from text fields, choices, and lists. To submit the data, you need to extract the input field values into postfield instances and define an event handler, go, that submits the fields to the server.

You need to add a card, place, in productview.jsp to allow the user to place the bid while viewing the item information shown in Listing 11.8. Figure 11.13 chronicles the steps performed by the user nicks in making a bid on the item.

Listing 11.8   productview.jsp: Generating the Form for Accepting User Data

```
<card id="place" title="Place Bid">
<do type="accept" label="Submit">
    <go method="post" href="bid.jsp">
        <postfield name="amount" value="$(amount)"/>
        <postfield name="name" value="$(name)"/>
        <postfield name="prod_id" value="<%= item.getProd_id()%>"/>
    </go>
```

Listing 11.8   continued

```
</do>
<p>
Enter your bid:
<input type="text" name="amount"
       value="<%= (hiBid.getAmount() + item.getMin_bid_inc())%>"/>
Your name:
<input type="text" name="name"/>
</p>
</card>
</wml>
```

Figure 11.13

Bidding on an item. Figure 11.13 (a) provides the link to the specific card in the navigation menu; Figure 11.13 (b) shows the bid form for the item; Figure 11.13 (c) accepts the user name; and Figure 11.13 (d) shows the option for submitting the form.

Displaying the Status of the Bid

You need to modify the controller, bid.jsp, to forward the request to the WML-generating JSP if the request originated from a WML browser. This JSP forwards the request to either successbid.jsp or failbid.jsp. You can modify both these files to generate WML decks. Listing 11.9 contains the source for successbid.jsp, and Figure 11.14 displays the deck if the bid has been registered.

Listing 11.9   successbid.jsp: Displaying the Success Status if the Bid Has Been Registered

```
<%@ page contentType="text/vnd.wap.wml"%><?xml version="1.0"?>
<!DOCTYPE wml PUBLIC "-//WAPFORUM//DTD WML 1.1//EN"
        "http://www.wapforum.org/DTD/wml_1.1.xml">

<wml>
  <card id="card1" title="Success">
    <do type="options" name="do1" label="default">
      <prev/>
    </do>
    <p>
```

11

Listing 11.9   continued

```
      Your bid has been recorded.
      <b>Item #: </b>
      <% String prod_id = request.getParameter("prod_id");%>
   <a href="/wap/auction/product.jsp?prod_id=<%= prod_id%>">
   <%= prod_id%></a>
   <br/>
   <b>Your Bid: </b>
     <%= request.getParameter("amount")%>
   </p>
   </card>
</wml>
```

Figure 11.14

A bid being registered successfully

WML Decks from Scratch?

One of the areas of concern in generating the WML decks from scratch is the lack of maintenance of the two sets of JSPs, one each for HTML and WML. Changes to JSP expressions, scriptlets, and declarations would require changes to be made to both the JSPs that can be pretty risky if the changes are large.

In most cases, WML decks can be generated by a transformation of the HTML pages generated by one set of JSPs. This has brought forth the use of *transcoders*, like *Websphere Transcoding Publisher*, to generate content. These transcoders convert HTML into WML decks by applying some transformation rules specified by the user.

Specifying these rules may be tricky if you expect to make major modifications, such as dividing the HTML page into different cards as we did for the item information display page.

Deploying the Web Application on Another Server

After you have developed your Web application, you might want to deploy it on another server. This can be accomplished by packaging the files of the Web application in the webapps folder and copying it to the deployment machine.

Packaging Web Applications in WAR Files

Web applications can be packaged in Web Archive or WAR files. This allows them to be stored and easily installed on another server. WAR files can be created using the `jar` command or using a zipping utility, and providing them with a .war extension.

To create the WAR file for the AuctionStation application, launch a command window, set the current working directory to `<jakarta-tomcat>/webapps/AuctionStation`, and enter the `jar` command as shown following:

```
jar -cvf AuctionStation.war *
```

This creates a WAR file, AuctionStation.war, in the current directory. To run AuctionStation on another server, you only need to copy AuctionStation.war in the `<jakarta-tomcat>/webapps` folder of that server. When you start Tomcat, the contents of the WAR file are automatically extracted. The WAR file can be consumed by other JSP 1.1-compliant servers based on their deployment process.

Extra Modifications Required

To run the application without a hitch, you also need to do the following:

- Set the root context as AuctionStation
- Add WAP MIME types in the server configuration
- Add index.wml to the welcome file list in web.xml
- Add a system data source for the Auction database to allow ODBC access

If you use another database, you will also need to create the tables used in the AuctionStation application.

Summary

In this chapter you learned some of the elements of WML such as text, images, tables, links, variables, and event handlers. You also learned to generate WML decks using JSPs and to reuse components built using the command pattern or MVC design.

This brings to an end our journey of learning about JSPs together. Throughout the course of this book, you have seen specific examples such as the calendar and auction applications. Even if you don't intend to develop such applications, you can easily reuse many of the design techniques for other applications. For example, the auction item catalog can be easily converted into a product catalog for an e-store. You can also convert it into a bulletin board containing messages and replies if you examine the similarities between the two applications.

11

I would love to hear your comments about the book, whether you are a Web designer, JSP tag developer, server-side programmer, startup braniac, or venture capitalist. You can reach me by email at maneesh@maneeshsahu.com.

Happy Web-application developing!

Appendix A

Online Material and Information

This appendix gives you sources for finding additional material online that will be helpful to you with your JSP projects.

Cascading Style Sheets (CSS)

- www.w3.org/Style/CSS

  The World Wide Web Consortium's (W3C) extensive collection of links to books, online resources, browsers, and editors for CSS.

- www.w3.org/TR/REC-CSS1

  and

  www.w3.org/TR/REC-CSS2

  W3C's Recommendations for Cascading Style Sheets.

Enterprise JavaBeans (EJB)

- java.sun.com/products/ejb/index.html

  Sun's pages containing the EJB specifications and related information.

- www.redbooks.ibm.com/abstracts/sg245429.html

  An IBM redbook, "Enterprise JavaBeans Development Using VisualAge for Java SG-24-5429-00," that I co-authored along with Joaquin Picon, Martin Weiss, Alain Dessureault, and Patrizia Genchi.

- http://www.redbooks.ibm.com/redpieces/abstracts/sg245754.html

  Another IBM redbook, "Design and Implement Servlets, JSPs, and EJBs for IBM WebSphere Application Server, SG-24-5754-00," co-authored by Joaquin Picon, Regis Coqueret, Andreas Hutfless, Gopal Indurkhya, and Martin Weiss.

JavaMail

- java.apache.org/james/

  Java Apache Mail Enterprise Server.

- java.sun.com/products/javamail/index.html

  Sun's pages on JavaMail specifications, API, and related information.

- java.sun.com/beans/glasgow/jaf.html

  Sun's pages on the Java Activation Framework specifications and related information.

- www.alphaworks.ibm.com/ab.nsf/bean/SMTP

  A suite of beans developed by IBM to visually develop mail-based applications.

JavaScript

- developer.netscape.com/tech/javascript/

  Netscape's repository of information on JavaScript.

Java Server Pages (JSP), JDBC, and Servlets

- jakarta.apache.org

  The Apache Software Foundation's Jakarta Project Web site and the Tomcat reference implementation.

- java.sun.com/products/jsp/index.html

  Sun's pages containing the JSP specifications and related information.

- java.sun.com/products/servlet/index.html

  Sun's pages containing the Servlet specifications, API, and related information.

- java.sun.com/products/jdbc/index.html

  Sun's pages containing the JDBC specifications, API, and related information.

- www.software.ibm.com/vadd

  The VisualAge Developer Domain, which contains a wealth of information about IBM's VisualAge for Java IDE. There are some excellent articles on using Tomcat in VAJava and designing Web-based applications.

Linux

- www.ibm.com/linux

  IBM Application Developer's Kit for Linux.

- www.developer.ibm.com/devcon

  Obtain tools like DB2 Universal Database, IBM WebSphere Application Server, Linux JDK, and VisualAge for Java for Linux.

Wireless Access Protocol (WAP) and Wireless Markup Language (WML)

- www.ibm.com/pvc

  IBM's Pervasive Computing site.

- www.forum.nokia.com/index.html

  Nokia's WAP developer forum. You can also download a WAP emulator.

- www.wapforum.org

  Delve deep into WAP, WML, and WMLScript.

eXtensible Markup Language (XML)

- www.w3.org/XML

  W3C's XML specification, recommendations, links, and other resources.

- www.alphaWorks.ibm.com/ab.nsf/bean/XML+Beans

  A suite of JavaBeans that I co-developed for processing, viewing, and editing XML documents.

- www.alphaWorks.ibm.com/tech/xmlviewer

  A Java-based tool that I developed for viewing XML documents in different perspectives.

- www.alphaWorks.ibm.com/tech/xeena

  A Java-based tool developed by the IBM Haifa Research Laboratory for visually editing XML documents.

- www.alphaWorks.ibm.com/tech/xml4j

  IBM's Java-based XML parser.

- www.redbooks.ibm.com/abstracts/sg245479.html

  An IBM redbook, "The XML Files: Using XML and XSL with IBM WebSphere V3.0 SG24-5479-00," written by Luis Ennser, Christophe Chuvan, Paul Fremantle, Ramani Routray, and Jouko Ruuskanen.

A

- www.ibm.com/developer/xml/

  A wealth of information on XML and related technologies.

- xml.apache.org/

  The Apache Software Foundation's XML project site. Contains various open-source XML projects for XML parsers (Xerces), XSLT style-sheet processors (Xalan), XML and Java-based Web publishing (Cocoon), XSL formatting objects (FOP), dynamic server pages (Xang), and the Simple Object Access Protocol (SOAP).

eXtensible Stylesheet Language (XSL)

- www.w3.org/Style/XSL/

  W3C's XSL specification, recommendations, links, and other resources.

- www.alphaWorks.ibm.com/tech/lotusXSL

  Lotus' Java-based implementation of the XSLT and XML Path recommendations.

- www.zvon.org/ZvonHTML/Zvon/zvonHomepage_en.html

  Some fantastic online tutorials on XML, XSL, and CSS, developed as a part of the Zvon project.

Miscellaneous

- http://www.ibm.com/hci

  IBM's Ease of Use site for Human Computer Interaction (HCI).

- http://www-3.ibm.com/ibm/easy/eou_ext.nsf/publish/572

  Web Design Guidelines at the IBM Ease of Use site.

Index

Symbols

I

IBM Application Framework
for e-business, 213
IBM DB2, 29
IBM HTTP Server, 28
IBM VisualAge for Java, 26
IBM VisualAge Team
Coordinator, 25
IBM Web site, 380
IBM WebSphere Application,
29
IBM WebSphere Studio, 24
identifying users, 324
IDEs (Integrated
Development
Environments), 25
IBM VisualAge for Java, 26
Inprise JBuilder, 26
Oracle JDeveloper, 26
Symantec Visual Caf, 26
testers, 26
IIS (Microsoft Internet
Information Server), 28
image editor, 24
tools, 24
Adobe Photoshop, 24
CorelDRAW, 24
GIF, 24
JASC PaintShop Pro, 24
JPEG, 24
Macromedia
FreeHand/Fireworks, 24
NetStudio 2000, 24
images
banner images, adding to
wireless applications,
360-361
hyperlinking documents, listings, 37
Web interface development,
35
img tag (WML), 361
implicit objects, developing
calendar application, 54
import statements,
MonthBean, 92
include directive, 47
include tag
developing calendar application, 59-60
JSP footer, 48
info card (auction application),
370-371
info tag element, 132
Informix, 29

inheriting CSS (Cascading
Style Sheets) rules, 300
initialization fullselect, 231
initializing applets, 347-348
Inprise JBuilder, 26
input fields, 68-71
HTML fields, defining, 72
HTML pages
buttons, 71
check boxes, 70
drop-down lists, 70
list boxes, 71
option buttons, 70
option menus, 70
password fields, 69
text area, 70
text fields, 69
user data, 69
input JSPs (Calendar application), 114-115
input page
error.jsp (error page) listing,
77
input.jsp Enhancing the
Generate Month, 83
input.jsp listing (yearly calen-
dars), 84
input.jsp Source listing, 74
input.jsp Validation listing,
79-83
month.jsp (extract parameters scriptlet) listing, 76
input pages, 68. *See also*
HTML pages
calendar application version
1.1
developing, 68-73
enhancing, 75-84
troubleshooting, 76
HTML pages
HTML forms, defining, 68
input fields, choosing, 69
developing, 68
input properties
JavaBeans, 89
MonthBean, 95
input.jsp Enhancing the
Generate Month, listing, 83
input.jsp Source (input page),
listing, 74
input.jsp Validation
(JavaScript), listing, 79
input.jsp Validation (JSP), listing, 82-83
InsertItemCommand bean,
281-282

installing
plug-ins, 337
Tomcat, 43
deploying Auction Station,
45
instance variables, session
scopes, 270
Integrated Development
Environments. *See* IDEs
interfaces
command-line, DBMS,
153-154
graphical user, DBMS,
153-154
tag
as-taglib.tld (error tag)
listing, 140
as-taglib.tld listing, 146
as-taglib.tld (today tag)
listing, 132
customtags.jsp listing, 147
email tags listing, 142
EmailTagHandler.java
listing, 144
error.jsp listing, 147
ErrorTagHandler.java
(BodyTag Interface)
listing, 137-138
ErrorTagHandler.java
(redefining) listing, 139
FromTagHandler.java list-
ing, 145
methods, 128-133
TodayTagHandler.java
(doStartTag method)
listing, 130
TodayTagHandler.java
(inheriting methods/fields)
listing, 131
Web, development of, 32-38
internationalization (Web
applications), 50
IP addresses, 27. *See also* host
names
iPlanet Application Server, 29
item card (auction application), 370
item catalog module, com-
mand beans
developing, 227-240
GetCategoryHierarchyCom
mand, developing, 230-235
GetCategoryHierarchyCom
mand, testing, 235
GetCategoryItemsCommand,
developing, 236-239

W

What's on the CD-ROM

Source Code Application

The CD-ROM includes the complete source code to build and implement a Web site for a hypothetical auction house from beginning to end. Use the code found in the Source Code directory on the CD-ROM to learn how to program Java Server Pages and how to build effective servlets.

Software Library

The *Java Server Pages from scratch* CD-ROM contains a collection of evaluation software to use in conjunction with the book. You may utilize these software versions to apply the techniques and knowledge you will learn by reading the book.

IBM's Websphere Studio 3.0 Entry Edition

`http://www-4.ibm.com/software/webservers/studio/`

In the struggle to get your information, your business, your service out on the Web and available to all your customers, IBM© WebSphere™ Studio makes your job easier. As part of the WebSphere family of products, Studio provides a complete environment that simplifies every aspect of Web application development—from designing and building to testing and publishing.

WebSphere Studio 3.0 brings together a suite of tools in a common interface, letting everyone on a multidisciplinary team work on the same projects and have access to the files they need. But the real goal of Studio is to help you create applications for WebSphere Application Server using the most advanced Web technologies. With Studio on your desktop, you can start with static HTML pages and progress to dynamic Web sites that include Java servlets, JavaServer™ Pages (JSPs) components, and JavaBeans.

IBM's VisualAge for Java 3.0 Entry Edition

`http://www.ibm.com/software/ad/vajava`

IBM VisualAge for Java™ is an award-winning, integrated development environment for creating Web-enabled enterprise applications. It delivers the industry's most advanced support for building, testing, and deploying 100% Pure Java applications, JavaBeans components, servlets, and applets. A key element of IBM's Application Framework for e-business, VisualAge for Java allows developers to build Java applications for today's most demanding e-business environments.

VisualAge for Java helps developers achieve exceptional productivity with advanced, easy-to-use functions that slash development time, enable a high level of code reuse and allow for integrated team development. It is the only Java development environment that supports the creation of Java applications that can scale from Windows NT to OS/390 enterprise servers. VisualAge for Java provides easy, fast, and secure access to data and extends existing applications to the Web.

IBM's DB2 Universal Database Professional Edition v6.1

`http://www-4.ibm.com/software/data/db2/index.html`

IBM's object-relational database for Windows 95, Windows 98, and Windows NT— DB2 Personal Developer's Edition provides all the tools for one software developer to develop desktop business tools and applications for DB2 Universal Database Personal Edition.

Tomcat Reference Implementation v3.1

`http://jakarta.apache.org/index.html`

Tomcat is a servlet container and JavaServer Pages™ implementation. It may be used stand alone or in conjunction with several popular Web servers.

Tomcat User Guide: `\.jakarta-tomcat\doc\uguide\tomcat_ug.html`

Developing Applications with Tomcat Index:
`\.\jakarta-tomcat\doc\appdev\index.html`

TOMCAT Version 3.1 Release Notes: `\.\jakarta-tomcat\doc\readme`

Frequently Asked Questions (FAQ) on Tomcat: `\.\jakarta-tomcat\doc\faq`

The Apache Software License, Version 1.1: `\.\jakarta-tomcat\License.txt`

NetObject's Fusion Demo Version

`www.netobjects.com`

NetObjects Fusion is the fastest, easiest way to build business Web sites. Create, manage, and update effective sites quickly and efficiently in its WYSIWYG environment. Build and update your site structure quickly in the drag-and-drop SiteStructure Editor. Place assets precisely where you want them in the WYSIWYG Layout Editor. Add e-commerce functionality and dynamic database access to your site without programming.

NetStudio 2000

www.netstudio.com

NetStudio lets business users, without an art degree, easily create professional-looking Web sites. NetStudio is a picture processor, a revolutionary new Web graphics program that's as easy to use as a word processor. With NetStudio, insert a Web button with one click, customize it with one click, and drop it into your Web site. NetStudio is easy to use, designed specifically for the Web, and integrated with Web page editors.

Nokia WAP Toolkit Product Information

www.nokia.com

Nokia WAP Toolkit—To assist developers in producing WAP applications and WAP services, Nokia has developed a toolkit. The Nokia WAP Toolkit provides a development environment for people who want to provide Internet services and content for mobile terminals. It will allow developers to write, test, debug, and run applications on PC-based simulations of both the Nokia 7100 series phone as well as a Nokia concept phone prototype.

The Nokia WAP Toolkit is free software and is available for downloading for all developers registered in the Nokia WAP Developer Forum. Open the HTML Product Information page on this CD-ROM for links to download the WAP Toolkit or further information about Nokia products and services.

The Product Information Page is on the CD-ROM in the following location:

```
CD-ROM Drive\Software_Library\Nokia\NokiaWAPToolkit.htm
```